Named in remembrance of

the onetime *Antioch Review* editor

and longtime Bay Area resident,

the Lawrence Grauman, Jr. Fund

supports books that address

a wide range of human rights,

free speech, and social justice issues.

The publisher and the University of California Press Foundation gratefully acknowledge the generous support of the Lawrence Grauman, Jr. Fund.

TAKING
CHILDREN

TAKING
CHILDREN

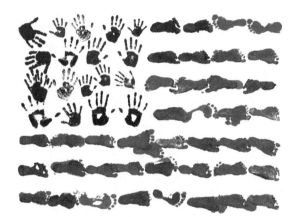

A HISTORY OF
AMERICAN TERROR

LAURA BRIGGS

 UNIVERSITY OF CALIFORNIA PRESS

University of California Press
Oakland, California

© 2020 by Laura Briggs

Library of Congress Cataloging-in-Publication Data

Names: Briggs, Laura, 1964– author.
Title: Taking children : a history of American terror / Laura Briggs.
Description: Oakland, California : University of California Press, [2020] |
    Includes bibliographical references and index.
Identifiers: LCCN 2020000732 (print) | LCCN 2020000733 (ebook) |
    ISBN 9780520343672 (cloth) | ISBN 9780520975071 (epub)
Subjects: LCSH: Child welfare—United States—Decision making. | Child welfare—
    Central America—Decision making. | Juvenile detention—United States. |
    Juvenile detention—Central America.
Classification: LCC HV6250.4.C48 B74 2020 (print) | LCC HV6250.4.C48 (ebook) |
    DDC 362.7/79145610973—dc23
LC record available at https://lccn.loc.gov/2020000732
LC ebook record available at https://lccn.loc.gov/2020000733

Manufactured in the United States of America

28 27 26 25 24 23 22 21 20
10 9 8 7 6 5 4 3 2 1

This book is dedicated to all children unjustly taken from their kin and caregivers, especially those who died in US immigration detention in 2018 and 2019 or immediately after their release:

Jakelin Caal Maquin, 7, from Guatemala
Felipe Gomez Alonzo, 8, from Guatemala
Wilmer Josué Ramírez Vásquez, 2, from Guatemala
Carlos Gregorio Hernández Vásquez, 16, from Guatemala
Darlyn Cristabel Cordova-Valle, 10, from El Salvador
Juan de Leon Gutiérrez, 16, from Guatemala
Mariee Juarez, 1, from Guatemala

Contents

Introduction

American Amnesia

The public debate about asylum seekers in 2018 and 2019 was raw. Members of the Trump administration and its supporters considered the asylum process a farce, a ruse that allowed people who transparently had no right to be in the United States to enter. Trump's people regarded them as illegal immigrants who were trying to manipulate the law by calling themselves refugees, and they complained that special rules on the treatment of children made bringing a child with you basically a get-out-of-jail-free card. They celebrated their strategy of deterring "illegals" by taking squalling children from their parents and caregivers, calling it "zero tolerance." "Womp, womp," said former Trump campaign manager Corey Lewandowski, mocking in high frat boy form the story of a child with Down's syndrome separated from her mother.[1] Administration officials made no effort to relieve overcrowding and squalid conditions in Border Patrol shelters that continued to house thousands of children even after a court order demanded the end of the child separation policy. When influenza and mumps ripped through shelters, killing three children, they announced that they would not offer vaccinations.[2]

Activists and journalists who opposed the policy protested in ways that were no less emotional. Protestors held up photos of children and parents separated from each other, downloaded pirated audio of children crying in shelters as Border Patrol officers laughed at them, and carried their own babies to demonstrations. The sounds and images of sobbing mothers and babies torn from their arms were everywhere.

In all this emotion, opponents of the policy in particular were repeating a very old move, reaching directly for historical parallels. Consciously and not, they borrowed one of the most successful tactics from the movement to abolish slavery. They tried to compel any audience they could get to imagine the fear and grief that stalked children and parents at the moment they were separated from each other and for the rest of their lives. They put that vulnerability and terror alongside the ugliness of the political ends of those who took babies and children.

In fact, some critics deliberately pointed out relationships between taking children of asylum seekers at the southwest border and the histories of slavery, Indian boarding schools, Japanese internment, mass incarceration, and anti-Communist wars against civilian populations in Latin America. Lance Cooper, a Flint water activist, tweeted what became a viral image of an enslaved mother reaching for a child being carried away by a white slave trader, writing, "Don't act like America just started separating children from their loving parents." DeNeen Brown wrote in the *Washington Post* about the parallels: "A mother unleashed a piercing scream as her baby was ripped from her arms during a slave auction," she said, reviewing an exhibit that the Smithsonian had pointedly put up on the history of child taking. "Even as a lash cut her back, she refused to put her baby down and climb atop an auction block." Catholic clergy and laity holding a mass protest in a US Senate office building carried large images of children who died in immigration detention in 2018 and 2019, a deliberate echo of the protests in the 1970s and '80s by mothers of the disappeared in Latin America. In Oklahoma, Japanese American, Black, and Native activists protested the opening of a detention camp for immigrant children on the site of a former World War II Japanese internment camp and, before that, an Indian boarding school.[3]

These kinds of activism sought to fill a void in public memory about the history of separating children from parents. One of the refrains that too often punctuated the liberal response to the policy was "This isn't America. We don't separate parents and children." ("There's nothing American about tearing families apart," Hillary Clinton tweeted.[4]) This kind of exceptionalist claim for an American moral high ground was as unhelpful as it was untrue.

On the other side, the supporters of the Trump-era border policy, including the president himself, also gave the policy a false history. Trump insisted dozens of times that the Obama administration had also separated children from parents at the border. Except that it had not. Obama's administration took pride in the fact that it detained parents and children together. It also deployed other harsh tactics against immigrants and asylum seekers; there was a reason La Raza head Janet Murguía called him the deporter-in-chief. His administration expelled record numbers of immigrants in each of the first five years of his presidency, numbers even the Trump administration did not match. It housed unaccompanied minors at military bases, detained small children and their mothers in camps, urged expedited removal for unaccompanied children without asylum hearings, and even attempted to put children in solitary confinement to punish their mothers for engaging in a hunger strike to protest their seemingly endless detention.[5]

Trump's misstatement seemed designed to assail Democrats in order to defend his own party. What he was evading was that it was a Republican administration, George W. Bush's, that had first separated asylum-seeking parents from their children. The Bush administration, as it securitized its immigration and refugee policies after September 11, 2001, also stepped up its punishment of children. It opened the notoriously abusive T. Don Hutto Center in Texas, where children were allegedly beaten by guards, separated from their parents, and held indefinitely until the administration was forced to stop by an ACLU lawsuit.[6] Bush's predecessors—Reagan, the first Bush, and Clinton—vanished into the haze beyond the horizon of the conversation, although they, too, had put immigrant and refugee children in detention camps.

As a historian, I found the deliberate attempt to sow confusion and the failure of most people to be able to fill in the blanks or correct the misinformation in the public conversation extraordinarily frustrating—and surprising. For decades, I have been writing about events that were not exactly obscure: the taking of children under slavery, in Indian boarding schools, in to the foster care system as a punishment visited upon "welfare mothers," in anti-Communist civil wars in Latin America, in the moral panic about "crack babies," and in the context of mass incarceration. In 2012, in a book entitled *Somebody's Children,* I even wrote that taking the children of immigrants was the next crisis on the horizon, in the vain hope that a history book could somehow stop it.[7] Gore Vidal once called out the "United States of Amnesia," complaining about our collective inability to remember even recent history. "We learn nothing because we remember nothing," he said. But this was something more even than that. The national debate was clogged with both forgetting and deliberate disinformation.[8]

Meanwhile, Central America—the original home of nearly all of the asylum seekers targeted by the Trump administration to lose their children—was astonishingly missing almost entirely from the public conversation. A few remembered that the United States had been involved in fighting civil wars in the region for four decades in the middle of the twentieth century. But the wars' aftermath—the fact that criminal organizations, including Mexican drug cartels and Los Angeles gangs, had spent a decade taking over civic spaces in Guatemala, Honduras, and El Salvador, sowing violence in small towns and big cities alike—was nowhere to be heard in the US conversation. Neither was the role of US military aid in Plan Colombia in pushing the multibillion dollar drug industry from Colombia and the Caribbean to far more lucrative routes through Central America and Mexico, all culminating in the massive US market.[9]

Decades of intervention by international financial institutions, the World Bank, the InterAmerican Development Bank, donor nations, and nongovernmental organizations (NGOs) to shrink and replace the functions of federal states in Central America had, by design, dramatically weakened Central American governments in order to promote free markets. Power abhors a vacuum, and the cartels rushed in. In many places, local officials, the police, gangs, and international crime syndicates increasingly blurred into one. Murder rates skyrocketed for impoverished people at the hands of all these groups, as punishment for failing to pay "la renta"—extortion money—for the privilege of, say, driving a taxi or running a store, or for real or imagined loyalty to rivals. People of humble means— particularly women, queer and trans folk, youth, and children— fled in droves, seeking asylum in the United States and Mexico.[10]

We need a different conversation about the separation of children from their kin and caretakers. This conversation needs to be grounded in the histories of how we got to camps on the southwest border. These places—sometimes the literal land on which tent cities were erected—have a history of detaining other children. There is in this hemisphere a powerful racialized haunting: generation upon generation of children who have lost parents, and parents, children. Sometimes this has looked like preventing even the existence of children, as in the nineteenth century, when Asian American "bachelor societies" came to be the form of immigrant communities in the United States as US policies deliberately created an extreme gender imbalance to prevent the creation of the only kind of families that officials could imagine: heterosexual, married, nuclear. They wanted sojourners who returned home, not babies, not elders.[11]

More often, missing and disappeared children were the direct product of state repression. Separating children from parents is more than just another version of a larger mistreatment of immigrants and asylum seekers or enslaved and indigenous people. Taking people's children participates in a very brutal kind of political punishment, a symbolism—and reality—that is meant to be starkly tangible, crude, and cruel. By its own account, the Trump administration took the children of Central American asylum seekers in an effort to terrorize them into staying in Guatemala, Honduras, and El Salvador or withdrawing their petitions for asylum. The international asylum system functions only to the extent people are able to petition for refugee status.

We cannot understand child separation and detention without paying attention to what art historians call pentimento. Sometimes old paint on canvas becomes transparent, allowing a glimpse of another sketch or image underneath. A prone body becomes upright; a woman is revealed to have been taller and looking boldly

forward instead of demurely down at the floor. It is called *pentimento* because the artist "repented" and changed his or her mind.
History can be pentimento, something beneath the surface but giving shading and form to things happening decades, even centuries
later. The fight over the Trump administration's child separation
policy was haunted in this way. When journalists captured photos
of children reaching for their parents to put a face to the Trump
administration's child separation policy and Twitter users published abolitionists' images of enslaved mothers' babies being torn
from their arms, it is not too much to say that the past was being
activated—beyond living memory, yet vividly alive.

The past stalks the present, the ghost in the machine of memory. This is why history writing matters; it gives us ways to understand the specters already among us and to assemble tools to
transform our situation. Things change; the epidemic of child taking in the context of mass incarceration is quite different from separating refugees from their children at the border, but you cannot
track the differences without a map of what happened. Writing histories is also a defense against the efforts to implant false memo-
ries, the insistence that things happened that did not. The Obama
administration did not have a policy of separating children from
their parents. Telling history's story is a way to define it, to put limits on the infinite range of things that might have happened.

Taking children has been a strategy for terrorizing people for
centuries. There is a reason why "forcibly transferring children of
the group to another group" is part of international law's definition
of genocide.[12] It participates in the same sadistic political grammar
as the torture and murder that separated French Jewish children
from their parents under the Nazis and sought to keep enslaved
people from rebelling or to keep Native people from retaliating

against the Anglos who violated treaties to encroach on their land. Stripping people of their children attempts to deny them the opportunity to participate in the progression of generations into the future—to interrupt the passing down of languages, ways of being, forms of knowledge, foods, cultures. Like enslavement and the Indian Wars, the current efforts by the Trump administration to terrorize asylum seekers is white nationalist in ideology. It is an attempt to secure a white or Anglo future for a nation, a community, a place.

Part of the reason this theater of cruelty at the border worked was precisely because of its history. But that is also why it faltered, in the sense that it generated passionate and angry denunciations of, for example, immigrant child detention centers as "concentration camps."[13] We are primed by memory—by bits of stories handed down across generations, conversations, things read and half-remembered, formal histories, activists' words and actions, and lies and distortions—to react in certain ways to events in the present. It is not that the histories of child taking repeat or that one set of events parallels another; it is that the past is brought to life in the present. William Faulkner famously evoked this sense of history when he wrote, "The past is never dead. It's not even past."[14]

Yet for all the anger the policy engendered, the demand for it to end also failed. The administration found a work-around that continued to separate children from their kin and caregivers. Instead of saying that children were being taken because parents were applying for asylum, the Trump administration began saying that it was because they were "neglectful" or dangerous to their children, often with the flimsiest of evidence—a diaper not changed quickly enough, a past criminalized disruption that caused $5 in damage. This, too, was about a failure of historical memory, as opponents failed to mobilize sufficient opposition to the ugly history of the use of "child neglect" to take the children of insurgent communities of color. The administration was reprising a tactic used against welfare mothers, who faced a definition of "child neglect" in the 1950s and '60s that included having a common-law marriage, a boyfriend sleep over, or an "illegitimate" child. The Trump administration also used the Obama-era tactic of detaining immigrant children with their parents. It called parents criminal—either through a (failed) strategy of naming crossing outside regular border checkpoints to apply for asylum a crime, which courts repeatedly said it was not, or through the more successful efforts to call acts felonies that would be trivial administrative matters if people weren't migrants, like giving a wrong name to the police. Other immigrants and asylum seekers in fact had criminal records. In the absence of a strong movement to protect the parental rights of those who are or were incarcerated in the United States—immigrants or not—the administration's work-around, too, served to demobilize the movement to reunite refugee and immigrant children with those who cared for them. Opponents of the policy failed to understand the deep history of the criminalization of parents of color, the way foster care had become a state program of child-taking, and to realize how easily refugee parents could be transformed from harmed innocents to dangerous criminals.

While international and US law make much of the difference between immigrants and refugees, the Trump administration sought to collapse that distinction. Asylum for refugees was a product of the post–World War II response to German concentration camps, and states don't like it much. Unlike regular immigration, which can to some degree be metered according to the labor needs of a nation or an economy—changing laws to allow more immigrants when more workers are needed, fewer when they aren't—asylum is understood in international law as a right that follows from being persecuted for one's ethnicity, race, or political view. The model is Jews under the Nazis, and it was extended to groups like the Hmong in Laos, who were forced to flee because of their aid to the Americans in the war in Southeast Asia. The international asylum system, however, has never worked well in the United States (or a great many other places), and Cold War refugees from politically unpopular left-wing governments, like those from Castro's Cuba, have been massively favored over refugees from right-wing governments, like those who fled El Salvador in the 1980s. In the eighties and nineties, activists argued that race was a factor as well, with Reagan and the first Bush administration refusing Haitian refugees while accepting largely white Cubans. (Ironically, by 2019, many of the refugees sitting in Mexican shelters awaiting asylum hearings were Cuban. The favoritism did not last.[15]) Bill Clinton campaigned against the distinction that allowed Cubans but not Haitians to petition for asylum in US courts, arguing that everyone had a right to go before a judge to make their case. As soon as he was elected, however, he too began to insist that Haitians couldn't apply for asylum because they had not reached the land border of the United States, sending them instead to Guantánamo Bay, the US naval base in Cuba. Indeed, Clinton made a mockery of the entire notion of asylum, signing legislation that allowed "expedited" review of such claims, which ensured that people did not set foot in front of a judge but, rather, made their case to an INS (Immigration and Naturalization Service, later ICE) official whose expertise was enforcement, not the finer points of the law.[16] George W. Bush and Obama steadily expanded the use of expedited removal, to the point where, by 2013, it accounted for 44 percent of all deportations, compared with only 17 percent that went before a judge.[17]

Taking Children is a book about how we got here. It tells the stories of the detention of children at the US-Mexico border since the presidency of Ronald Reagan, and it also explores four other contexts in the past four centuries where the US state has either taken children as a tactic of terror or tacitly encouraged it. The first is the taking of Black children, beginning with the centuries of racial chattel slavery. Chapter 1 examines slavery and its aftermath through the decades after World War II, when white supremacists sought to dull the moral force of demands for the end of segregation by drawing attention to families and households they tried to paint as pathological: single mothers and their so-called illegitimate children relying on welfare. With the cooperation of the federal government, Southern cities and states put Black children in foster care as punishment for Black adults' activism against segregation. Chapter 2 investigates the taking of Native children, beginning in the closing decade of the Indian Wars, designed to quiet further revolt. Child taking continued through the emergence of movements for sovereignty and against tribal termination in the middle of the twentieth century. Again, states responded with an aggressive discourse about welfare and illegitimacy, resulting in removal of one in three Native kids from their homes. In response, from 1969 to 1978, tribal councils, the Association on American Indian Affairs, and Native newspapers, newsletters, and radio shows began a campaign for an Indian Child Welfare Act, calling the taking of children the latest episode in centuries of settler colonialism—and they won.

The third episode of children being ripped from their parents and communities I examine in the pages ahead unfolded in the anti-Communist wars in Latin America and their aftershocks. After reprising the better-known cases of disappeared children in

Argentina and the Southern Cone, chapter 3 tells the story of Central America: how governments in Guatemala and El Salvador took the children of suspected Communists and placed them for adoption or in institutions to an extent that is still being unearthed. In Honduras, the Reagan administration backed the Contras, a mercenary force seeking to overthrow the government of Nicaragua that happened also to be working with cocaine and marijuana traffickers from Colombia and Mexico, which set in motion much that followed. Within the United States, it sparked the "crack" epidemic, the subject of chapter 4. Crack cocaine justified the launching of a new campaign of harassment of drug *users,* not just dealers, including massive testing of Black pregnant women and taking their children into foster care in the name of protecting "crack babies." Native women were caught in a parallel "crisis" that sent them to jail for drinking during pregnancy and sent their children to foster care.

The expansion of cocaine consumption also vastly empowered and armed drug cartels, launching the events that would end in the waves of refugees and asylum seekers that arrived at the borders of the United States in significant numbers beginning in 2013, as we will see in chapter 5. Central America's Northern Triangle— Honduras, Guatemala, and El Salvador—had became increasingly unlivable for impoverished people, particularly youth, as the cartels and gangs claimed their neighbors in an ever-accelerating spiral of extortion, kidnapping, violence, and murder.

Taking Children is about a long history in the Americas of interrupting relations of care, kinship, and intimacy, and about how disrupted reproduction produces new regimes of racialized rightlessness. Child taking is, I am arguing, a counterinsurgency tactic has been used to respond to demands for rights, refuge, and respect by communities of color and impoverished communities, an effort to induce hopelessness, despair, grief, and shame.

This is not the whole story, however. There is also a fierce tradition of protesting this practice by the targeted communities and by those who acted in solidarity with them. Many people have found these policies repulsive and abhorrent, and activists, lawyers, and policy makers have sought to reform them. When we forget about the ways that governments have taken children, we also lose a powerful history of communities standing up against that practice, one that has often been quite successful, and provides resources for how to imagine doing it even now. Walter Benjamin wrote urgently about understanding the power of history in this way: "To articulate the past historically does not mean to recognize it 'the way it really was.' It means to seize hold of a memory as it flashes up at a moment of danger."[18] Benjamin's point was that we will never see the past as those who lived it saw it, never grasp it whole, but we don't have to be troubled by this partial vision. In his view, we need memory—history—for something else, for the way it is useful in the present, in a crisis (he was thinking of fascism).

This work is inspired by social movements' responses to crisis, including one that Black feminists in the United States have started calling reproductive justice. In recent years, we have seen new protest movements coalesce around missing children—sparked by the mothers (especially, but also fathers and grandparents) of unarmed Black and Latinx youth shot by police or vigilantes—Trayvon Martin, Michael Brown, Freddie Gray, Aiyana Stanley-Jones, Jessie Hernández, Tamir Rice, Rekia Boyd, Antwon Rose, and so many others.[19] In Mexico, a nationwide movement to end state- and police-sanctioned killing by criminal organizations coalesced around the demand by the parents of the young adults disappeared from the Ayotzinapa teacher-training school that they be returned alive. For forty years, some of the most effective opposition to the political right in Latin America has come from family members of the "disappeared," those arrested or kidnapped by police and paramilitary forces. While most opposition to right-wing governments was dismissed as the work of Communists and "terrorists," groups like the Comité de Madres Monsignor Romero (Comadres; Committee of Mothers) in El Salvador claimed moral authority by speaking on behalf of disappeared sons and daughters literally in the name of Archbishop (now Saint) Óscar Romero, who was killed by the military while celebrating mass in 1980. In the 1990s, despite Central America's truth commissions initially refusing to believe that disappeared children and infants were not dead, parents' groups like Pro Búsqueda began searching for, and sometimes finding, children who had been taken to orphanages and boarding schools—and sometimes adopted abroad. These parents, kin, and caregivers cast the war and the taking of children in a new light, while continuing to fight for a full reckoning for the crimes committed in the name of anti-Communism.

This is the legacy that we carried into the twenty-first century. In the United States, both Democratic and Republican administrations have sought to deter those who lawfully sought asylum by punishing parents *as parents* and their children. The US government sought to terrify people into not asking for a review of their asylum cases by putting their children in camps, even as it enacted policies that ensured they would come in ever greater numbers. In the pages that follow, this book builds out these stories about how taking children came to seem reasonable, a kind of pain that kept the peace or maintained the status quo, and how people again and again stood up to that violence. Taking children may be as American as a Constitution founded in slavery and the denial of basic citizenship rights to Native people, African Americans, and all women, but activists in every generation have also stood up and said it did not have to be.

1   Taking Black Children

For more than two centuries, children in the United States were sold away from their enslaved kin and caregivers. The decision by the Trump administration to follow this precedent and separate the children of parents and other relatives applying for asylum was more than an accidental similarity. There are real parallels. The architects of the border policy are hearkening back to the racial nationalism of a country that until at least 1865 could imagine itself as white. African, African-descended, and sometimes indigenous people who were resident in it were held in slavery. Only "free White persons," in the words of the 1790 naturalization law, were guaranteed the right to become citizens if they immigrated. Then, as in the twenty-first century, taking children was part of a broader effort to terrorize those who resisted regimes of dehumanization to keep down those whom the state was trying to keep ineligible for citizenship. To understand the policy of separating children from parents at the border, we first need to attend to the way the practice worked to terrorize enslaved people in the first three hundred years of US history and how those who fought to abolish slavery turned it against slaveholders.

Abolitionists made the dehumanizing practice of separating children from their parents a key weapon in their antislavery arsenal. They repeatedly told the stories of mothers and children separated—just as immigration activists did in 2018 and 2019. The association between enslavement and losing one's kin or one's children was so firmly welded together in the antislavery imagination that when Congress began the formal, legal process to end slavery with the passage of the Thirteenth Amendment, Republican Senator James Harlan of Iowa spoke for it by saying that slavery was responsible for "the abolition practically of the parental relation, robbing the offspring of the care and attention of his parents, severing a relation which is universally cited as the emblem of the relation sustained by the Creator to the human family. And yet, according to the matured judgement of these slave States, this guardianship of the parent over his own children must be abrogated to secure the perpetuity of slavery."[1]

For decades, abolitionists reminded people throughout the English-speaking world and beyond that enslavement meant children separated from those who cared for them, particularly their mothers. In etchings, pamphlets, slave narratives, newspapers, and sermons, abolitionists tried to ensure that no one could turn away from wrenching scenes of weeping mothers and children reaching for each other as they were parted by heartless slaveholders and slave traders, and this, perhaps more than anything else they did, brought enslavement to the conscience of the nation.

The extent of the taking of children should not lull us into believing that people did not think it was wrong. On the contrary, when slave owners defended themselves in relationship to the images of weeping mothers separated from their children, they often did so by denying that such things happened, suggesting that even they understood perfectly clearly that it was wrong and cruel. What distinguished this era was not a failure to understand the heartbreak of child separation. It was that those with power, government and slave owners, found that pain to be a reasonable path to putting down rebellion. Taking children wounded people fiercely, and it was meant to hurt and terrify them into submission.

Separating mothers from their children was so foundational to slavery that Saidiya Hartman titled her extraordinary book on the long history of kidnapping, slaving, and enslavement in Europe, Africa, and the Americas *Lose Your Mother*.[2] Historian Martha S. Jones underscores the terror that losing children was meant to—and did—instill in people in North America, where the eventual banning of the slave trade from Africa meant that women born in the New World often survived to, and were encouraged to, reproduce: "Among the tools of coercion employed by slaveholders, as they sought to render enslaved people compliant, was the threat of separating families," writes Jones. "Historians of slavery emphasize that no threat . . . was more potent and more feared than the threat that reluctant, resistant, or otherwise non-compliant slaves would be sold. Instilling the fear of separation might be used as a weapon."[3]

Indeed, the threat that children could be taken from kin and caregivers was one of the "essential features" of enslavement, as the sociologist and Black radical theorist W.E.B. DuBois wrote a generation after slavery's end.[4] It was what made slavery different from other kinds of unfree labor like indenture in the United States; enslavement was the only condition that entailed the possibility of one's children being sold. In 1662, the Virginia colony enacted a law stating that the status of an enslaved woman's children would follow that of their mother and that therefore they would be enslaved themselves. This principle made slavery racial, and indeed made race itself into a category that carried a pretense of heredity, as if it were something other than a political category. Selling children thus became a source of cash, a kind of property that white owners could use to settle debts, pass on to heirs, or use to enrich themselves. As many abolitionists pointed out, it also made sexual violence against enslaved women profitable, enabling rape's offspring to be sold. It was a deviation from the major legal traditions that governed the Americas, including English common law, which held that children followed the status of their fathers.[5]

Freed people spoke and wrote about the threat of losing children, or of children losing a mother, constantly. In 1851 the itinerant preacher Sojourner Truth gave a speech that we still quote about her experience when she was enslaved in New York, saying at a woman's rights congress, "I have borne thirteen children and seen most all sold off into slavery, and when I cried out with a mother's grief, none but Jesus heard." She was expecting that those in the room with experience in the abolition movement—and there were many; even Frederick Douglass was there—would be familiar with such stories. Sojourner Truth, in fact, had spent years fighting for those children, becoming the first Black woman in New York State to successfully sue an owner to force him to honor a promise to free her child, even after he had sold the boy to a slave owner in Alabama.[6]

Slave narratives—the huge genre of autobiography written and dictated by people who were formerly enslaved, running to thousands of texts—dwelt often on the question of child taking. It was in these books and pamphlets that African Americans held in slavery theorized the dehumanizing effects of separating children from parents and its role in keeping enslaved people in subjection. Frederick Douglass's *Narrative of the Life of Frederick Douglass, An American Slave,* written in the rich prose of a brilliant orator, tells a moving story of the refusal of enslavement first through literacy, then escape; it is credited with inspiring the abolitionist movement and has been read by generations as a foundational American story. It begins with his separation from his mother, Harriet Bailey, "before I knew her as my mother." Douglass suggests he was probably cared for by her for some of his first year of life but was then passed into the care of an elderly woman who had formerly worked in fields as a slave, because "it is a common custom, in the part of Maryland from which I ran away, to part children from their mothers at a very early age." Thereafter, he saw her only "four or five times in my life," when she would walk the twelve miles between the plantations where they worked to lie next to him in the night. When he was seven, he said, "I received the tidings of [my mother's] death with much the same emotions I should probably have felt at the death of a stranger."[7] Here, as throughout his autobiography, Douglass underscores that slaves are not born, they are made. He was made to understand his nakedness in the world, the absence of sheltering kin, his subjection to the will of others. He locates his mother's absence as foundational to his becoming aware of himself as a slave. In a different context, Saidiya Hartman writes:

> Douglass establishes the centrality of violence to the making of the slave and identifies it as an original generative act equivalent to the statement "I was born." The passage through the blood-stained gate is an inaugural moment in the formation of the enslaved. In this regard, it is a primal scene. By this I mean that the terrible spectacle dramatizes the origin of the subject and demonstrates that to be a slave is to be under the brutal power and authority of another.[8]

Here, Hartman is talking about a scene where Douglass watches his Aunt Hester being whipped and the terror it instilled in him. But she could just as well be talking about the scene of separation from his mother that immediately preceded that whipping and the terrible lessons visited on him and other children who were deprived of parents. By such means, enslaved children and their mothers were instructed by slave owners that they were not to be treated as people, the subject of the care and work that passes cultures down from one generation to another, but instead were bodies, flesh, cultivated for the labor they could do.[9] Still, theirs was a body that could remember, dread, and learn fearful lessons from loss.

Another slave narrative, Harriet Jacobs's *Incidents in the Life of a Slave Girl,* has a somewhat more fortunate story to tell. Jacobs, too, sees taking children as a crucial part of what makes it possible to turn someone into a slave. Jacobs's narrative has been read and reread by Black feminist scholars in recent decades for its ability to imagine a "loophole of retreat," a space of freedom within slavery, offering a prefigurative politics of freedom and self-possession that also speaks to the disappointments, in the end, of a freedom that, while vastly better than the condition of slavery, still was no Jubilee.[10] Jacobs narrates the presence of children and family members to each other as central to how the project of producing the subjectivity of a slave can fail. "I was born a slave; but I never knew it till six years of happy childhood had passed away." She writes of living under one roof with her mother, father, and brother in a home her grandmother owned for those six years. "I was so fondly shielded that I never dreamed I was a piece of merchandise, trusted to them for safe keeping, and liable to be demanded of them at any moment."[11] In these lines she sets in motion her notion of a loophole of retreat: a space of refuge where it is possible to think oneself outside the grim realities of being, legally, chattel, someone's property. It is only a partial kind of freedom, constrained by the possibility of the "demand" of slaveholders, but real.

As an adult, Jacobs's relationship to her own children emerges along these same lines; she tries and only partially succeeds at shielding them from their own condition of slavery. They are sold away from her, a possibility so awful that her grandmother faints from her encounter with it, but the slave trader is a subterfuge organized by Jacobs, and the children are sold to their father, a white doctor who frees them and sends them to live with their grandmother. By this time, however, Jacobs has "escaped." Having listened to the admonitions not to leave her children without a mother for years, she finally was unable to bear her condition any longer. However, she made it only as far as her grandmother's attic. While just a few trusted friends knew where she was, she could get no farther from the watchful eye of a master who wished to make her his unwilling sexual partner through rape. For seven years, she occupied a tiny space, barely able to move her limbs— but by pressing an eye to a knot in the wood, she could see her children. She had not lost them, yet she had; they were free, but they were removed from their mother like enslaved children. Although they were separated by only a few feet of air above their heads, they did not know where she was, and so it might as well have been a continent.

The book concludes on this note, too, capturing how her loophole of retreat works as a not-quite freedom for mothers and children. Jacobs finally escaped to the North with her son and daughter, and a sympathetic white friend bought her freedom from her master's daughter—against Jacobs's wishes, because she refused utterly to concede that she could be property. For all that was wrong with her purchase, though, freedom was sweeter than enslavement or the dangers of fugitivity. "Reader, my story ends with freedom; not in the usual way, with marriage. I and my children are now free! We are as free from the power of slaveholders as are the white people of the north." Recalling the political struggles against wage slavery, she adds, "though that, according to my ideas, is not saying a great deal, it is a vast improvement in my condition." Still, Jacobs, recalling all the ways her and her children's lives had been transformed by the fact that her grandmother owned her own house, hastened to point to the inadequacies of her financial circumstances—the poverty that followed her and so many people out of enslavement, as the fruits of their labor were taken by their former owners. "The dream of my life is not yet realized. I do not sit with my children in a home of my own. I still long for a hearthstone of my own, however humble." This compact assessment of the politics of wages and the poverty of unpropertied freedom was framed in her next sentence in terms of what can be passed down to a next generation: "I wish it for my children's sake far more than for my own." Inheritance of both parental care and property was crucial to her understanding of freedom.

It was not just slave narratives that put the question of children's separation from their family at the center. Harrowing accounts of child taking circulated in abolitionist pamphlets passed around the North. Silas Stone wrote about this scene from Charleston, South Carolina, in 1807:

[There] was a stage built, on which a mother with eight children were placed, and sold at auction. . . . The sale began with the old-est child, who, being struck off to the highest bidder, was taken from stage or platform by the purchaser, and led to his wagon and stowed away, to be carried into the country; the second and third were also sold, and so on until seven of the children were torn from their mother, while her discernment told her they were to be separated probably forever, causing in that mother the most agonizing sobs and cries, in which the children seemed to share. The scene beggars description.[12]

Consider too the famous image from Harriet Beecher Stowe's *Uncle Tom's Cabin* captioned "The Separation of the Mother and Child" (figure 1). Images like these were staples of abolitionist literature. Slaveholders' attempts to persuade white people in the North—where slavery had been gradually ended—that enslavement was an essentially benevolent institution outraged abolitionists. Abolitionists insisted that slavery was wrong and dehumanizing, not just because of the lash, rape, and other kinds of torture, not just because of the horrors of the Middle Passage, the treatment of people as property, or the denial of freedom, but because separating mothers from their babies was cruel. Arguably, it was these images more than any others that brought the moral crisis of slavery to the fore and enabled abolitionists to demand its end in the context of the Civil War. To speak of child separation under slavery was to be against it. Together with stories about the rape of enslaved women by white men, often their owners,[13] stories about the selling of children away from their families, especially their mothers, animated abolitionist literature.

Slave owners did not so much defend the practice of child separation as deny it, although some, like proslavery legal scholar Thomas R. R. Cobb, were brazen enough to claim that the Black mother "suffers little by separation" from her children, claiming

FIGURE 1. *The Separation of the Mother and Child* by George Cruikshank. From *Uncle Tom's Cabin* by Harriet Beecher Stowe.

that she lacked maternal feelings.[14] More often, though, slavery's defenders sought to deny that child separation happened and to portray slavery as a benevolent institution in which owners provided food and shelter for African and African-descended people in exchange for work from the able-bodied members of their families. It was better than the poorhouses in the North, they argued, where immigrants and other poor people wound up when they could no longer work to support themselves. "I hold that in the present state of civilization, where two races of different origin, and distinguished by color, and other physical differences, as well as intellectual, are brought together, the relation now existing in the slaveholding States between the two, is, instead of an evil, a good–a positive good," said John C. Calhoun, Andrew Jackson's vice president and then senator from South Carolina, in a famous speech from the Senate floor. He continued:

"I may say with truth, that in few countries so much is left to the share of the laborer, and so little exacted from him, or where there is more kind attention paid to him in sickness or infirmities of age. Compare his condition with the tenants of the poor houses in the more civilized portions of Europe—look at the sick, and the old and infirm slave, on one hand, in the midst of his family and friends, under the kind superintending care of his master and mistress, and compare it with the forlorn and wretched condition of the pauper in the poorhouse."[15]

This position grew ever more difficult to maintain as slavery was relentlessly hammered for twenty years by abolitionists' images of children being torn from their mothers. So, in the 1850s, Southern states began to outlaw taking infants from their mothers, seeing it as a limited reform that would enable their states to continue to protect the institution of slavery.[16]

When Congress ultimately abolished slavery after the Civil War with the Thirteenth Amendment, child separation was, as we have seen, part of what was on their minds. Indeed, it was frequently invoked. Republican Senator Henry Wilson of Massachusetts, for example, said: "When this amendment to the Constitution shall be consummated . . . the sharp cry of the agonizing hearts of severed families will cease to vex the weary ear of the nation. . . . Then the sacred rights of nature, the hallowed family relation of . . . parent and child, will be protected by the guardian spirit of that law which makes sacred alike the proud homes and lowly cabins of freedom."[17]

When slavery was made into an issue of separating children from their mothers, then, abolitionists were powerfully successful in insisting that it had to be ended, that it was a moral and spiritual evil and had to be opposed.

Reconstruction

Despite the hopes of the drafters of the Thirteenth Amendment, Reconstruction did not mean the end of child taking. Regimes of apprenticeship for Black children often meant separating them from their families. For many African Americans in the south, labor systems changed little from the era of slavery even to the 1950s. Children went to work very young, usually between the ages of 5 and 8. Immediately after emancipation, some former slave owners apprenticed children, generally from 12 to 14 years old, sometimes as young as 6, insisting that their families could not support them (while leaving them with the problem of supporting younger children, often destroying the economic viability of the family as a whole by removing potential wage earners).[18] As with so much about the conditions of Black freedom, the continued loss of children was crushingly disappointing. "We were delighted when we heard that the Constitution set us all free, but God help us, our condition is bettered but little: free ourselves but deprived of our children. . . . It was on their account we desired to be free," said one freedwoman in Maryland. A freedman from Alabama wrote, "I think very hard of the former owners for trying to keep my blood when I know that slavery is dead."[19] Even the Freedmen's Bureau itself apprenticed Black children whom it decided were orphans, indenturing them rather than placing them with their free extended family members.[20]

Some African Americans moved out of the South, and others bought their own land, shops, and wagons. Many, though, when

Reconstruction drew to a close, found themselves in a substantially similar situation to that of slavery: working in agriculture, often on the same plantations, with the police patrolling for "vagrants"— even children—who could be arrested for idleness and put with other prisoners on a chain gang. The Ku Klux Klan forcefully ended the hopeful promises of Reconstruction with a campaign of terror, lynching, and mob violence against African Americans who tried to vote, who owned businesses or land. For half a century, they forced many Black families back to work planting and picking crops for white owners. Black workers—"free" and prisoners alike— often picked cotton under the shadow of guards with guns.[21] Under such a system, Black children continued to be separated from their parents, including in prisons and on chain gangs.

Taking Black Children (Again) at Midcentury

In the early twentieth century, some African Americans began the Great Migration north, hoping to leave behind the regimes of share-cropping, the chain gang, and child taking. For a moment during the war mobilization of the 1940s, many Black mothers found good jobs in war industry factories in the North, while fathers often were drafted or volunteered for the military. However, the end of the war brought rising Black unemployment, as Black women in particular but also Black men were a fired as part of a policy to make way for returning (white) soldiers. As prosperity generally increased for whites in the postwar period, through GI Bill education, subsidized mortgages, and the building of new housing in the suburbs, Black people, generally excluded from this government largesse, found their economic situation little changed. The rising tide lifted only some boats—and poverty, once shared by many whites and immigrants, was increasingly racialized. The situation was particularly acute for Black single mothers. Those jobless mothers who were also widowed, divorced, or separated found themselves in increasingly precarious circumstances, often in the North or West and far from kin, insecurely housed and fed. Some turned to Aid to Dependent Children—welfare—to feed their kids. Those who had stayed in the South through the Depression were less likely to get access to welfare, and when they got it, they faced even more contempt and disparagement. Being on welfare also opened households up to losing their children in new ways. If women were "on welfare," local officials impugned their sexual morality and their parenting and threatened to find that they were keeping an "unsuitable home" in which to raise their children, opening up Black households to new ways of losing their children.

Welfare programs for mothers and children had been a political football since their inception as mothers' pensions in 1909. The United States has never liked giving cash money to poor folks who might be unworthy, and women were potentially the worst. Critics charged that mothers' pensions were just a reward for immoral behavior: failed marriages, the inability to manage money in a thrifty way, drunkenness, laziness, carrying on with a man, or even having an illegitimate child. Reformers who sought to keep impoverished children out of orphanages and in their own homes dealt with this political problem by agreeing that only those women who kept a "suitable home"—only "fit" mothers—would receive benefits. (It is remarkable how enduring these campaigns proved to be; today, the only time we regularly use the eugenic language of "unfit" is in connection with parents, usually an "unfit mother.") Chaste widows fared best under suitable-home rules, as the only ones who were apparently blameless for their predicament.

They also had to be white. A 1931 study found that 96 percent of welfare recipients were white, and the majority of Black recipients were in only two states, California and Ohio. Only two Black mothers in all of the South received payments—one in North Carolina, the other in Florida.[22] A welfare field supervisor in the late 1930s explained that the goal of withholding welfare from Black mothers was to keep them in the workforce rather than home caring for their own children:

> The number of Negro cases is few due to the unanimous feeling on the part of the staff and board that there are more work opportunities for Negro women and to their intense desire not to interfere with local labor conditions. That attitude that "they have always gotten along," and that "all they'll do is have more children" is definite. . . . There is hesitance on the part of lay boards to advance too rapidly over the thinking of their own communities, which see no reason why the employable Negro mother should not continue her usually sketchy seasonal labor or indefinite domestic service rather than receive a public assistance grant.[23]

This unnamed field supervisor was unusually blunt in explaining what everyone knew: that the push coming from the federal government to end discrimination against African Americans in welfare was a problem for the South, because the region had counted on Black women's labor in the fields and in other people's homes for centuries.

In the post–World War II period, welfare for mothers and children expanded and was renamed as Aid to Dependent Children. As funding for the program increased, however, so did the political backlash against it, with state after state opening investigations into fraud, charging that Democratic administrations from Roosevelt to Truman had overseen an expansive empire of indolent welfare cheats. One critic of these 1950s efforts to prove fraud noted, "There have been many demands for further humiliation of welfare recipients, apparently based on a strong conviction that the poor are carrying out some sort of conspiracy in a depressing world where vast numbers of chiselers and slug-a-beds buy not only whisky but automobiles with their relief money."[24] Especially but hardly exclusively in the South, the women suspected of immorality and fraud were likely to be Black.

The 1950s and '60s also saw an irruption of Black rebellion against the Jim Crow caste system in the South and its less legally formalized counterparts in the North, but this too was met with new regimes of child taking. Children were in the front lines of this insurgency, not only as participants in marches and demonstrations but also in the legal strategy to end segregation. For decades, the NAACP Legal Defense Fund cast around for a case that would overturn Jim Crow segregation in public accommodations— in restaurants, on trains and busses, and at swimming pools, amusement parks, and other public places. The NAACP lawyers settled on schools and children. On the one hand, this was a stroke of brilliance, shifting the conversation from Black men like Homer Plessy (of *Plessy v. Ferguson*, the 1896 case in which the Supreme Court had affirmed segregation), whom white supremacists claimed were criminals who menaced white women—seemingly by the simple fact of being Black men. *Brown v. Board of Education* changed the focus to small and unthreatening third graders like Linda Brown, who only asked to go to her neighborhood school.[25] Black children dramatically and forcefully become some of the most visible warriors of the Black freedom movement, as participants in marches and demonstrations and especially in desegregating schools.

At the state level, white resistance to desegregation often punished the children who were most vulnerable—those on welfare. The more African Americans fought for civil rights, the more officials cut welfare. US Senator Robert Byrd, who coined the term "massive resistance" (to school desegregation) also gave us "welfare abuse." He argued in the Senate that 60 percent of welfare cases were fraudulent, offering evidence that women on welfare were working—as domestics, child minders, and prostitutes—and that they had men ("paramours") in their homes and beds who should be supporting them and their "illegitimate" children.[26]

In the years between 1957 and 1967, the city of Birmingham decreased its total expenditures on welfare from $31,000 to a mere $12,000 a year.[27] These were, not incidentally, the years of Black Birmingham's rebellion; of police chief Bull Connor;[28] of the Children's Crusade that brought down Connor when he turned dogs and firehoses on little kids on the nightly news; of the Klan bombing of the Sixteenth Street Baptist Church on Youth Sunday, killing four little girls;[29] and of their contemporary Angela Davis, living in a neighborhood where so many Black businesses were bombed by white supremacists that it was known as "dynamite hill."[30]

In 1954, within days of the Supreme Court ordering the desegregation of schools in *Brown v. Board of Education,* the Mississippi state legislature attached a rider to an appropriations bill cutting children off welfare if their mothers failed to keep a suitable home. "Listed among the recognized functions of the family are the passing on from one generation to another of the special ways of life that make up the civilization of the nation," the statute read, reverting to an old language of civilization and savagery to characterize the unsuitability of African American women's and children's homes. "Parents are expected to help each child to develop moral and social standards through example, training, and education." It went on to outlaw common-law marriage—poor people's marriage—as "an illicit relationship or promiscuity."[31]

This campaign to punish the most impoverished Black households for the NAACP's desegregation work caused real suffering. Between 1954 and 1960, according to the *Clarion Ledger-Jackson Daily News,* Mississippi cut 8,392 children off welfare, almost all of them Black, because they or a sibling were illegitimate. The NAACP cried foul and insisted that there was a political agenda at work. In the Delta, an NAACP representative claimed that among Southern whites, "The white landlords are being overheard to say now more and more when Negroes ask for assistance, 'Let the NAACP support you this winter.'"

At the height of the struggles over school desegregation and voting rights, the abrupt decline in welfare eligibility—and the resulting increase in child taking—was no coincidence. The state legislature sought several things when they cut children from the welfare rolls: to drive Black mothers and children out of Mississippi and to Northern cities and to prevent "bastard" children and their siblings from attending school. Certainly the legislators meant to threaten mothers who had children while on welfare with being cut off and even facing legal action for welfare fraud, because, welfare officials said, if they got pregnant, their children had a "substitute father," which made them ineligible for payments.[32] They also sought to shame the respectable civil rights folks in their Sunday best by pointing to promiscuous mothers and illegitimate children.

The reason given for taking children from insurgent Black communities was the problem of illegitimacy, but that fooled no one. A study conducted by several colleges in Mississippi in 1957 found only three white families among the 323 they contacted that had been cut off welfare for reasons of illegitimacy. They also found that being denied welfare grants (alongside the larger context of Black poverty, poor health care, and substandard housing in Mississippi) had left mothers and children in desperate straits. For example,

> Viola is in dreadful circumstances. . . . The house is the nearest thing to nothing this interviewer has ever seen human beings live in. Holes . . . planks off . . . windows out. Viola had a rusted bunkbed with fertilizer sacks sewed together and filled with a thin layer of cotton for a mattress. . . . The children wore rags and no shoes. . . . She said she had not been able to get any work in four months. They have existed on what "one and another" gave them."[33]

Another case study noted the sexual violence that resulted in the birth of some of the "illegitimate" children that the "massive resistance" apparatus of Mississippi was condemning so forcefully: "This former recipient of ADC is in very severe circumstances. . . . Her house is located in the middle of a cotton patch, and as is typical of such houses, it is old, crudely constructed, and rotting away. Seven of her children are known to be illegitimate. The oldest child, one of the two legitimate ones, was raped at school and now has an illegitimate child of her own." The report goes on to note extensive health issues that the mother and children endured. But just as Viola had help from the Black community ("one and another"), the mother in the second case was not abandoned. The trouble was just that everybody around her was painfully impoverished, too. Although she and her ex-husband were separated, he, a sharecropper, planted and worked a crop for her and the children. As the caseworker noted, "When the mother was in the hospital, some of her colored neighbors sent her an occasional fifty cents. . . . She was not so worried about clothing [because her sister sent her hand-me-downs], but when the children cry for food, that does bother her."[34]

The Mississippi legislature actually tried, but failed, to enact even more draconian measures, threatening to sterilize Black women in the civil rights era in the name of illegitimacy and resistance to segregation. Its efforts were stopped only by nationwide publicity by another civil rights group, the Student Nonviolent Coordinating Committee. Every year from 1958 to 1964, the state's legislature debated bills on sterilization and illegitimacy. The 1964 bill, for example, made bearing an illegitimate child a felony, punishable by sterilization or three years in the state penitentiary. The sponsor of the 1958 bill claimed that "during the calendar year 1957, there were born out of wedlock in Mississippi, more than 7,000 negro children, and about 200 white children. The negro woman, because of child welfare assistance, [is] making . . . a business . . . of giving birth to illegitimate children. . . . The purpose of my bill was to try to stop, or slow down, such traffic at its source." Some said the legislation was the work of the White Citizens' Councils, founded to stop desegregation.[35] In floor debate in the state legislature on the 1964 bill, one state legislator argued that "when the cutting starts, [Negroes will] head for Chicago."[36] Voting rights activist Fannie Lou Hamer, founder of the Mississippi Freedom Democratic Party, famously called sterilization "the Mississippi appendectomy," an operation targeting Black women.

Within a handful of years, five other states—Georgia, Florida, Virginia, Arkansas, and Texas—followed Mississippi's lead, using welfare and child taking to respond to the civil rights "crisis." In Arkansas in 1957, at the height of the school desegregation fight at Central High School in Little Rock, Governor Orville Faubus enacted a "suitable home" rule to remove Black children from their mothers on welfare. He argued that ADC "rewarded sin." Looking back at his administration in 1960, he proudly asserted that "8,000 illegitimate children were taken off the welfare rolls during my term of office" as a result of the suitable home regulation.[37]

In addition to the fact that welfare offices were exclusively targeting Black single mothers, it was also true that having an "illegitimate" child was a fate that white women could avoid much more readily than Black women could. In the 1950s, according to one federal government estimate, about 70 percent of white "illegitimate" children were given up for adoption, many through unwed mothers' homes, but only between 3 and 5 percent of nonwhite children were. Virtually no agencies would accept African American children for adoption, and no unwed mothers' homes welcomed pregnant Black girls and women, although the National Urban League, for a time, ran a demonstration project that showed that Black babies were adoptable.[38]

"Voluntary Placement"

Florida and Tennessee were the first states to explicitly rely on taking children to punish Black women for the civil rights rebellion. In 1959 in Tennessee and 1960 in Florida, state legislatures enacted new "suitable home" statutes. In Florida, common-law marriages previously recognized by the state became "illicit relationships," and "illegal cohabitation"; children conceived with another partner while a woman was legally married, previously considered to be the legal children of the husband, were retroactively made "illegitimate." Both statutes relied on case workers to pressure mothers to "voluntarily" release their children to a relative if they were denied welfare. If mothers refused, their cases were referred to juvenile court for neglect proceedings. Florida conducted a study in 1960 of the effects of the law. From it, we learn that state welfare workers challenged the suitability of 13,000 families; of these, only 9 percent were white, even though white families made up 39 percent of the total caseload. In the first year of the policy, 2,908 were asked to relinquish their children to relatives (while a similar number were given trial periods to reform the "moral environment").

To the surprise of white welfare workers, reared on the old, self-justifying belief from slavery times that Black women had little maternal feeling and that it was customary among African Americans to circulate children among relatives, only 186 families of the 13,000 the Florida law targeted gave in to the pressure to relinquished their children. Welfare workers may have believed that many mothers would be relieved to be free of the desperate situations they were in, but on the contrary, 3,000 "voluntarily" withdrew from the welfare program rather than have their "suitability" evaluated and run the risk of losing their children. Welfare workers reported that mothers responded to the new rules about sexual morals with anger, hysteria, and despair; that they felt it was an invasion of privacy and hearkened back to an "old-fashioned and unrealistic attitude toward adult morality," as one woman bravely told a caseworker. Even more, most simply had no idea how to feed or clothe their children without help from the men they loved—and neither did welfare workers.[39] While we have fewer records of what happened in Tennessee, the "voluntary relinquishment" program worked the same way: mothers could keep their children by withdrawing their application for ADC. While the situation in these states was dire for the families involved, the policies generated very little national attention.

All of that changed in Louisiana. When confronted with a court order to desegregate schools in New Orleans in 1960, which allowed four little Black girls to attend first grade in two schools in the then-white Lower Ninth Ward, Louisiana governor Jimmie Davis and the legislature went into special session and announced a "segregation package" of new laws designed to stop the order and terrorize African Americans. Nearly all the bills were immediately struck down by a judge, but a "suitable-home" rule that would cut 23,000 "illegitimate" children from the welfare rolls was allowed to stand, following as it did seven other states in which the Social Security Administration had permitted such plans. This was nearly a third of the state's welfare caseload, and the overwhelming majority of those targeted were Black. Only 5 percent of those affected were white. Among the state's Black residents, the proposal was clearly understood as retaliation for school desegregation. If Black Louisianans wanted to rewrite a social contract based on patronage, in which they accepted second-class status in exchange for (very inadequate) charity from on high, they were going to pay. They could try to win an education equivalent to that of whites, or they could receive the benevolence of the white power structure in the form of a welfare check of about $23 a month per child (worth $200 in 2019 dollars)—which is to say, not enough to keep body and soul together. An African American child welfare worker described the legislature's mood as "vindictive." According to her, the Black community absolutely understood that legislators were intent on hurting them in retaliation for school desegregation.[40]

Even though the Louisiana law did not specifically require welfare workers to urge foster care for the children of those who lost their aid—as the Tennessee and Florida laws did—that was the effect. One Black child welfare worker remembered forty years later that

> we would get referrals [to take children from their homes and put them into foster care] after public assistance cut them off, and they weren't able to feed their kids. I remember several families who were referred—the women had to give up their kids if they couldn't care for them. I never removed kids from their families because of poverty—but I know other workers who did. I remember one woman who loved her kids. She didn't want to give them up, but ended up having to. Families didn't understand why this was happening. I am haunted by a woman who had to give her child up. The resolution for many families was that they gave their children away.[41]

Suitable-home laws may have sounded like a statement of community morality to some, but their practical effect was to take children, coercively if necessary, and to try to break the will of resistant Black communities and turn people against one another.

Through the work of activists in New Orleans, cutting "illegitimate" children off welfare in Louisiana became a national and international scandal in a way previous states' efforts did not. Cutting off children to punish them for school desegregation efforts became known simply as the "Louisiana incident." While Governor Davis was slandering welfare mothers as "prostitutes" and "promiscuous women," New Orleans Urban League president J. Harvey Kerns was mobilizing national and international networks to feed their children so they could keep their families together and support the civil rights effort.[42] He travelled to New York and asked the annual National Urban League convention for help. This event, on the occasion of the Urban League's fiftieth anniversary was particularly well attended, with the Rev. Dr. Martin Luther King Jr. speaking, and it launched a nationwide campaign for the welfare mothers Louisiana had cut off: Operation Feed the Babies. Food, clothing, and cash flowed to New Orleans, with Illinois welfare workers donating almost $4,000. Locally, the Urban League coordinated dozens of groups, helping Louisiana's Black churches (especially the Baptist Emergency Relief Committee) and community groups, including local Black businesses and labor, that were mobilized to feed people. At its height, the effort helped three hundred people a day and distributed thousands of pounds of food. Local activists brought groceries, meals, clothing, and rent to those who had lost their welfare assistance.[43] Black newspapers around the United States spread the word about hungry children " 'cry[ing] for food' in New Orleans" in response to the governor and legislature's "segregation package."[44] Kerns issued appeals for assistance to the federal government. Emphasizing the widespread suffering, Kerns threatened to approach the United Nations if US funds did not materialize. He also enlisted the support of Moise Cahn, former president of the National Council of Jewish Women, to launch a publicity campaign for Operation Feed the Babies.[45] In a move that was particularly designed to embarrass President Eisenhower, who was refusing to get involved because segregation was a "states' rights" issue, a group of white councilwomen from Newcastle upon Tyne, England, airlifted food, money, and clothing to the "starving babies" of New Orleans. In the state, the Urban League, social welfare activists, and black church and community groups pressured Louisiana's legislature to reinstate the "innocent children" to the welfare rolls.

The outcry had an effect. The federal government was paying attention to school desegregation and was not amenable to seeing the state flout the federal court's school desegregation order by punishing the local Black community, nor was it appreciating the widespread scrutiny of hungry African American children in Louisiana. It responded with a hearing by the Department of Health, Education, and Welfare (HEW) to consider whether the state's suitable-home provision was permissible under federal rules. The ACLU and the national Urban League filed amicus briefs asking for a finding that it was not in conformity, and so did the American Legion, the Child Welfare League of America, and others.

Unfortunately, they lost. HEW, having allowed virtually every other Southern state and Michigan to pass suitable-home rules, could not find a reason to stop Louisiana's. Still, Arthur Flemming, the head of HEW, expressed regret, acknowledging that this measure was, in intent and in effect, racially discriminatory. The following day, Flemming—as a member of an outgoing Republican administration about to be replaced by John F. Kennedy's appointees—announced a new rule that took a well-meaning but ultimately disastrous step. It instructed the states that, going forward, welfare programs could not limit their benefits to "suitable homes" without taking appropriate measures to rehabilitate the home. If the home could not be "rehabilitated," state welfare programs would be required to remove the children. In a move subsequently made into law, Flemming provided federal funds to put children in foster care.[46] Almost immediately, Louisiana and Mississippi enacted statutes, borrowing heavily from Florida's, encouraging "voluntary" placement or referring those who did not volunteer to relinquish their children to juvenile court, where judges could take them from their families and place them in foster care.[47]

With this new rule, HEW gave city and state official license to engage in the wholesale terrorizing of unmarried Black mothers. In subsequent decades, tens of thousands of Black families lost their children to foster care, and the federal government largely paid for it.[48] These policies were not limited to the South, either. Outside New York City, the city of Newburgh sought to displace Black residents and reduce welfare costs by taking children, issuing rules that "prior to certifying or continuing any Aid to Dependent Children cases a determination shall be made as to the home environment. If it is not satisfactory the city shall take such children and place them in foster homes in place of welfare aid to family adults."[49] With federal funding and a mandate to ensure that homes that received Aid to Dependent Children were "suitable," foster care expanded dramatically. In 1961 alone, 150,000 children were placed in out-of-home care.[50] So many Black children entered the child welfare system in the next decade that some described it as "the 'browning' of child welfare in America."[51] In 1960, only about 20 percent of Black children in care had been put into orphanages, group homes, or foster care—54 percent of Black children in out-of-home care were in juvenile detention, in contrast to 20 percent of white children.[52] While federal officials decried "the recurrent suggestion of asking the courts to take all illegitimate children away from their mothers and place them in foster care homes" in 1962, once Congress authorized federal funding, it could not stop local officials from doing just that.[53] In the course of a few years, as legal scholar Dorothy Roberts argues in *Shattered Bonds: The Color of Child Welfare*, foster care went from being a system that ignored the needs of Black children to one that seemed primarily designed to break up Black families.[54]

In subsequent years, welfare rights became more explicitly a civil rights issue with the founding of the National Welfare Rights Organization (NWRO) in 1966, which lasted as a national organization until the mid-1970s, and some local groups persisted until welfare itself was ended during the Clinton administration. At its height, it had 25,000 members, and many more joined big demonstrations, like the 1966 national mobilization or the Poor People's Campaign in 1968. From its inception, the NWRO had multiple strategies—fighting locally for welfare rights by struggling for service provision, including extra grants for school clothes or winter coats, through street demonstrations and legal action. One of its most important victories was at the Supreme Court in 1968, where, in an Alabama case, *King v. Smith*, lawyers finally put an end to the hated moral restrictions against sex by welfare recipients. It challenged a law that allowed termination of welfare grants if a recipient "cohabited" with a man. Numerous states defined *cohabitation* to include even casual relationships. (In Alabama this had resulted in 16,000 children being dropped from AFDC.) The court struck down the provision as inconsistent with federal statutory definitions of *parent,* opining that the provision punished a woman for engaging in sexual relations and was unrelated to Congress's intent to provide aid to needy children. Citing the Flemming rule's call for rehabilitation, the court finally put an end to a welfare application itself being a reason to take children from their families. At least for single mothers applying for welfare, the fight that began in Louisiana to both keep their children and receive benefits in a post-desegregation world had finally been won—for a while.[55]

Without losing sight of the real victories by activists against slavery and its aftermath—the fights for abolition, for school desegregation, for welfare rights that also of necessity became struggles to keep Black children together with their mothers, other kin, and caregivers—it is also true that that across four centuries, the broadest story is that Black families in the United States have overwhelmingly been vulnerable to losing their children. Unlike in the Caribbean, where for much of slavery's history people were essentially worked to death at young ages and then replaced with other enslaved people brought from Africa, in the United States, slavery was a reproductive project.[56] Having children, however, made enslaved people vulnerable to loss, and provided one avenue through which slaveholders tried to keep their slaves fearful and intimidated, to prevent the slave rebellions that were a ubiquitous threat where whites were outnumbered, particularly after the model of Haiti's Black Republic, born in 1804. When African-Americans did rise up, notably during the Civil War, Reconstruction, and the fights for civil rights and the Poor People's Movement, whites responded as they had during slavery, taking children as a strategy for tearing the heart out of Black rebellion. Those who seek to stop children from being taken from immigrants seeking asylum at the Southwest border are, whether they realize it or not, struggling in the context of this long history of taking Black children.

2 Taking Native Children

In the 1870s, the US federal government began separating Native American children and taking them, under the watchful eye of soldiers, to Indian boarding schools, which were, among other things, military-run detention centers. In fact, Indian boarding schools were the direct legal precursors of the detention camps that held migrant and refugee children in the late twentieth and early twenty-first centuries, as scholar Maggie Blackhawk argued in the *New York Times*. Indeed, the doctrine that created boarding schools was cited by the second Bush, Obama, and Trump administrations to justify not only detention centers but the whole conduct of the war on terror—insisting that it is exempt from judicial review because of the plenary power doctrine, which gives the executive branch unfettered power over Indian matters. If we want to understand how the detention of immigrant and refugee children came to operate so far outside what would seem to be Constitutional parameters, we have to pay attention to how the Indian Wars were conducted and their aftermath in the taking of Native children.

Notwithstanding our preferences for believing that at least since the end of Jim Crow, the United States has not had race-specific laws, it is worth noting that Indian law can be read that way. Notably, Hitler was an admirer of Indian boarding schools. In fact, some have speculated that they were a model for the Third Reich's concentration camps. One Nazi legal theorist, Heinrich Krieger, provided a memo detailing US federal Indian law and Jim Crow for a National Socialist meeting on the Nuremberg laws that set out the special limitations on Jews, including stripping them of citizenship. Krieger published extensively on US race law, mostly in Germany. In one article in English, he argued that the best way to understand US reservation policy (including those founded as camps for prisoners of war), the denial of US citizenship to American Indians (until 1924), the denial of the right to vote in elections (still not won by the time Krieger wrote in the thirties), and the whole contradictory character of Indian law was to see it as a species of race law: "The proper nature of the tribal Indians' status is that of a racial group placed under a special police power of the United States." Whether this was the only or best understanding of Indian law, it is clear that boarding schools *could* be understood as a special instance of race laws under federal military power. As Blackhawk argues, one problem is that the plenary power doctrine is still good law that continues to be cited, whereas other race laws have been overturned, like *Plessy v. Ferguson* and *Dred Scott* (even the *Korematsu* case that allowed Japanese American internment during World War II has been cast as suspect).[1]

Indian boarding schools were created by the military and operated under military authority. Richard Pratt was a colonel in the infantry when he was appointed to create the first Indian boarding school in Carlisle, Pennsylvania (which is now part of the US Army War College, if its military character was ever obscure). Pratt's model was his experience in controlling and even torturing Native prisoners at Fort Marion, Florida. From the federal government's perspective, Indian schools were to be places that would destroy children's Indianness, that would "kill the Indian to save the man," as Pratt famously put it. Taking children as a means of ensuring peace, Pratt removed children from the Plains and then the Southwest and relocated them in Pennsylvania. His efforts, in fact, were designed to put a final end to the Indian Wars by disrupting the passing down of indigenous languages and the organization of tribal nations. For a time, boarding school attendance was both mandatory and enforced by the military. In the end, generations of Native kids spent time in them.

However, as with slavery, activists finally successfully demanded an end to taking children and putting them in boarding schools, and Native kids and teachers themselves transformed them into complex and contradictory spaces where some youth and ways of being Indian actually thrived. In the 1920s, an organized campaign publicized the abuses of boarding schools and demanded the attention of government, concluding an era of legal challenges. Activists, lawyers, and eventually, in the 1930s, government officials as well fought to bring children home again. They insisted that tribal nations and individual parents had a right to determine what happened to their children, that children and youth should be educated in day schools on reservations, and that the boarding schools' high rates of mortality, low rates of literacy, brutal work requirements, and inadequate nutrition militated for their immediate closure.

Native American Child Separation

Consider the images in figure 2. While much of our material on slavery and child separation—now as then—comes from abolitionists, much of the visual archive of Native kids and their separation from their parents comes from the other side, from those who sup-

FIGURE 2. Tom Torlino (Navajo) "as he entered the school in 1882" and "as he appeared three years later." From John N. Choate, *Souvenir of the Carlisle Indian School*, 1902. Courtesy of the Carlisle Indian School Digital Resource Center.

ported it. The photographer John Choate was commissioned by the Carlisle Indian Industrial School to make portraits of the students, the famous before-and-after photos of Native children at boarding schools that circulated like trophies among Anglo Americans, similar to the photos and mementos of lynchings that would circulate several decades later. These pictures and others like them showed children shorn of their long hair and having shed their traditional dress for the trappings of "civilization." These photographs also showed a change in skin tone—and this is remarkably consistent—such that it appeared that the children were literally becoming white. Here we see imagery produced by the victors, those who fought against indigenous people.

Indian boarding schools had originally been proposed in the 1860s by the Indian Peace Commission, which was the first to argue for boarding schools as a way to end the Indian Wars. The US federal government was warring with Plains Indian tribes in order to secure frontier settlements, land for agriculture and railroads, and mining and mineral rights. The commissioners' report described numerous social and legal injustices to Indians, including repeated violations of treaties, settlement on their land, acts of corruption by many local agents, and employees of the railroad shooting down Indians "in wanton cruelty." However, the report also insisted that the root problem was "the tribal or clannish organization" of Native people and their failure to speak English, both of which the report insisted could be remedied by boarding schools. Tribal nations would be extinguished, and Native children would become English speakers.[2]

The transformation in the US approach to Indian policy from warfare to schools that could exterminate indigenous languages and teach children to farm was not finally accomplished until 1879, after open warfare between the Sioux (Dakota/Lakota) and the US Cavalry had flared up again in a dispute over the Black Hills, sacred to the Lakota, including the 1876 defeat of the Seventh Cavalry at the Battle of the Little Bighorn ("Custer's Last Stand," known to the Lakota as the Battle of the Greasy Grass), and just before the Wounded Knee Massacre of 1890, which was the mass killing of hundreds of unarmed Lakota men, women, and children by US cavalry. Despite whatever veneer of humanitarianism cloaked the founding of boarding schools, their aim was not to educate children but to make them a useful weapon in persuading indigenous people to end their warring over violated treaties: in the words of the War Department, children should be taken as "hostages for tribal good behavior."[3]

In order to accomplish this, the War Department ordered Pratt to go to Sioux Territory to begin the work of Indian education.[4] Pratt was chosen because of his experience with American Indian prisoners in what was essentially the Guantánamo Bay prison of his generation, Fort Marion, in St. Augustine, Florida. During his tenure there, the Fort Marion prisoners came from the Southern Plains Indian War (Comanche, Kiowa, Cheyenne, Arapaho, Caddo) in Oklahoma and the Apache Wars in the Southwest. These tribal nations were considered particularly "uncivilized" and fierce. Pratt succeeded in "pacifying" them by cutting their hair, teaching them English, compelling them to clean and cook, instituting military drills and tribunals (in which some prisoners sent others to the dungeon), and forcing them to attend church. He also participated in torturing and killing them.[5] In 1879, while still on active duty, he opened the Carlisle Indian School in Pennsylvania, using many practices from Fort Marion: taking children far from home and teaching them English, running military-style drills, enforcing corporal punishment, and capturing and incarcerating runaways to enforce his educational methods. Epidemics of cholera, influenza, and tuberculosis devastated children's numbers there, and many were buried at the school.[6]

This history is condensed in the two group portraits in figures 3 and 4, taken at the Carlisle Indian Industrial School. The first shows Apache children at the time of their arrival in November 1886, and the second four months later, in March 1887. This group belonged to the Chiricahua Apache tribe, whose leader, the famous Geronimo, had surrendered with his followers in Arizona at Cochise Stronghold in September 1886, marking the end of the

FIGURE 3. Chiricahua Apache children on arrival at Carlisle Indian School in November 1886. *Back row (l to r):* Hugh Chee, Bishop Eatennah, Ernest Hogee. *Middle row:* Humphrey Escharzay, Samson Noran, Basil Ekarden. *Front row:* Clement Seanilzay, Beatrice Kiahtel, Janette Pahgostatum, Margaret Y. Nadasthilah, Frederick Eskelsejah. Photo courtesy of the Carlisle Indian School Digital Resource Center.

Apache wars. The band, including its children, was taken prisoner and sent to Fort Marion; the children were then sent to Pratt's Carlisle School in Pennsylvania.

Following what Anglo-Americans saw as the success of Pratt and the War Department, Christian missionaries and civil society "Friends of the Indian" groups began opening more boarding schools in the 1880s. In 1881, Congress declared school attendance for Indian children compulsory and authorized the Indian Bureau to deny benefits guaranteed by treaty if children failed to attend; it

FIGURE 4. Chiricahua Apache children at Carlisle Indian School in March 1887. *Back row (l to r):* Hugh Chee, Frederick Eskelsejah, Clement Seanilzay, Samson Noran, Ernest Hogee. *Middle row:* Margaret Y. Nadasthilah. *Front row:* Humphrey Escharzay, Beatrice Kiahtel, Janette Pahgostatum, Bishop Eatennah, Basil Ekarden. Photo courtesy of the Carlisle Indian School Digital Resource Center.

was to "withhold rations, clothing, and other articles from those parents who resisted sending their children to school."[7] Indian boarding schools spread through the West and Midwest. "Before and after" photos were popular throughout the United States to show the process of "civilizing" Indian children. American Indian Studies scholar Tsianina Lomawaima writes, "The famous 'before and after' pictures of Carlisle students are as much a part of American iconography as the images of Custer's Last Stand. 'Savages' shed buckskin, feathers, robes, and moccasins; long black hair was shorn or bobbed or twisted into identical, "manageable" styles; pinafores, stiff starched collars, stockings, and black oxfords signified the 'new woman.'"[8]

Removing Native children was also linked to enhancing the wealth of non-Indians, particularly through attacks on the notion of tribal self-determination. The end of the Indian Wars opened up Native lands for extractive capitalism. The General Allotment Act of 1887 inaugurated a massive grab for Indian territories. Congressional and Bureau of Indian Affairs (BIA) efforts allowed non-Indians to develop the natural resources of Native lands: oil, water power, minerals, tourism. The federal government, corporations like the railroads, and private individuals systematically violated treaties. The US federal government was empowered to act as a trustee for Native people, but it consistently failed to act in or even consider Native best interests. There was also a conflict of interest inherent in locating the Bureau of Indian Affairs in the Interior Department, which also managed natural resources.[9]

The process of separating Native children from their parents was often violent. One witness, writing in 1930, reported on conditions on the Navajo (Diné) reservation:

> In the fall the government stockmen, farmers, and other employees go out into the back country with trucks and bring in the children to school. . . . The wild Navajos, far back in the mountains, hide their children at the sound of a truck. So stockmen, Indian police, and other mounted men are sent ahead to round them up. The children are caught, often roped like cattle, and taken away from their parents, many times never to return. . . . Some, especially children who ran away, would be taken across the country and not return until they were 16 or 18.[10]

Tribes and occasionally even Anglo lawyers and courts were shocked by the violence of the Pratt system of Indian education and the removal of Native children. In 1899, a federal district court granted an Iowa tribe a writ of habeas corpus that forced the return of a Native child from the Carlisle School, suggesting an alternative trajectory that might have ended boarding schools much sooner had it been followed. The court found that tribes had to consent to the removal of a child.[11] Sometimes, individuals withdrew their consent by running to Canada (though it had its own residential schools), as in this narrative from Lone Wolf (Blackfoot) in Montana:

It was very cold that day when we were loaded into the wagons. None of us wanted to go and our parents didn't want to let us go. Oh, we cried, for this was the first time we were to be separated from our parents. Nobody waved as the wagons, escorted by the soldiers, took us toward the school at Fort Shaw. Once there our belongings were taken from us, even the little medicine bags our mothers had given us to protect us from harm. Everything was placed in a heap and set afire. Next was the long hair, the pride of all the Indians. The boys, one by one, would break down and cry when they saw their braids thrown on the floor. All of the buckskin clothes had to go and we had to put on the clothes of the White Man. If we thought that the days were bad, the nights were much worse. This was the time when real loneliness set in, for it was then that we were all alone. Many boys ran away from the school because the treatment was so bad but most of them were caught and brought back by the police. We were told never to talk Indian and if we were caught, we got a strapping with a leather belt. I remember one evening when we were all lined up in a room and one of the boys said something in Indian to another boy. The man in charge of us pounced on the boy, caught him by the shirt, and threw him across the room. Later we found out that his collar-bone was broken. The boy's father, an old warrior, came to the school. He told the instructor that among his people, children were never punished by striking them. That was no way to teach children; kind words and good examples were much better. Then he added, "Had I been there when that fellow hit my son, I would have killed him." Before the instructor could stop the old warrior, he took his boy and left. The family then beat it to Canada and never came back.[12]

Nevertheless, federal agents and missionaries continued to promote off-reservation boarding schools, in some places until the late 1970s.[13] Few Native children lived at home. Even visits home were seen to impede the assimilation process and were discouraged as a matter of policy.[14] Instead, children across the country were "farmed out" in the summers, boys working as ranch hands and farm laborers, girls doing domestic labor.[15]

Regimens at boarding schools were harsh. Children were punished, often beaten, for speaking indigenous languages; dress was carefully monitored and checked by staff.[16] Some scholars and activists have suggested that sexual abuse of children was rife in boarding schools; an investigation into boarding schools in Canada in the 1970s resulted in 3,400 complaints of sexual abuse. No similar investigation took place in the United States, although some have argued that any full inquiry into the crimes in US Indian boarding schools would find not only sexual abuse but starvation, medical experimentation, involuntary sterilization, and physical punishment that amounted to torture.[17] A 2012 survey of boarding school attendees found that nearly 30 percent reported that they had been sexually abused at their school.[18]

Yet there was one official inquiry in the United States that took boarding school policy seriously as something that harmed Native children and communities. Throughout the 1920s, Indian-policy reform advocates ran ever more far-reaching campaigns about the horrors of American Indian policy, including ongoing land theft, detribalization, and the suppression of Native culture, language, and religious practices; they insisted that child separation and boarding schools were the keystone of all these other processes. As a result of this public pressure, the secretary of the interior commissioned an independent investigation.

The 1928 report, known as the Meriam Report, suggested that things were, if anything, worse than the press accounts had reported. Its description of boarding schools were particularly powerful. Investigators found children living in overcrowded dormitories, sometimes without even adequate toilet facilities, subject to appalling health conditions, ill-clad, ill-fed, and ill-housed. Boarding schools "operated below any reasonable standard of health and decency," Lewis Meriam wrote. (In a rather striking echo in 2019, physician Dolly Lucio Sevier reported on refugee children in tents and warehouses serving as children's detention camps in Texas with "extreme cold temperatures, lights on 24 hours a day, no adequate access to medical care, basic sanitation, water, or adequate food."[19]) Children in Indian boarding schools suffered high rates of illness and death and were subject to a curriculum of little value; the report noted high rates of illiteracy. They had virtually no leisure time and, in violation of child labor laws, were forced to do manual labor to support the school.

The Meriam Report urgently recommended that children be returned to their parents and communities: "The continued policy of removing Indian children from home and placing them for years in boarding schools largely disintegrates the family and interferes with developing normal family life," its authors held.[20] The Meriam Report put pressure on the Hoover administration to close boarding schools. The report also discredited allotment: the 1887 Dawes Severality, or General Allotment Act, which had legally eviscerated many Native nations, eliminating the basis for holding land in common and for tribal jurisdiction over Indian affairs. Allotment and related legislation had led to the legal breakup of many reservations, the parceling out of tribal lands to individual households in an effort to create nuclear families. US citizenship was awarded to the small number of indigenous people who became "successful" farmers and ranchers (which the absence of key resources like water rights made unlikely).[21]

The effect of the Meriam Report was electric—as close as the United States ever came to publicly repudiating Indian child-separation policy. President Hoover immediately announced an increase in the federal funding to boarding schools for food and clothing for children. Within a few years, Hoover was voted out of office and President Franklin D. Roosevelt appointed an Anglo activist in the Indian reform campaign, John Collier, to head the Bureau of Indian Affairs. Collier introduced significant changes designed to recognize tribal organization, end laws that prevented the practice of Native religion, including dances deemed obscene, and halt the reduction of the land base of Indian Country. (He also thoroughly irritated many Native people by requiring a form of tribal governance that included rule by simple majority rather than, for example, 75 percent, which many saw as an arbitrarily imposed standard that resulted in sharp factionalism within tribal nations.) Collier also closed many boarding schools in favor of day schools, and in 1934, the federal policy requiring compulsory boarding school attendance was lifted. Still, some boarding schools persisted into the 1970s, and a few still exist, albeit with a much revised mission.²²

Boarding schools were complicated places. On the one hand, if they had never existed, it is likely that a number of indigenous languages would not have declined precipitously. Children who suffered sexual abuse at boarding schools would not have. In 2006, mental health professionals documented continued harms; they surveyed nearly five hundred Native American adults and youth and found not only that those in the group who had attended boarding school had much higher rates of suicide attempts, alcoholism, and drug abuse, but also that they passed their trauma to their children. The harms persist across generations, touching even those who never went to a boarding school. People raised by boarding school attendees "are significantly more likely to have a general anxiety disorder, experience posttraumatic stress disorder symptoms, and have suicidal thoughts in their lifetime compared to others."²³

Boarding schools may have begun with the goal of the extinction of Indian communities and languages, but the Native genius for survival made them something more. Because the history of generations of Native people, youth, and educators ran through these institutions, they also became important spaces of indigenous survival, resistance, and culture. Charlotte Kelley (Assiniboine) reports:

> I've heard really bad stories about people that left their reservation and went to boarding schools, but that wasn't my experience. I really enjoyed it for a lot of reasons. One reason is . . . the home that I had where I grew up, we didn't have running water or electricity. And, so when we went to boarding school, we had all of that and

that, to me, was, you know, really important to me. The teachers and the people that worked in the dormitories, the support staff . . . they were all good to me. . . . There was never any kind of abuse or anything in that way. And so I can't, you know, say anything bad about the boarding schools. And I think that if I didn't have the opportunity to go to a boarding school, I would not have had the opportunity to finish schooling and go on to do something else.[24]

Many recent histories of boarding schools by Native people stress some of the ways they became space of resistance. For example, the American Indian Movement (AIM), a key part of the Red Power insurrection of the 1960s and '70s movement for tribal sovereignty, was born out of the intertribal pride fostered by Indian boarding schools, which helped forge an "Indian" identity that was broader than any individual tribal nation.[25]

Taking Native Children and Fighting for the Indian Child Welfare Act

As in the Black community in the South, Native people in the 1950s and '60s fought state welfare workers who tried to take their children. The context was tribal termination (the administrative term for reversing federal recognition of tribes) and ongoing depredations of Native land, livelihoods, and people—again, especially children. With the expansion of welfare programs to Native households beginning in the 1930s and termination policies, reservations became places where state social workers went. Before termination, when Indian land belonged to tribes and was under treaties with the federal government, those who worked for states had rarely trespassed on it. Welfare, however, was a program administered by state governments (with usually about half the money coming from the federal government). With state-controlled welfare came state foster care. If the 1928 Meriam Report had worked to reduce the number of children at boarding schools, foster care took them from their mothers and households again, and in large numbers. The Spirit Lake Dakota Nation, for example, had by 1968 done everything possible to resist losing its children to the state-run foster care system in North Dakota. It sought instead to run child welfare programs through the tribe and keep children on the reservation or, if elsewhere, at least with Native families. While mothers of "illegitimate" children were losing their children to welfare workers in Mississippi and Louisiana, Mrs. Elsa Greywind was standing in the doorway of her home in North Dakota to prevent a welfare worker from taking her grandchildren and putting them in a white foster home. She stood firm even when the police came and took her to jail. Mrs. Fournier may not have been directly related to the Dakota foster boy she was raising, but that didn't matter. When a welfare worker drove onto the reservation to take the child to a white adoptive home in Fargo, she said they would have to take him away from an Indian community over her dead body, and she meant it. She took the boy in her arms and refused to let go, even as the social worker grabbed him and tried to pull him away. Other Native foster families responded similarly to state social workers' efforts to take children. You could spot a social worker because she drove a new car, not one of the fleet of ancient Indian cars, and children were hidden under beds or in the woods or sent fleeing with their parents through the reservation's back roads.[26]

Despite the courage and toughness of women like these and the high value Native peoples placed on cultural survival, especially through the rearing of children, tribal nations lost a lot of their children to welfare agents like these. Welfare workers disparaged the poverty of reservations and shamed unmarried mothers and others who cared for children because they thought heterosexual nuclear families were the only proper homes for children. They refused to acknowledge indigenous kinship systems and the important role of elders and other adults in child rearing. For example, welfare workers took a child named Ivan Brown and placed him with a white foster family because they saw no relationship between him and the woman who by Dakota tradition was his grandmother (although she hadn't given birth to either Ivan's mother or father), and they said that at 63, she was too old to be babysitting for a child.[27]

Tribal chairman Louis Goodhouse made getting children back from the state a priority. The Devil's Lake Sioux had taken welfare officials to court over and over in the 1950s and '60s, insisting they had no right to be on the reservation at all. Whether the children were being properly cared for was a matter for tribal leadership, and state welfare workers were trespassers. Goodhouse even had a court order to prove it: tribal members had gone to the North Dakota Supreme Court to establish that tribal courts had jurisdiction over the nation's children, and they won their case in 1963. Still, welfare workers kept coming, insisting that as long as women were receiving the state's welfare money to care for children, they had a right— a responsibility, in fact—to make sure the children were all right.[28]

Louis Goodhouse then went to the Association on American Indian Affairs. They sent Bertram Hirsch, a young, long-haired Anglo lawyer, to get Ivan Brown back to his grandmother. Over the months of filing motions and trying to extract Ivan from the picture-perfect white foster family, Hirsch went house to house and found that a quarter of the children born to families on the reservation were in white foster or adoptive homes or at off-reservation boarding schools. He continued gathering data until the mid-seventies, eventually producing the well-known statistic that 25–35 percent of Native children were in some kind of out-of-home care. He talked about the importance of understanding that this was a problem affecting a lot of people. When he began collecting statistics, he said that many Native people were shamed by losing their kids to the foster care system and thought, "'This is my problem.' They didn't know that the family a mile down the road . . . or over the next butte . . . was experiencing the same thing. Everybody was feeling shame about it and was not talking about it. They thought it was their own personal circumstance. . . . So people kind of kept it to themselves and they did not seek out assistance from their own tribes."[29] Investigating further, he found that although Native people constituted less than 2 percent of North Dakota's population, their kids were 50 percent of the state's foster population.[30]

In this spirit, in 1968 a defiant Devil's Lake Tribal Council passed a resolution prohibiting county officials from removing children from the reservation under any circumstances.[31] The county responded just as the South had to Black community refusals—by halting all welfare payments to the tribe, despite a 90 percent unemployment rate. Even though the Devil's Lake Sioux reservation and its headquarters at Fort Totten were three hours from the capital in Bismarck by car, they thoroughly irritated state officials. The reservation had fewer than two hundred households,[32] but a lot of them were on welfare, and that offended state officials, even though the money came from the Bureau of Indian Affairs. North Dakota even passed a law that made "chronic dependency" (by which they meant long-term use of welfare) evidence in itself of keeping an "unsuitable home" and a reason to place a child in foster care.

Over the next few years, another North Dakota group, the Three Affiliated Tribes (or the Mandan, Hidatsa, and Arikara Nations) of the Fort Berthold Reservation and three Lakota tribal nations in South Dakota—the Sisseton-Wahpeton Sioux, the Standing Rock Sioux, and the Oglala Sioux—all joined the organized resistance to the state taking their children and putting them in foster care. All five nations passed tribal council resolutions denouncing the manner and the rate at which children from their nations were being placed in off-reservation foster homes. Together with the Three Affiliated Tribes, these Lakota nations were finding more and more ways to resist state officials, following a tradition that has virtually defined Sioux/Dakota/Lakota people throughout the region, starting in the nineteenth century with the Plains Indian Wars, the demand for accountability for the Wounded Knee massacre, and the Ghost Dance "crisis"; continuing into the twentieth century with the insistence on compensation for lands lost to the Pick-Sloan irrigation and hydroelectric schemes and the demand for an end to corrupt tribal leadership allied with the FBI and US Marshals Service in the 1972–73 standoff at Wounded Knee (about which more later); and into the twenty-first century with the "Water Is Life" Standing Rock protests against the Dakota Access oil pipeline crossing rivers on treaty lands.[33]

Like a number of other states that had a lot of land under Indian control, North Dakota aggressively pursued the implications of tribal termination, the federal efforts to "get out of the Indian business." The state built dams and rerouted waterways with no regard for flooding on tribal lands; the Standing Rock and Cheyenne River reservations lost 200,000 acres of their best agricultural and grazing lands in the 1950s and '60s, were deprived of their water rights, and saw more than 150,000 of their members relocated, their homes newly under the Missouri River. Those bottom lands, J. W.

Thompson testified to a US Senate subcommittee, were "our heart lands. No similar lands are for sale. We depend on our land for our livelihood; it furnishes our income. To take our land is to take our homes and income, and a part of our history and heritage."[34] Governments in other western states, including Nevada, Arizona, and New Mexico, fiercely resisted assuming any responsibility for the support of Native children and single mothers: Arizona in fact evaded paying any benefits to anyone until 1960. And in the 1940s and '50s, Nevada likewise had no welfare program for anyone in order to resist paying benefits to Native mothers.[35] Arizona's state government argued that unmarried Native mothers on reservations were not citizens because they did not pay taxes or speak English, so they were ineligible for welfare.[36] But like North Dakota, other states that did allow unmarried Native women to receive welfare benefits took their kids into foster care in unconscionable numbers and often placed them in adoptions.[37]

Other Native mothers faced forced sterilization by state welfare workers as a condition for keeping their children. Betty Jack (Cheppewa) from the Lac du Flambeau Reservation in Wisconsin testified before the Senate Commission on Indian Affairs in April 1974 about two cases in her community. One woman was told that unless she consented to sterilization, she would lose her four children. A welfare case worker took her out of state for the operation. Another woman who became pregnant while on welfare was also taken from the Lac du Flambeau Reservation, this time to Keshena Women's Prison (on the Menominee Reservation), where she was sterilized. The welfare worker also forced her to relinquish her baby for adoption.[38] Norma Jean Serena, a Pittsburg mother of five, also charged that welfare officials compelled her to be sterilized without her knowledge and consent after the birth of a baby, whom they placed in an adoption. Previously, she said, welfare officials had also placed two of her children in foster care, claiming that they were ill and needed medical treatment. Her understanding was that they would be returned, but, she charged, welfare officials had no plan to return them.[39]

The Association on American Indian Affairs, unable to find justice in North Dakota or in Washington, DC, through the Bureau of Indian Affairs, sought to halt the taking of Native children by jumping scales: they took it to the foreign press at the height of the Cold War.[40] Executive director William Byler told reporters:

> The Devil's Lake Sioux people and American Indian tribes have been unjustly deprived of their lands and their livelihood, and now they are being dispossessed of their children. Nothing exceeds the cruelty [to children] of being unjustly and unnecessarily removed from their families. Today in this Indian community a welfare worker is looked on as a symbol of fear rather than of hope. County welfare workers frequently evaluate the suitability of an Indian child's home on the basis of economic or social standards unrelated to the child's physical or emotional well-being and Indian children are removed from the custody of their parents or Indian foster family for placement in non-Indian homes without sufficient cause and without due process of law.[41]

Goodhouse, Greywind, Fournier, and three other women who had become activists for the nation's children at Devil's Lake—Alvina Alberts, Annie Jane DeMarce Leftbear, and Genevive Hunt Longie Goodhouse—were also there at Byler's press conference. Native social worker Evelyn Blanchard joined the movement somewhat later, but she was a stalwart advocate for the movement for legislation that eventually became the Indian Child Welfare Act. Although we don't remember their names alongside the icons of the Red Power movement like Russell Means (Oglala Lakota) or Dennis Banks, the movement for the defense of Native children they launched was critical not only to the futures of Native kids but also to the defense of sovereignty of tribes, their ability to conduct their own affairs and control their land without interference from states or even the federal government. And while the fight for legal respect for tribes as autonomous entities with rights enshrined in treaties and the unceded sovereignty of autonomous nations to govern their own people was—and is—an ongoing struggle, the minimal requirement of self-government was surely what most white households expect as a baseline: the freedom to raise their own children. The movement that began at Devil's Lake resulted in the passage of the Indian Child Welfare Act a decade later. Where North Dakota sought to make an example of the Devil's Lake people for their obstinate insistence on the right of their tribal nation to control the placement of their own children, these activists launched a movement that was ultimately a powerful building block—indeed, some would say *the* most powerful building block—toward reclaiming tribal sovereignty.

The fight that began at Devil's Lake was remarkably successful. The delegation went from New York to Washington and began negotiations with the BIA about addressing the welfare and family dissolution that had brought them there and what it would take to build a system that worked. This was also the year just before a wave of radicalism from Native youth, including the occupation of Alcatraz in San Francisco Bay by Indians of All Tribes, a Red Power group—which is to say, the activists of Devil's Lake and the Association on American Indian Affairs never acted alone in their struggle for child welfare. Still, what they accomplished was ultimately nothing less than a complete transformation of the relationship between the tribe and the federal government—with the tribe acting autonomously and state officials completely out of the picture. They got the BIA food stamp program rerouted through the tribal government rather than the county. They also finally succeeded in having child welfare cases go through the tribal court rather than the bureaucracy of the county welfare department.[42]

Wounded Knee

Not incidentally, the emerging fight over Native child taking unfolded in rebellious communities that were resisting the status quo of settler colonialism. As in Black communities, the state was moving to take children in response to activism. The Dakotas were a region of particular importance to the Red Power movement, including a seventy-one-day standoff in 1973 between members of the American Indian Movement (AIM) and the Oglala Sioux Nation against federal marshals, members of the National Guard, and the FBI. AIM and members of the tribal nation sought a restoration of treaty rights and the impeachment of a corrupt tribal chairman, Dick Wilson, whom elders had sought to remove. Wilson had a private police force that he called the Guardians of the Oglala Nation (the GOON squad) that had harassed his opponents and joined the feds in shooting at AIM and members of the nation in the standoff. Treaty-rights activists and members of other tribes flocked to the area, but a perimeter of federal officials attempted to stop any food or medical supplies from reaching the occupiers. There were frequent firefights, and two Oglala men were killed, and a federal marshal was seriously injured. The events were a tipping point in Native activism for treaty rights and tribal sovereignty.[43]

However, the more radicalized the region of the Great Sioux Nation became, the more of its children welfare officials took. The AAIA litigated more than twenty child-taking cases in the Dakotas, and while it won them, countering a wholesale policy one at a time was time-consuming and labor-intensive, and the group knew that it wasn't finding all of them. For example, a welfare caseworker took 4-year-old John because his mother, Cheryl Spider de Coteau of the Sisseton-Wahpeton Sioux sometimes left him with his great-grandmother, Melinda Spider, who was 69 and thus, in the caseworker's view, too old to care for a 4-year-old. The welfare department later came back for his sibling without even bothering with legal authorization. In June 1972 alone, welfare official took twenty-two other children from the Sisseton-Wahpeton Sioux, claiming that households marked by poverty, inadequate housing, lack of indoor plumbing, and overcrowding were not fit places for children.[44]

In 1973, Delphine Shaving Bear of the Standing Rock Sioux asked the South Dakota State Department of Public Welfare to take temporary custody of her 1-year old son, Christopher, so she could hitchhike several hundred miles in a successful weeklong quest to recover custody of her other two children. When she returned, the welfare department refused to give Christopher back because his foster parents wanted to adopt him. Shaving Bear insisted that she had not relinquished him, pointing to a statement on the form she had signed that said, "I understand that this does not give the Division of Child Welfare the right to place my child for adoption." It took a year and half for her to get her baby back.[45]

In another case, Benita Rowland, a 3-year-old Oglala Lakota child from the Pine Ridge reservation in South Dakota was taken on January 1, 1972, and "adopted" by two women from Wisconsin. The lawyer for Rowland's father, Frederick van Hecke, recalled,

"There was not only no adoption, there was no *pretense* of adoption, no color of law. These people had absolutely no legal right to take that little girl."[46] In a letter to Rowland's mother, the pair wrote of the religious basis for the adoption: "We have not taken Benita from you; you gave her physical birth, which we could not give, and we can give her opportunities which you could not give—so she belongs to both of us. But far more, she belongs to the Lord."[47] When the AAIA got involved on behalf of Rowland's father, the group found that the pair also had another child from the reservation, Vina Bear Eagle, an infant from Wounded Knee. Ten months later, Rowland's father went to court in Milwaukee and got Benita back, and the couple also returned Vina Bear Eagle.[48]

Even AIM got caught up in efforts to take Lakota children. When the FBI sought to prosecute AIM members for the standoff at Pine Ridge, they sought to arrest Leonard Peltier for the deaths of two agents. Initially, Peltier fled to Canada to avoid being arrested, proclaiming his innocence but saying he couldn't get a fair trial in the United States.[49] Peltier was extradited based on testimony by Myrtle Poor Bear that she was Peltier's girlfriend and that she saw him kill the agents. Later, she withdrew her testimony and said that the FBI wrote it and coerced her to sign: "They started threatening me about my daughter, that's Marty. They said that they were going to take her away from me and I wasn't ever going to see her again, and that I had to cooperate with them. They said, 'You're going to say this, we're going to make you say it, and if you don't say it, then you aren't going to see Marty no more.'"[50] Peltier was ultimately convicted for their murder, although he continues to maintain that he was framed. He is serving a life sentence in federal prison.[51]

After Benita Rowland, after Ivan Brown, Vina Bear Eagle, Christopher Shaving Bear, and all the other children that the courts said had been improperly taken from their families among the Dakota—to say nothing of the tribal council resolutions of the Sisseton-Wahpeton, Devil's Lake, and Standing Rock Sioux—it turns out one of the most famous AIM prosecutions was also made possible by threats of child taking.

The Indian Child Welfare Act

Throughout this period, the AAIA played a coordinating role across tribal nations and lobbied Congress for federal protection from state officials taking Native children through what would eventually become the Indian Child Welfare Act (ICWA) of 1978. Congressional hearings about American Indian children being taken by state officials were held in 1974, 1976, and 1977, producing volumes of testimony. Mostly those testifying were Native women and girls who were organizing around this issue within many tribal nations and across the United States, persuading families that these were not individual, isolated, and shameful events but a coordinated wave of child taking that could be resisted. Sexism was also a factor; with some exceptions, male tribal leadership had trouble seeing child taking as an important issue, especially early on. Most of the Congressional testimony was explicitly about taking the children of "unwed" mothers—those who were divorced, separated, or never married. While Native men may have had trouble thinking about it, the issue was significant: what counted as kinship. Social workers' relentless focus on heterosexual nuclear families and the proper age of caregivers (that is, that elders should not be in charge of children) was central to the fight for ICWA. The Native women who testified made the case that Native communities had to have sovereignty over their children not only as a matter of simple justice, but also because Anglos failed to understand indigenous meanings of kin.[52]

ICWA, finally enacted in 1978, sought to keep Native households together by making tribal courts the only jurisdiction that could remove a child of an Indian family that lived on a reservation, and generally, off the reservation as well.[53] The act created a preference for keeping children with kin and community that was often not the norm in Anglo family court proceedings, though in subsequent years, it became so in more progressive states. The preference was elaborated as follows: to keep Indian children with their own extended family first, other tribal members second, and other Native people third. The act sets the evidentiary standards higher than for non-Native children in dependency hearings (where parents might lose custody of their children to, say, foster care) or termination of parental rights. There is a requirement that the family be offered crisis intervention services before a child can be taken. Unfortunately, Congress did not allocate money for the enactment of ICWA, creating an endlessly renewed fight for funding.

ICWA didn't solve all the problems of Native child welfare. For one thing, compliance is a huge and ongoing problem, with some states trying harder than others to identify whether kids are eligible for tribal enrollment and hence covered by the ICWA. For example, in Maine, a state sufficiently committed to doing right by Indian children that the governor and the five tribal chiefs authorized a Truth and Reconciliation Commission (TRC) to untangle the state's long history of child taking from Wabanaki people (the First Nations and Native American confederacy in the region). Though the TRC sought to "promote individual, relational, systemic and cultural reconciliation," a 2015 report by the TRC still found that less than half the children in the system had their Native heritage verified.[54] In addition, some tribal courts and social services work better than others. While some are well run and seek the best solutions for children in crisis, others, especially in small rural communities, are riven by family factions, underfunded, understaffed, and affected by the brain drain that lures some people with education away—just as their non-Indian counterparts outside reservations are. It is bitterly ironic that in recent years the Devil's Lake Sioux (now known as the Spirit Lake Sioux, as the original name was a mistranslation into English) are better remembered for a *Frontline* documentary, *Kind Hearted Woman,* that highlighted one family's resistance to the ongoing failure of the tribal court and social services to respond to child sexual abuse, than as the tribal nation that demanded federal action for *better* care of its children in the 1950s.[55] While the fight for ICWA was an important protest against states taking the children of politically rebellious communities, it's unclear whether it actually reduced the number of children taken from their homes. One federal study found that by the mid-1980s, the rate of Native children in out-of-home care remained at one-third. Ironically, states that are in better ICWA compliance, like Washington, may nevertheless show steadily rising rates of Native children being taken because they are continually getting better at identifying ICWA-eligible children.

The middle of the twentieth century saw the birth of the modern foster care system, with its preponderance of Black and, in the West, Native children. It is the legacy of the fight to desegregate public schools and the demand for tribal sovereignty over land and water that states took the children of rebellious people and put them in foster care. It wasn't just the aftermath of the "discovery" of child abuse by emergency room physicians looking at children's x-rays and finding multiple old fractures, as some historians have said; that happened later.[56] "One hundred years from now," wrote legal scholar Dorothy Roberts in 2002, "today's child welfare system will surely be condemned as a racist institution—one that compounded the effects of discrimination on Black families by taking children from their parents, allowing them to languish in a damaged foster care system or be adopted by more privileged people."[57] The contemporary foster care system was born in these episodes of punishing Black and Native insurgencies in the context of the Black freedom movement and the Red Power calls for tribal sovereignty.

More recently, child taking has emerged as a strategy for a quite different kind of conservative: the Goldwater Institute—a Koch-brothers-funded think tank—began intervening in ICWA cases while supporting non-Indian gaming. Casinos, apparently, were too lucrative to be left to tribal nations, and so targeting photogenic children with their wealthy white foster parents was a strategy (together with attempting to deny tribal governments the right, under the Violence Against Women Act, to prosecute Anglo men who raped and beat Native women) for once again abrogating indigenous sovereignty—creating an opening in Indian law that would disrupt the consideration of Native people as separate, sovereign nations.

By the middle of the twentieth century, child taking had outgrown its original form as part of the centuries-long brutalization of indigenous people in the United States in the service of a vision in which Indians were the enemy, and then captive nations. The period of trying to disrupt tribal relations, destroy indigenous languages, and take away traditional dress and livelihood closed with the end of boarding schools. Child taking grew into a more flexible grammar of counterinsurgency. With the challenge to tribal termination policies represented by the Red Power movement, the movement to stop welfare workers from taking Native children from their homes and communities grew in importance, for both sides. For Native people, the Indian Child Welfare Act became a cornerstone of tribal sovereignty, with tribal courts having genuine power to oversee their own children. For the FBI in its efforts to put down the Red Power movement and for states that sought control of tribal assets—from land to federal aid—the ability to take children from their mothers, kin, and caregivers was another site in the struggle over resources.

Even though there were few political sanctions for ignoring and abusing treaty obligations through termination policy, flooding people's lands, taking their livelihood, providing inadequate health care and sterilization abuse at Bureau of Indian Affairs hospitals, and there was plenty of social support for fathers who failed to support their children or abused their partners, the women and children who were downstream from all this were punished. Child taking had been transformed into a form of structural violence and a cover story for other kinds of harm. Child taking had become part of the warp and weft of the US social fabric, public life, politics, and history. As we will find in chapter 4, the twenty-first century has seen not only conservative groups but also sometimes liberal ones taking aim at ICWA. But before we think about the next chapter in Native and Black child taking, we need to turn to Latin America and 1980s anti-Communism. US foreign policy in the region in the late twentieth century is the other history that we need in order to see what set the stage for children being put in detention camps on the Southwest border.

3 Taking Children in Latin America

In order to understand the Trump-era policy of taking children from refugees and immigrants, we need to ask how Central Americans were made into people who could be dispossessed of their children. How did it come to be in the spring of 2018 that immigration officials walked the Bridge of the Americas between El Paso and Juárez, Mexico, and picked Central Americans out of the crowds of people from every country, continent, and island on that sky bridge? Why were Central Americans in particular told that the United States was "full" and they could not cross? "If you look indigenous and you look Central American, they will stop you," said Ruben Garcia, the director of a nonprofit that helps immigrants, describing how officials tried to circumvent the asylum law and who they targeted. "They never ask why you are coming. They just say we can't receive you."[1] This policy did not spring fully formed from the head of a Trump administration official in 2017. It has a history in the anti-Communist civil wars of the latter part of the twentieth century, when Central Americans first began losing their children to state terror.

Latin America in the 1960s, '70s, and '80s provides perhaps the clearest example of child taking for political ends. There, in the space between Henry Kissinger and Ronald Reagan's America, fascist Spain, and Latin America's own autochthonous nationalism, militarism, and right-wing Catholicism, an increasingly paranoid anti-Communism sought to rigidly control not only the present but the future. Military dictatorships up and down Latin America, from Guatemala to Argentina, directed campaigns of torture, assassination, and disappearance. While initially these right-wing military dictatorships targeted armed left-wing guerillas, their victims grew more diverse as actual militants were quickly overwhelmed—and largely killed. From the revolutionaries, the dictatorships turned to people who supported anything even vaguely socialist, from unions to students to agrarian cooperatives. Then they took their children, hoping to ensure that the very young who might have been touched by their parents' leftist ideals were violently uprooted and reeducated in conservative adoptive families or outside the country.

This right-wing dream of killing ideas by burying their proponents and taking their children was a failure. As the extent of torture and especially kidnapping of children became known to ever-wider circles, opponents made efforts to prosecute them. In 2006, Jorge Rafael Videla, once the most powerful man in Argentina as its military dictator, went to prison with a number of his collaborators *not* for the tortures, murders, and disappearances they had directed but for kidnapping children and running an illegal adoption ring. Although the Argentine Congress had tried to grant a general amnesty to the former leaders to prevent their prosecution for the crimes they had committed as they oversaw hundreds of torture centers and ordered the military to kill civilians, a judge found that the official pardon didn't cover child kidnapping because it was an ongoing crime, continuing after the final date on the amnesty. Kidnapping infants and children turned out to be the crime they could be prosecuted for, and it is what held them in prison until the amnesty was repealed in 2005.[2]

Although the repressive right-wing regimes up and down Latin America that used the state apparatus to take children for political purposes was different from that in the United States, I discuss it here for two reasons. First, the contemporary political debate about taking children in the United States centers around Latin American immigrants and refugees, particularly from Central America. They are refugees *from* something that was born in relationship to the right-wing anti-Communism I am discussing here—not in the limited sense of being a direct cause, but in a broad sense of the often grotesque violence and the wide availability of guns and other weapons being a product of this post–World War II era of militarism and torture. Second, the United States was very involved in the production of forms of terror and repression in Latin America in this period. Child taking emerged in this period as a transnationally produced grammar of terror against insurgent populations (and contemporary asylum seekers are insurgent, at least in the minimal sense of engaging in mass action to protest their location in the world economy and the ways they have been marked for death in regimes that scholars have called "necropolitical"). This was also the period in which Latin America's current role as a labor reserve for the United States took its contemporary form—one in which laborers engage in temporary migrations to the United States to work for low wages in its service sector, in private homes, construction sites, and fields, but they are supposed to leave their children and elders in Latin America. You can't get to 2019 at the Southwestern border of the United States without going through Cold War Latin America.

Argentina (and Paraguay, Uruguay, Bolivia, Chile, and Brazil)

Argentina probably has the best-known story about the far right and disappeared children, in large part because of the hard work of activists to reconstruct what happened. Perhaps because the US government was not overly involved, it was willing to turn over all its documents to help scholars and activists, a gesture that is unlikely to be repeated with respect to places like Chile or Central America.[3] From 1976 to 1983, an Argentine military junta conducted the Dirty War against the left, beginning with guerillas of the People's Revolutionary Army (ERP), a Trotskyite group of a few hundred people, and the Montoneros. The Montoneros had started out as followers of President Juan Perón, but after a massacre of Perón's left supporters, they turned to revolutionary activities and violence, saying they wanted to unmask the fascism of Perón and usher in a worker's state. What they got instead was massive repression from the right. When a military coup put Jorge Rafael Videla in power in 1976, the state quickly arrested and "disappeared" the members of the armed guerillas, putting an end to their bombing campaign and other revolutionary violence and killing most of them in the first eighteen months. Over the seven years that it was in power, however, the military junta turned to a campaign to stop leftist and antinationalist influence in general, arresting and torturing tens of thousands of people in hundreds of detention centers around Argentina. They killed an estimated 30,000 people, most of whom were not guerillas at all, but union members, students, homosexuals, countercultural hippies, or atheists.[4]

The children of accused leftists and countercultural fellow travelers were taken from their mothers and placed in adoptions, including those born in prisons and those "disappeared" with their mothers. Many infants and children were placed with those who supported the regime, a surreal kind of reward for those on the hard right who were struggling with infertility. Other children were dropped off in orphanages. The family members of the disappeared organized to oppose the regime—most famously as the Madres de Plaza de Mayo, but other groups as well—and they began looking for the disappeared children.

It soon became clear to activists that the Argentine military had coordinated with other extreme right-wing governments in South America: initially Paraguay, Uruguay, and Chile, and later also Bolivia and Brazil. Prisoners were moved across the six countries, and intelligence and "antiterrorist" measures were shared, including forms of torture. People faced beatings, electric shocks with wires or cattle prods, cold, hunger, cigarette burns, and prolonged periods of darkness. Many were taken on "death flights"—pushed out of planes over the ocean.[5] Women—and men—were raped, and those who could often became pregnant. Out of deference to the Catholic Church's position on abortion and the innocence of fetuses, pregnant women were often allowed to live until after their babies were born. Then they were killed.

Rumors that the children of those disappeared and detained were being kept alive and placed in adoptions were proven true when the first disappeared children were found in 1979. Anatole Julien Grisonas and his sister, Victoria, who had been disappeared in 1976 with their mother at the ages of 3 and 1, respectively, turned up, adopted, in Chile. They were found by the Abuelas (Grandmothers) de Plaza de Mayo with the help of the Committee for Human Rights of the Countries of the Southern Cone (CLAMOR, for its initials in Portuguese) and the Archbishop of São Paolo, Brazil—and the adoptive family had no idea about the children's origins. The children, in fact, had been found wandering, abandoned, in a park in Valparaiso (Chile) before they were adopted. While the children stayed with their adoptive family after learning their history, they also began to have extensive contact with relatives of their birth mother. In 1980, the Abuelas found two more children, this time in Argentina, as a result of passing around pictures and their own detective work. Again, the adoptive family had no knowledge of their background, and so the children stayed with the adoptive family but maintained contact with their birth family. During the process of legally restoring the children's original names and identities, however, a sympathetic but cautious judge asked a critical question: how could the Abuelas prove that the children were who they said they were?[6]

This question set in motion a multinational search for scientists and methods to establish a relationship between a child and a possible grandmother. In 1980, DNA paternity testing was still in its infancy, although one of the Abuelas stumbled upon a mention of it in a newspaper in La Plata. Over the next several years, the group contacted a number of scientists, particularly in the United States, including Eric Stover of the American Academy for the Advancement of Science, who had himself been briefly detained in Argentina in 1976, and Mary-Claire King at the University of California, Berkeley. They believed that a "grandparentage" test, akin to a paternity test, could be developed.[7]

The following year, in 1983, the Dirty War ended with the election of Raúl Alfonsín as president. Forensic anthropologists began to unearth mass graves, and the National Commission on the Disappearance of Persons began its investigations for the report that would be called *Nunca Más* (Never Again)—which now seems bitterly ironic. Based on King's mathematical formulas for grandparentage, the group was able to identify Paula Logares, adopted by a policeman, as the granddaughter of one of the Abuelas, and she was returned to live with her grandmother.[8]

Two years after the junta fell, a film, *The Official Story* (1985), was released in Argentina and internationally. It told the story of the placing of children of accused leftists with the junta's sympathizers. Although these kinds of stories had been circulating all over Argentina, this was the first time that international audiences were confronted with them. In subsequent years, the Madres and the Abuelas de Plaza de Mayo identified nearly three hundred children that had been taken by police, military, and torturers from prisoners and detainees. An estimated five hundred children were born in detention during this period; many remained missing.

Taking children wasn't an accident, a bureaucratic exigency in a complicated and confusing time. The government believed it was repressing "a [political] minority which we do not consider Argentine," as Videla put it. General Ibérico Saint-Jean, the governor of Buenos Aires explained, "First we will kill all the subversives; then we will kill their collaborators; then . . . their sympathizers, then . . . those who remain indifferent; and finally we will kill the timid."[9] The political right didn't just want to stop those it called terrorists; it wanted to destroy any element of Argentine culture that might not support its "tradition" and the hard-right elements in the Catholic Church—anything, indeed, that could allow the flourishing of a left. The right did not want children growing up in the kinds of families that had already produced their subversive parents.[10] Indeed, the taking of children was often perfectly legal, even when their living relatives did not consent to it, simply because judges declared it legitimate. Since the parents had been "terrorists," these juvenile-justice judges insisted, the grandparents had been negligent or allowed leftist beliefs to flourish in their children and thus had no right to their grandchildren.[11] If the children grew up with their parents or grandparents, they would take up their politics (particularly after the right wing killed their relatives). The junta was ruthlessly efficient in eradicating not just leftists but the "cultural" elements that it believed had contributed to their rise, the vaguely Marxist intellectuals, university professors, Jewish communities and businesses,[12] and union members. By taking children, the junta intended to eradicate the next generation of subversives as well.

Ultimately, the Argentine right failed spectacularly to create the future in its own image, perhaps precisely because of its extreme violence. The Argentine and international left spent the forty years after the junta fell exposing its torture, murders, and censorship. The fearless journalist and newspaper publisher Jacobo Timmerman's memoir of his torture, *Prisoner Without a Name, Cell Without a Number,* has been continuously in print since 1981. Above all, the left has exposed the taking of children.

El Salvador

Fighters for historical memory, human rights, and accountability in El Salvador and Guatemala have sought to ensure that we know and never forget the children whom military and paramilitary forces abducted. These activists have created opportunities for the adults who were disappeared as children to meet the families that lost them, although they have not followed the lead of the Madres and Abuelas de Plaza de Mayo and instituted a legal process to dissolve their relationships with adoptive families that collaborated with the right-wing regime. Or, perhaps more accurately, they have lacked the political power and cultural authority to do so.

El Salvador by the end of the 1970s was a deeply unequal society with an economy grounded in coffee for export and the landlessness of the majority. Over the course of the twentieth century, its economically disenfranchised majority had exhausted all the nonviolent routes to reform—the military was in power, elections had been repeatedly hacked and corrupted, and its feckless leaders had been unable to accomplish even the limited land reform they had promised. Protest was repeatedly met with violent massacres, and paramilitary death squads terrorized the country. Food prices were sky-high in this agricultural nation, and education was out of reach for many rural children, with illiteracy rates for 10-year-olds at about one-third.[13]

Nevertheless, the late '70s were also full of optimism for change in El Salvador. Everyone was organizing: teachers and community educational initiatives, unions, students, Christian base communities, women's collectives, peasants, and agrarian cooperatives were providing concrete means through which people were taking control of their own lives and the direction of the country. People were poor, to be sure, and the wealthy and the government were repressive and corrupt, but there was a felt sense that the future was theirs to create, and life would be different for the next generation. People were in the streets in 1977, demanding free and fair elections and meaningful change, when security forces opened fire, gunning down as many as 1,500 people.[14]

With other paths to reform foreclosed, people turned to support the leftist military guerillas. In the United States, the Carter administration (to a small degree) and then the Reagan administration (massively) gave El Salvador support in the form of training for the military, weapons, military "advisors," and aid—ultimately about $1 million–$2 million a day—to prop up a brutal and massively unpopular government.[15] The Salvadoran state held power through terror: detentions and disappearances, death squads that left bodies in the street as a warning to others about opposing the government, torture, and massacres of civilian communities that were suspected of support for the guerillas. During the armed internal conflict, an estimated 75,000 civilians were killed in a country of only 5 million people. The overwhelming majority died at the hands of the military.[16]

Military and paramilitary forces in El Salvador also took between 800 and 1,000 children.[17] During the armed internal conflict, the military sought to eliminate the "social base of the guerilla." Drawing on the experience of Vietnam, it sought to eliminate the "water" that the guerilla "fish" swam in, engaging in a scorched earth campaign against civilians in areas where the guerillas were strong and creating model villages surrounded by barbed wire and guarded by military and paramilitary units in place of autonomous communities.[18] Their goals included breaking people's will to resist the military by sowing terror, including taking children, and as in Argentina, controlling the future by refusing to allow those suspected of being Communists from raising a next generation. Sometimes children became lost in the confusion when military threat forced communities to flee. Others were picked up in front of their parents, and there were cases when they were literally ripped from their mother's arms. According to its research and the reconstruction of cases from the stories of surviving relatives, the Asociación Pro-Búsqueda attributes 90 percent of the cases to the military and 10 percent to the guerillas. These included cases when members of the guerilla were forced to leave their children in "safe houses," which resulted in permanent separation.[19]

During the government-sponsored La Quesera massacre in 1981, for example, 350–500 civilians were killed and 24 children were disappeared. One survivor, Milagro Martínez, the mother of Marisol and Nicolás Arnoldo, recalls:

> When the authorities came into the villages we would run and hide, because if we stayed in the houses, they would kill us. Many people died that way. So some of us were afraid, and we decided to flee with the children. When the invasion came, we fled into the hills with the children. We fell into an ambush set by the Armed Forces; they trapped us. They shot at us, and they chased us until they caught us. And they took our children away . . . You can never forget a loved one. I only forget when I am asleep. But I always hold on to the hope of meeting my son or daughter some day. Even if it's during the last moments of my life, I would love them with all my heart.[20]

In late May and early June of 1982, in the events that became known as the Guinda de Mayo (the May Flight), people fled their homes because they were tipped off that paramilitary groups and the army were planning to come to their homes and kill them, believing that they were supporters of the guerillas. The military called this Operation Cleanup (Operación Limpieza); it was designed to wipe out communities in northeast Chalatenango. People ran from one community to another with soldiers on their heels who killed anyone they found, slaughtered animals, and destroyed homes and crops.

These forces also took at least eleven children, including Ernestina and Erlina Serrano Cruz, ages 3 and 7. When the Serrano Cruz family was tipped off that the military was close by, they began running. The mother and a brother made it past the military barricade and went in one direction, while the father, Dionisio

Serrano, brother Enrique, and sisters Suyapa, Ernestina, and Erlina went in another. After three days of walking, they made it to a settlement, Los Alvarenga. They hid there for another three days without food and water, but finally Dionisio and Enrique went to search for water. Ernestina and Erlina, finding themselves alone, began to cry, tipping off soldiers to their presence. Suyapa was not far away, but since she had a six-month-old baby, she had tried to protect her family by hiding separately, in case the baby cried. She later reported that she heard one soldier ask if they should take Ernestina and Erlina or kill them. Another replied that they should take them. When she no longer heard the soldiers, Suyapa went and searched for her sisters, but they were gone. When their father and Enrique returned, they all looked for the girls all over the area, but they were never found.[21]

The mother of José Adrián Rochac Hernández did not realize that soldiers and members of the National Guard and paramilitary were nearby in time to flee. They went to her house in a village called San Martín in 1980 and said they were looking for arms. They searched the house but found nothing. They took away the mother, María Silveria Rochac and her oldest son, Sergio, 12, and killed them. According to witnesses, the soldiers went back to the house and took 5-year old José Adrián. He was led away to the village of San Bartolomé Perulapía, but that is the last time he was seen.[22]

After the war ended in 1992, family members gave testimony to the Truth Commission about the disappearance of their children, but it merely recorded them as among the dead. Jon de Cortina, a Jesuit priest, helped the families of missing children begin to organize to support each other and try to find the children. They formed La Asociación Pro-Búsqueda de Niños y Niñas Desaparecidos (Association for Searching for Disappeared

Children). As in Argentina, members of the group began with a word-of-mouth campaign, circulating photos and talking about what was known of the circumstances of their children's disappearance. Pro-Búsqueda insists on accountability for the missing children and supporting the family members who are still searching, looking for a grown child, a grave, or at least a story, if nothing else. After the war, the association began taking cases to court, demanding that the military and the state take responsibility for accounting for the kidnapped children. In 1994, Pro-Búsqueda found the first children. Since then, it has found about five hundred and continues searching.[23]

While it took decades of work for Pro-Búsqueda's lawyers, the case that ultimately broke open the impunity surrounding the paramilitary and military child taking was that of Erlinda and Ernestina Serrano Cruz. The Interamerican Court of Human Rights ruled in 2005 that the state was responsible for their disappearance and demanded that it open its records to help find them and form a National Search Commission, which it did (albeit not until 2011). The court also found that the military unit that took the girls was the infamous Atlacatl Battalion, responsible for numerous massacres and other atrocities during the war.[24] This is particularly significant for the still-unanswered question of whether US military and intelligence advisors, widely believed to have trained Salvadorans in torture and in planning the scorched-earth strategy, were also involved with Salvador's child-kidnapping policy. The Atlacatl Battalion was trained by the US military in the School of the Americas in North Carolina and was directly advised by them once it returned to El Salvador. The *New York Times* called the battalion "the pride of the United States military team in San Salvador."[25] Even if US advisors did not directly urge child taking—

and we do not know whether they did or not—it is difficult to believe that they never heard anything about it. Some children were even living in military barracks, and every child who was adopted transnationally to the United States passed through the US embassy in San Salvador. Robert White, US ambassador to El Salvador in 1980 and '81, said of the efforts of the Reagan administration and to a lesser extent the Bush and Carter administrations to cover over the horrors of what the Salvadoran leadership and military were doing, "The Salvadoran military knew that we knew, and they knew when we covered up the truth. It was a clear signal that, at a minimum, we tolerated this." If they knew and didn't speak against it, US officials aided and abetted child taking.[26]

Guatemala

Although Guatemala shares a border with El Salvador, the countries are quite different, and their civil wars had very different dynamics. One could say that about the Central America region as a whole. In Nicaragua, the guerrillas won; in El Salvador, they almost won; in Guatemala, they had an uphill battle but were stopped by genocide when they were beginning to make progress; and in Honduras, in part due to US military aid and presence, they never got off the ground.

El Salvador is a small, relatively homogeneous country (especially following a massacre of the indigenous people in the 1930s) that had a lot of support for left movements, including the guerillas. Guatemala is a much larger nation, with more than twenty languages. About half its people are indigenous, some of whom live in remote communities in the highlands that are a day's walk from a road. If El Salvador is finally coming to a reckoning with child taking in the 1980s, Guatemala's encounter with its Cold War horrors is still ongoing. El Salvador has a relatively complete counting of the hundreds of children that were lost during the war, and many have been found; Guatemala lacks anything like a comprehensive account of the five thousand or more children that were disappeared.

The roots of Guatemala's civil war date to a right-wing military invasion in 1954 planned and funded by the CIA to unseat a popularly elected president, Jacobo Arbenz Guzmán. Right-wing military rule followed, and in the early 1960s, a small group of Marxist guerrillas arose to challenge the regime. The nation's first wave of guerrillas was quickly defeated, but they regrouped and spread into the Mayan highlands—the mountainous regions where the indigenous population lives—in the 1970s. By that time, a broad-based popular movement had arisen, giving voice to the people's longings for a different future. Like the guerrillas, unions, teachers, Christian base communities and lay catechists, peasant cooperatives, and other social justice groups were targeted on a massive scale for assassination, torture, and imprisonment. The military killed or disappeared an estimated 200,000 people; there were only about 2,000 guerillas.[27] It was as if a nuclear bomb had been used to eliminate an anthill. A 1981 Reagan administration directive ensured the involvement of the CIA even when the State Department and Congress tried to halt it; the agency was to supply "training, equipment and related assistance to cooperating governments throughout Central America in order to counter foreign-sponsored subversion."[28] The word for people who have been disappeared, who occupy the uncanny, ungrievable space of terror and absence without resolution—*los desaparecidos*—comes from Guatemala.

A paranoid Ladino ruling class feared the autonomous, non-Spanish-speaking, indigenous Mayan communities of the highlands. Some (like the Ixil-speaking Maya of a remote region of the highlands) were identified as a subversive group, guerilla sympathizers or worse, and targeted for elimination. Although the military rulers denied it to the world and most Guatemalans in the major urban areas tried to pretend it wasn't happening, the military was committing atrocities and massacres in the highlands, slipping into communities in the early morning hours and killing everyone, destroying crops, killing animals, burning homes; it reveled in gruesome ways to end the life in a human body, whether man, woman, or child. The military massacred and razed 440 communities, with the intimate and extensive cooperation of the US military advisors and CIA.[29] Where they didn't assassinate, they captured people and disappeared children.

The effects of taking small children and disappearing them are similar everywhere: the exquisite pain of the loss of a loved one compounded by the uncertainty of what happened to him or her and the agony of having failed someone who was so dependent on you.

My name is Feliciana Raymundo, and I remember that after they disappeared José in 1982, they killed my husband and disappeared my other sons. . . . I became ill from the pure sorrow and suffering. During the following 18 years, I was able to find three of my sons, but I wasn't able to learn about my José. I didn't know what had happened. Sometimes I thought that maybe he had died and other times I felt that he was alive, I always kept alive that hope and I wondered, "Who does my son live with? Could he be married? Where would he be living?" Other days sadness would get the better of me and I would think that it would have been better if I hadn't left him with someone [a place she thought was safer], if I had done other things in those days, surely José would not have been lost.[30]

Survivors grieve without end, without resolution.

Although the armed forces and the paramilitaries certainly murdered children,[31] they also took them to other indigenous communities for adoption or dropped them off at orphanages or took them to towns and cities. One of the tactics of the vast bureaucracy of the military and intelligence, which effectively encircled the entire nation through its network of *orejas* (informants and spies), was to pit indigenous peoples against each other. The goal of disappearing children came from the logic of ideological *and* genocidal elimination: to disrupt the transmission of languages, ways of life, the practical arts of weaving *huipiles* (blouses), ways of thinking and acting. Sometimes, even during the war, people would learn that their children were still alive but growing up in a community that spoke a different language and was loyal to the government.[32] On the one hand, it was a relief to find them alive, but on the other, a sorrow to find that they were now, in some sense, also part of the enemy that might return to kill you and all your community.

The peace accords were officially signed in 1996, but the civic process of building peace is still ongoing. The now-grown children who were kidnapped are still searching for their families and communities, while parents and relatives keep looking for them. As elsewhere in Latin America, family members of los desaparecidos were a political force to be reckoned with, demanding that children who had been taken alive be found. Unlike in El Salvador, in Guatemala, the Truth Commission Report of 1999 documented the kidnapping of 183 children and demanded that the government form a commission to sift through its records and find them.[33] Unlike in El Salvador or Argentina, however, in Guatemala the same people who were found responsible for "acts of genocide" by the Truth Commission often stayed in power.[34] Two reports from the Archbishop's Commission on Human Rights, one in 1998, the other in 2000, collected testimony first on 216 children disappeared alive, then on 444.[35] The latter report, *Hasta encontrarte* (Until You Are Found), focused exclusively on disappeared children and suggested that there were many, many more cases. In 1999, a number of groups of relatives of the disappeared came together to begin the massive task of trying to reunite children with the families who lost them under the umbrella of Todos por el Reencuentro (Everyone for Finding Each Other). By 2008, they had organized 650 reunions, bringing together translators—often more than one, since so many monolingual speakers of indigenous languages were involved—and gathering the resources for the often long trips across the country on bus and on foot. These emotional reunions often brought out whole communities to celebrate, though the renewed connections were often fleeting in the face of expensive travel and the absence of shared language.

In 2003, two US journalists who had covered the war—Mary Jo McConahay and Patricia Flynn—released a documentary film, *Discovering Dominga*, through PBS's POV series that told the story of the forced disappearance of a child during the war and her adoption by a conservative Christian family in Iowa. It traces Dominga Sic's journey to find her community and then her activism to document the Rio Negro massacres in which she had lost them. Then it follows her as she works with them to demand reparations. The Rio Negro Maya-Achí communities had been flooded in a development project to build hydroelectric power with the Chixoy Dam, and the people had then been targeted by soldiers when they demanded resettlement and compensation.[36]

However, *Discovering Domingo* did not have the effect in the United States that the Argentine film *The Official Story* did. In part this may have been because *The Official Story* locates its fictional narrative about relatives of disappeared children searching for their lost ones in the context of the relatively well-known Argentine Dirty War, while *Discovering Domingo* worked to make US audiences aware that there even was a war in Guatemala involving massacres and disappeared children. Despite its proximity to the United States and the extensive involvement of US intelligence and military in Guatemala, the horrifying brilliance of the Guatemalan right-wing lay in its ability to flatly deny that anything at all happened. Guatemalan newspapers did not cover the war, and while many were aware of the inescapable presence of the military in the streets and people being hooded and carried off buses by soldiers, the lockdown on information and the murder of anyone who spoke out in this vast, largely rural, multilingual country made it possible to simultaneously be aware that something wasn't right and to put up barriers to knowing it for certain. In the United States, when Reagan said that military dictator Efrain Ríos Montt was getting "a bum rap" for human rights abuses, people could choose to believe that was true, even as Montt ordered genocidal acts against the indigenous people in the highlands with funding and support from Reagan's CIA.

People in the United States who adopted children from Guatemala—it was one of the top three countries for decades among US-based transnational adopters—may also have preferred not to know about the disappearance of children. In contrast to El Salvador, where adoptions to the United States were abruptly restricted after the end of the civil war when the military government was replaced with civilians, in Guatemala, transnational adoption numbers exploded after the 1996 peace accords. Many members of the militaries and PACs were only nominally demilitarized and became members of criminal enterprises, gangs, and cartels, and many political leaders stayed in power through the long, slow winding down of the war and its aftermath. Transnational adoption was a highly lucrative business, and as I have written elsewhere, children in Guatemala continued to be kidnapped and disappeared in transnational adoptions, primarily to the United States, despite the activism of organizations of family members of the disappeared to stop it. This continued until 2008, even as an online US adoption community continued to refuse to acknowledge the evidence that this was happening. For some parents and communities in Guatemala, especially single mothers, the war continued, at least in this one important respect.[37]

In 2008, however, a powerful coalition of human rights groups finally brought the issue of child taking to a head. A feminist group, Fundación Sobrevivientes (Survivors Foundation) began demonstrations with empty baby strollers outside the National Adoption Authority, the CNA (its initials in Spanish), that riveted the attention of the press. The highly respected Myrna Mack Foundation joined the Survivors Foundation in 2007 in producing a report on adoption and the disappearance of children entitled *Adoptions in Guatemala: Protection or Business?*[38] Even if the press could be—and for decades, had been—routinely discredited by transnational adoption advocates, Helen Mack and her colleagues at the Myrna Mack Foundation had a great deal of credibility in Guatemala and beyond as serious researchers. Sobrevivientes and Fundación Myrna Mack were joined also by a group with still more gravitas, the Archbishop's Office of Human Rights, author of a truth commission report and one of those who prosecuted high-ranking military officers for the murder of Bishop Juan Gerardi. The report was also the work of an NGO, Casa Alianza, the Social Movement for Children and Adolescents, and the Social Welfare Secretariat.

In *Adoptions in Guatemala,* investigators report on two different kinds of child disappearances—adoption cases and young people who wound up in sex work and pornography—and the 230 cases of kidnapped children reported to the Solicitor General of Human Rights in the first six months of 2007. Carefully footnoted, with detailed case studies, the report finally broke through the silencing and impunity around child taking that had begun during the war and continued through the years when Guatemala led the world in adoptions per capita. Although the adoptions were supposedly all of children who had been orphaned, abandoned, or abused, they weren't the right age to fit that demographic—Guatemala was known for its vast supply of infants and toddlers. The report told stories of a child trafficking ring and *jaladoras* (child procurers) who approached women when pregnant and vulnerable, in line to visit husbands and boyfriends in prison, or tricked them out of their babies in line at the Roosevelt, the public hospital. Pregnant women offered testimonials of being drugged, tricked, raped, kidnapped. When it became known in certain circles that babies could be given to lawyers and foster families with international connections for cash, as paid work disappeared and bare survival was at issue for many, the report found there were husbands, boyfriends, and rapists who convinced, coerced, or tricked women into relinquishing children. The report examined many kinds of material: adoption files at the PGN, the case files of these diverse organizations, international press accounts, and interviews conducted by the report's authors with those who alleged nonconsensual adoptions, exploitation, coercion, or kidnapping and could be located and had not been interviewed previously by these groups— the classic methodology of human rights groups in Guatemala during the war.[39] In 2007, a UN report, the *Report of a Fact-Finding*

Mission to Guatemala in Relation to Intercountry Adoption, began by noting that most of what could be said about adoption in Guatemala in 2007 had been said in international reports in 2000.[40] Finally in 2008, international adoption from Guatemala was shut down, ending the process of state-sponsored or -abetted child taking that had begun during the war.

Nicaragua

Honduras was the staging ground for the war against the government of Nicaragua by the Contras, a group that united disparate factions opposed to the elected Sandinista government. Although we do not have evidence that the Contras took children, there seems little doubt that they ran drugs—which, as we will see in chapter 4, was becoming important to how people were losing children in the United States; the only dispute was over how much the CIA knew about this sideline. From the outset, however, the extensive US federal government support for the Contras was largely run through the CIA. Congress and public opinion polls evidenced little support for the Contras, who were associated with widespread human rights abuses—including rape, kidnapping, and the execution of civilians. Americas Watch also claimed the Contras executed children captured in combat and that they kidnapped children and forced them to become soldiers.[41]

From 1982 to 1985, Congress restricted the use of CIA funds to prosecute the war against Nicaragua through the Boland Amendment, a prohibition that was apparently ignored. The CIA turned to other kinds of operations to pursue the war. One that became a cause célèbre was referred to as the Iran-Contra affair, which involved the sale of arms to Iran in exchange for the release of US hostages and then giving profits from the sale to the Contras to continue their war against the Sandinista government. Eleven members of the Reagan administration were convicted of unlawful activity associated with that operation.[42]

Congress was less successful in pursuing what was almost certainly the more extensive route through which the Contras were funded: cocaine trafficking. A number of journalists documented evidence that the Contras and those who worked with them were engaged in moving Columbian cocaine to Florida and California. The CIA set out aggressively to discredit reporting by the *San Jose Mercury-News* that linked its Contra operations to crack cocaine flooding South Central Los Angeles. The article series by Gary Webb claimed, in essence, that the CIA was involved with a criminal organization of Nicaraguan exiles who were responsible for selling crack to Los Angeles street gangs, one of the major epicenters of the spread of crack in US cities.

While the forceful debate over Webb's work has raised substantial questions about whether the CIA was directly involved with how cocaine got to the US mainland, as well as how it was distributed thereafter, that seems to obscure the larger issue. The undisputed fact, confirmed in government reports and Congressional hearings, is that the agency knew that a number of its operatives involved in supplying the Contras with weapons were paying for them with cocaine profits. The agency also interfered with efforts to stop cocaine trafficking, in both Latin America and California, which enabled drug runners in Mexico and Central America to get into the coke business and then to consolidate small-scale operations into region-wide cartels. These cartels were supplying some of the distributors who were fueling an emerging crack crisis in the United States.[43] The downstream effects of the Contra war were ultimately huge for the region as a whole, not only in a crack epidemic in the United States but also in criminal violence that spread from Mexico to Central America, setting off the refugee crisis that resulted in child separation and detention on the US Southwest border in 2018 and 2019.

The Question of Culpability

So who was responsible for the child taking in Latin America from the 1960s through the 1980s, 1990s, even 2008? On one level the answer is the military and sometimes the civilian leadership that ordered it. There has sometimes been a tendency in the United States to think of Latin American countries during the Cold War as carrying out an agenda that was not their own, making them dupes or puppets of the United States. This is not true; the extreme violence and hard-right political ideologies were very much their own Latin American Catholic, nationalist conservatism, even perhaps fascism.

It bears noting that Franco's Spain took children during World War II; this may have been the origin of some child kidnapping in Latin America, just as Mussolini's Italy and then Franco's Spain were a resource for rightist thought in the region. At Catholic hospitals across Spain, nuns and doctors told as many as thirty thousand mothers—most unmarried—that their babies had died in the period from the 1930s to the 1990s. These infants were placed with "approved" families: Catholic and married. The same thing happened in Chile during the military dictatorship, also in Catholic hospitals; they are known as the "children of silence."[44] Because the Catholic Church is a very transnational organization, with priests and nuns travelling all over the world, it is easy to imagine how the children who were called "bastards" until the 1970s were placed in what were considered more respectable families. Since the conservative Catholic Church had an elevated status under right-wing governments in Latin America, such influence could travel.[45]

In Central America, however, there is not much evidence for the influence of Spain or other European nations in what was clearly a policy of kidnapping children. Some elements in the Catholic Church gave a lot of support to the left and the poor, to the extent that in Guatemala, where there were significant ties between the military leadership and Evangelical Protestant churches, Catholic priests, nuns, and lay catechists were murdered at such high rates that a bishop ordered all of them out of the state of Quiché.[46] Catholic support for taking the children of unwed mothers was not a credible explanation in Central America. Furthermore, US influence in the region was huge. The United States was deeply involved in the day-to-day operation of the wars in El Salvador (especially the Atlacatl Battalion—best known in the United States for conducting the El Mozote massacre with US bullets—which was responsible for many kidnappings) and in Guatemala (whose war spilled into Honduras, as a staging ground for anti-Communist forces in El Salvador and Nicaragua).[47]

Historian Ben Cowan gives us a framework that is more useful and accurate: the political right up and down the Americas was closely networked and interrelated. The right wing in each country entered into these relationships for its own reasons, but the beliefs, ideas, and tactics were shared by militaries and intelligence services throughout the region,[48] especially at training centers like the School of the Americas at Fort Benning, Georgia.[49] The Reagan administration's willingness to circumvent Congress and even the

State Department to wage anti-Communist war in Central America (including the illegal Iran-Contra deal) was well documented. So, too, was the fact that the CIA was training Central American militaries in torture.[50]

The United States was less involved in operations in Latin America's Southern Cone. Nevertheless, Secretary of State Henry Kissinger declined to use the power he had to stop the kidnapping, torture, rape, and murder of those accused of being leftists in Argentina and the Southern Cone. We know from declassified documents obtained by the National Security Archive that Kissinger did give the green light to nonspecific human rights violations in Argentina. "Look, our basic attitude is that we would like you to succeed," Kissinger told the military junta and then tried to make a virtue of it:

> I have an old-fashioned view that friends ought to be supported. What is not understood in the United States is that you have a civil war. We read about human rights problems, but not the context. The quicker you succeed the better. . . . The human rights problem is a growing one. . . . We want a stable situation. We won't cause you unnecessary difficulties. If you can finish before Congress gets back, so much the better. Whatever freedoms you could restore would help.[51]

Some of the parents who adopted from Central America in the '80s were also scholars who wrote memoirs. One was Helen Fehervary, writing under the pseudonym Lea Marren. The stories of her adopted Salvadoran daughter about rape, murder, and the flying bullets of the military pushed Fehervary to try to learn more. She chronicled her gradually unfolding awareness about her daughter's stories of the civil war and concludes that the US embassy was aware of the origin of the children taken from those being punished for political reasons. Margaret Ward, a professor of German and Gender and Women's Studies at Wellesley College, adopted a child in 1983 from Honduras under the watchful eye of US ambassador John Negroponte—literally staying at his house, while his wife, Diana Negroponte, organized all the details of the adoption. (On Negroponte's watch in Honduras, death squads roamed the streets, while right-wing Honduran strongmen were receiving training from the CIA and the Argentine secret police. Negroponte was no traditional ambassador, but the overseer of a not-very-clandestine military training operation in torture and other forms of terror.[52]) Several years later, Ward and her partner, Tom De Witt, were contacted by Pro-Búsqueda, which told them that their child's mother was a Salvadoran militant who had been killed by Honduran security forces and that his family had been looking for him. What happened next was classic Pro-Búsqueda: a very moving story about how all the child's families, adopted and birth families, come to know, trust, and care about one another. But the evidence raises the question of how much the United States was involved in the disappearance of children. Apparently, a lot.

4 Criminalizing Families of Color

While the Reagan administration was waging war on Communism through the bodies of peasants and their children in Nicaragua, Guatemala, Honduras, and El Salvador in the 1980s, it was also rapidly expanding Nixon's war on drugs in the United States. This was painfully ironic, given that the CIA was simultaneously working with the cocaine dealers supplying the US market in order to fund the Contra war. In the United States, rates of incarceration skyrocketed as states and the federal government engaged in hyperpolicing of drug users, particularly targeting Black users of crack, rather than the dealers who had, in earlier decades, been the subjects of enforcement and now were protected by federal law enforcement who wanted to keep them in the Contra war business.[1] Mass incarceration of Black, Native, and Latinx people, in addition to its many ugly consequences, was also a child separation program. By 2015, one in nine Black children had had at least one parent in prison.[2] State and federal prosecutors aggressively targeted those who used drugs and alcohol during pregnancy—particularly Black and Latinx people who were using crack and Native people who were drinking—sending them to jail to protect fetuses. While many liberals supported these actions as earnest efforts to deal with increased Black infant mortality and what some claimed was an epidemic of fetal alcohol syndrome on reservations, the rhetoric of fetal harm was medically wrong and relied on baseless assumptions that pregnancy was healthy in prison and children and infants were better off without their parents. Furthermore, jailing people for fetal protection often left other children behind or sent them to foster care. Those who pushed the hardest to imprison pregnant people often had quite different motivations; they were antiabortion prosecutors who sought a legal basis to overturn *Roe v. Wade*, trying to assert a "right to life" for fetuses that could bypass the well-being of the people whose body carried them. Jailed pregnant women and their other children were an afterthought.

Mass incarceration was also an important history and backdrop for those who sought to defend the Trump administration's policy of separating the children of asylum seekers at the border. As Secretary of Homeland Security Kirstjen Nielsen put it, what Border Patrol was doing by taking the children of those who wanted to petition for asylum was "no different than what we do every day in every part of the United States when an adult of a family commits a crime."[3] Nielsen's critics rightly pointed out that requesting asylum is not a crime (and the efforts of the administration to invent one—like requesting asylum at someplace other than an authorized point of entry—failed repeatedly when tested in court).[4] Still, Nielson had a point. The vigorous criminalization of Black and brown people since the 1970s had normalized the separation of children and parents. Separating parents and children was, indeed, "no different than what [they] do every day in every part of the United States" to families of color, and for activism to get children out of immigrant detention to succeed, it needs to take up the question of mass incarceration.

Economic Divisions

The 1950s, '60s, and to some extent the '70s saw Black, Native, and Latinx and Latin American communities standing up against conditions of impoverishment and dispossession through collective action, law, and efforts to change consciousness and cultural production. Feminists and gay and lesbian people waged battles to change how we understand sexuality, the meaning of family, who could raise children, and racialized and gendered divisions of labor in unpaid and paid work. White supremacists, religious conservatives, and anti-Communists opposed these kinds of change, and their tools to stop these insurgent communities included taking their children and putting them in foster care or adoptions, or, in the case of divorce, using judicial patterns of awarding custody, insisting that certain parents (conspicuously gay and lesbian people, as I have written elsewhere[5]) are bad for children.

This began to change in the 1980s and '90s. It was a time of growing economic division, largely because of the work of a right-leaning social movement that espoused free-market fundamentalism, libertarianism, and small government—known as austerity politics or neoliberalism in some circles. Neoliberalism divided social movements, splitting the people with social and economic capital from those without it. By traditional measures of political and class power (offices held, influence in major parties, and so forth), some members of all these groups—racially minoritized communities, feminists, queers—did well in the '80s and '90s. But for the majority of all these groups that remained on the losing side, the bottom fell out. To a certain extent, giving some people a few seats at the table was a far more effective way to put down the rebellion of earlier decades than white supremacy or any of the rest of it.[6] The impoverished segments of all these groups lost children in unprecedented numbers to the war on drugs, violence, mass incarceration, the criminalization of maternal drinking, particularly on reservations, and the termination of welfare and most government support for households with dependent children.

The War on Drugs

Within a few years of Reagan's election, sentencing laws for drug crimes would explicitly name what had already begun to happen in courtrooms: a playing field tilting toward the incarceration of Black and brown people. Crack cocaine was cheap and being aggressively trafficked into impoverished Black communities, and its use and possession began entailing much longer sentences than the powder cocaine more often used by affluent and white people. In the 1980s, crack was changing the landscape of many impoverished urban communities, producing more petty theft, intensifying the presence of sex work, and even, some claimed, harming fetuses in their mother's womb. In her memoir *Men We Reaped,* Jesmyn Ward writes of the appearance in her Southern city of painfully thin people when she was a child, which is also a measure of the rise of the volume of cocaine trafficking through Mexico and Central America and into the United States.

> One day an older woman walked up to [my father], wearing white, her skin dark against the fabric. . . . It was hard for me to figure out that she was a woman; she was so skinny she had none of the curves I associated with all of the older women in my family. Her forearms were the same size as her upper arms. She smiled at my

father, and I saw that she was missing teeth, and those that were left were black at the gum line. And she was not alone. I looked at most of the people walking the street and saw that half the neighborhood looked as if they were starving. . . .

"Why is everybody so skinny?" I asked.

My father looked at me. He always talked to me like an adult.

"They're on crack," he said. "They're all crackheads." . . .

"All of them?" I said.

"All the ones you see that are skinny like that."

I frowned. The majority of the neighborhood was smoking crack. Skeletal men and women walked with jarring steps every day in an endless roam.[7]

As crack transformed working-class Black communities, the state was getting out of the drug treatment business, and treatment became much harder to find than it had been when heroin first hit in the 1970s, further intensifying the epidemic.[8]

If crack was a crisis for its effects on communities and bodies, it was made even worse by intensive policing of those who became addicted. By design, the war on drugs was a war on people of color and the left. Nixon advisor John Ehrlichman told Dan Baum of *Harper's* in 2016, "'The Nixon campaign in 1968, and the Nixon White House after that, had two enemies: the antiwar left and black people. We knew we couldn't make it illegal to be either against the war or black, but by getting the public to associate the hippies with marijuana and blacks with heroin and then criminalizing both heavily, we could disrupt those communities," Ehrlichman said. "We could arrest their leaders, raid their homes, break up their meetings, and vilify them night after night on the evening news. Did we know we were lying about the drugs? Of course we did."[9] By the Reagan era, the script had changed from heroin to crack, but anti-Blackness was still central.

Black and white people used (and still use) drugs at about the same rate, but African Americans were much more likely than whites to be imprisoned for drug use.[10] By the eighties, the US Congress and many state legislatures imposed mandatory minimum sentences on those convicted of drug crimes. The House of Representatives—with a Democratic majority—passed one such mandatory minimum law, the Anti-Drug Abuse Act of 1986, by an astounding 378–16 vote. That bill transformed the system of federal supervised release to drug treatment to one that instead added additional punishment. It created a sentencing disparity of 100:1 between amounts of crack and powder cocaine, which intensified racial differences in rates of imprisonment. One opponent, Mike Lowry (D-Washington) called the law "legislating by political panic."[11] This is what Michelle Alexander called "the new Jim Crow," the mass incarceration of African Americans, policing and then locking away a racialized group through the creation of a legal mechanism that both relied on and produced an infrastructure of inequality.[12] The excessive criminalization of crack was designed to put substantial portions of what was, economically, becoming a surplus population behind bars, as Black abolitionist scholar Ruth Wilson Gilmore points out.[13]

The war on drugs was also a war on Black children, who started to enter the foster care system at alarming rates as crack use put their parents in prison. At the same time, there was rapid growth in the number of Black children in the child welfare system for reasons of parental neglect—which often amounted to little more than poverty. Racist policing of parenting, Dorothy Roberts argues, was the companion to hyperpolicing of drug use.[14] As rates of incarceration for women doubled, then tripled in the 1980s, mothers were separated from their children by the state—80 percent of Black women who were incarcerated in the 1980s had children living with them at the time of their arrest. Some of these children went to live with fathers, grandparents, and other relatives. But a lot of them went into foster care. Experience in foster care also made it twice as likely that these children would enter the juvenile justice system themselves.

The figure of the "crack baby," the infant damaged by drugs, accelerated both mass incarceration and the growth of foster care. The crack baby was the war on drugs' perfect innocent victim in need of protection. The call for "law and order" had long been a right-wing dog whistle to justify putting African Americans in jail, but the crack baby brought even liberal Democrats into the fold, helping build the lopsided votes for crime bills that locked people away for decades.

In 1989, a couple pieces of news triggered panic about crack babies. One was a slight uptick in the rate of Black infant mortality—from 18.5 to 18.6 per thousand—while for white babies, it declined from 8.4 to 8.1.[15] It was the first time in fifty years that the infant mortality rate had risen for any group.[16] The second piece of news was preliminary research by Dr. Ira Chasnoff and a few other researchers in Chicago suggesting that 11 percent of pregnant women in hospitals tested positive for illicit drugs or alcohol and that cocaine use during pregnancy was associated with a whole host of negative outcomes: stillbirth, low birth weight, prematurity, and irritability in newborns.[17] Together, these two reports made it possible to believe that a sudden increase in crack use was resulting in higher-than-normal rates of Black infant mortality. But even if this were a plausible interpretation, journalists overreacted. A lot. Many researchers were finding that cocaine-exposed children developed normally, and for those who did not, it was not at all clear that cocaine was the cause, but this countervailing evidence was largely ignored.[18]

In 1989, major newspapers across the country ran articles about crack babies. Conservative writers offered suggestions like "put cocaine babies in protective custody," while liberals called crack babies "America's shameful secret."[19] Black and brown parents were "giving birth to a new underclass of disadvantaged youth like none seen before," as the *New York Times* had it.[20] The children in these stories had two major characteristics: they were woefully deviant (they don't even like toys![21]), and they were going to cost a lot of money (one federal report estimated health care and education for one "crack baby" to the age of 18 would cost $1 million[22]). They would all be in special ed, and they would mostly grow up away from their mothers and need adoptive parents.[23] In the media, the crack mother was usually a Black woman. One media researcher found that from 1988 to 1990, 55 percent of the women shown in network news in stories about crack were Black; between 1991 and 1994, the figure was 84 percent.[24]

Antiabortion Politics

The 1980s and '90s saw the consolidation of fights over sexuality, marriage, and family as *the* battleground between religious conservatives, feminists, and all those who sought a broader definition of household and family—this time, the issue was abortion, although welfare never went away. The crack baby was folded into fights about abortion. Ambitious prosecutors, especially in the South, used Black women's bodies to make bad law on abortion, using the pain of drug-addicted pregnant women to further a legal theory of "fetal personhood."

If the fetus could be recognized as a person as a matter of law—and pregnant crack users had been rendered by the press as particularly unsympathetic moral agents—then abortion could be criminalized as well. "The 'crack baby' became the poster child for one side in each of two heated controversies in the United States: the war on drugs and the struggle over abortion," wrote feminist public health researcher Wendy Chavkin in the *Journal of the American Medical Association:*

> Those opposing abortion generally have done so in the name of fetal personhood. This same assertion underlies the charges brought against women who used drugs while pregnant: child abuse/neglect, homicide, and delivery of drugs to a minor. . . . This concept of fetal personhood that derives from the abortion debate has led to the depiction of the pregnant woman as one whose selfish negligence or hostility toward the "innocent" fetus must be constrained by the outside intervention of the criminal justice system. These prosecutors have not been deterred by evidence from medical experts that many pregnant addicted women are very concerned about the consequences of their drug use for their future children and are eager for treatment, even though that treatment is difficult to access generally, and often specifically unavailable for pregnant women and for the incarcerated.

Prosecutors saw in the crack crisis an opportunity to blow up the medical and legal belief about abortion that, as Chavkin said, "maternal and fetal interests are intertwined and that the pregnant woman speaks for those interests."[25]

It was a familiar move. As we have seen, during the civil rights movement similar forces homed in on unmarried Black mothers and their "illegitimate" children to discredit respectable folk and the demand for desegregation and equal access to education. In the '80s and '90s, conservatives focused on crack babies to discredit the image of respectable and often white women making responsible moral choices about whether to continue or terminate a pregnancy through abortion.

Black Children and Protest

One of the reasons for conservatives to call Black babies "a biounderclass" or "uneducable" was to make the language of injury to Black children unavailable to Black protest, which it long had been. For example, Gil Scott-Heron complained about government priorities in his spoken-word poem "Whitey's on the Moon" on the 1970 album *Small Talk at 125th and Lenox,* released shortly after Apollo 11 first put humans on the moon. He put space flight in the context of the unremitting poverty of Black life and lack of access to health care. Echoing a discussion of rat-bite fever in *The Autobiography of Malcolm X,* he talked about poverty in terms of vermin and the health of children, "A rat done bit my sister Nell / With whitey on the moon / Her face and arms began to swell / And whitey's on the moon." He goes on to underscore the lack of state priority for health care, particularly for African Americans: "I can't pay no doctor bills / But whitey's on the moon / Ten years from now I'll be payin' still / While whitey's on the moon."

When, in the 1940s, Richard Wright described the ways landlords in Chicago killed the dream of freedom of the Great Black Migration, he talked about how they retrofitted old buildings as "kitchenettes," the smallest habitable unit, a tiny apartment with the bathroom down the hall. In "The One-Room Kitchenette," he says, "The kitchenette, with its filth and foul air, with its one toilet for thirty or more tenants, kills our black babies so fast that in many cities twice as many of them die as white babies."[26] In the '80s and '90s, as Black babies began to die at even higher rates, 2.5 times higher than white babies, conservative white commentators and even some African American intellectuals like Derrick Z. Jackson at the *Boston Globe* wrote that the cause was Black women using crack.[27]

Ultimately, though, it turned out that the concern about crack babies was vastly overstated, more effective at creating a case for taking children into foster care and making the fetus into a legal person than diagnosing the cause of rising infant mortality. "The crack-baby syndrome doesn't appear to be real," said Charles Bauer, professor of pediatrics, obstetrics, gynecology, and psychology at the University of Miami, in 1999. The principal investigator in a maternal lifestyle study that followed cocaine-exposed infants long term, Bauer said that earlier associations made between drug exposure and child development simply do not exist. "There was a frenzy in the 1980s. People were worried that the school system would be flooded with [developmentally disabled], uncontrollable children. That just didn't happen."[28] Or more dryly but authoritatively, the *Journal of the American Medical Association* reported, "The data are not persuasive that in utero exposure to cocaine has major adverse developmental consequences in early childhood— and certainly not ones separable from those associated with other exposures and environmental risks."[29]

Crack use during pregnancy *was* correlated with preterm births and sick infants, but it was not a cause. It was often a marker of multidrug exposure. People using heroin, alcohol, nicotine, *and* cocaine during pregnancy might have babies that did not do well, though it was not, apparently, the cocaine itself that was responsible. In addition, crack use during pregnancy was often correlated with houselessness and violence, including intimate partner violence.[30] However, the era saw the withdrawal of much of the support for women trying to escape from violent heterosexual relationships—including the end of welfare and the reduction of the availability of subsidized housing—and its replacement with criminalization. The Violence Against Women Act of 1994 was mostly a massive gift to police departments and prosecutors, an insistence that the only way to address domestic violence was criminalization, while welfare reform in 1996 took away the one program that had actually been extensively used by battered women.[31]

However, instead of understanding crack use during pregnancy as a marker that health care workers should screen for smoking, alcohol use, and domestic or other violence and offer drug treatment, housing, and other help to pregnant women, doctors, nurses, and law enforcement took their children. At the urging of federal drug czar William Bennett, many hospitals—especially those serving mostly Black patients—introduced routine screening for cocaine into delivery rooms, and mothers who tested positive lost their newborns on the spot; some even went to jail, still bleeding from labor.[32] More than two hundred women were sent to jail between 1985 and 2000 simply for being pregnant and using crack. Tens of thousands had their babies and older children taken by the state and put in foster care.[33] In the three years between 1985 and 1988 alone, the number of children in out-of-home placement—foster care, psychiatric institutions, and the juvenile justice system—increased by 25 percent.[34] The images were the familiar, almost archetypal, tropes of American history: African American women shackled in their beds, their children sometimes literally ripped from their arms.

Resisting Child Taking and Fetal Personhood

The ACLU Reproductive Freedom Project and individual plaintiffs who refused to swallow harsh treatment nevertheless won some victories. In a particularly well-known case, *Ferguson v. City of Charleston*, a Black woman named Crystal Ferguson was taken to jail after the birth of her baby, Annika, because the Medical University of South Carolina (MUSC) in Charleston was testing impoverished women for cocaine when they came in for prenatal care or to deliver a baby. Ferguson tested positive twice. She agreed to seek treatment, but when she called around, she found that no one would let her take her two children with her to inpatient treatment, and she had no one to care for them. When she enrolled instead in an outpatient treatment center, that was unacceptable to the nurses and doctors at MUSC, which had an agreement with local law enforcement and an ambitious local prosecutor who was interested in prosecuting fetal personhood and crack cases. So instead of going to treatment, she went to jail.

African American feminist legal scholar Patricia Ocen points out that the story of Charleston's drug-testing protocol for women seeking prenatal care or in labor became well known because, while many hospitals were engaged in prenatal testing, their practice was particularly clear and unmistakably racist (at least to everyone but the judge that dismissed the racial discrimination case). It was implemented at Charleston's only hospital serving primarily people using Medicaid. It was an agreement between the medical staff and a prominent, elected antiabortion prosecutor. And of the thirty people who went to jail under it, twenty-nine were Black and one was a white woman in an interracial relationship with a Black man. Crystal Ferguson—someone who was willing to tell her story to Lynn Paltrow and the ACLU Reproductive Freedom project and stand up to the city's prosecutor—became a plaintiff in a civil suit that sought to pursue the racial discrimination question. The case also raised the question about the point of child taking and prosecution rather than comprehensive drug treatment that would allow pregnant and parenting mothers to keep their children with them in inpatient treatment. It lost on the racial discrimination question, but the plaintiffs won an "unreasonable search" claim. While the victory was good for others who might have been drug-tested without the pushback, it didn't help Crystal Ferguson. Her fate is telling about the kinds of violence faced by women with as few social protections as she had: she was dead a few years later together with her 9-year-old daughter, the victim of rape, murder, and arson by a man whose advances she refused.[35]

Criminalizing Alcoholism

If the crack crisis sent alarming numbers of African American parents to jail or prison or into extended contact with the child welfare system, on reservations and among urban Indians, there was a related development: the idea that fetal alcohol syndrome (FAS) was blighting a generation of babies. The sense of looming tragedy was met by a related effort to imprison Native people who failed to stop drinking during a pregnancy. The frenzy was launched by an autobiographical polemic, a book entitled *The Broken Cord*. Written by Native scholar Michael Dorris, it was a memoir of his adopted son, whom he called Adam in the book, who suffered from pervasive disabilities caused by FAS. Published at the height of the sense of crisis about crack babies in 1989, the book told a painful story about the crashing to earth of Dorris's hopes for his young son.[36]

The emotional narrative launched a bestseller. It received unprecedented media attention, won a National Book Critics Circle Award, and eventually became an ABC-TV movie. The book helped popularize the belief that fetal alcohol syndrome was an emergency. Soon after its publication, with Dorris as a star witness, Congress held hearings and passed legislation that labeled alcohol with warnings against drinking during pregnancy.[37]

Dorris's book became a touchstone for the question of fetal rights—didn't those babies have a right to be born without disabilities?—both in the context of whether those who drink during a pregnancy could be jailed and in relation to abortion politics. Indeed, *Broken Cord* framed those precise questions, organized by Dorris's "rage that [Adam] was not born whole."[38] Dorris never really accepted who Adam was but took refuge in his dreams of a boy who might have been. Initially blaming himself for Adam's struggles, Dorris does not relinquish the sense that someone is to blame and moves on to the woman who gave birth to him. "My ultimate allegiance was to that person Adam was not allowed to be, to the baby carried by every woman who wouldn't . . . or couldn't . . . stay alcohol-free for nine crucial months."[39] This vision of a pregnant woman stubbornly clinging to drinking even as it harmed a future child builds throughout the book. Dorris compares her drinking to an assault: "If she had come after him with a baseball bat after he was born, if she had smashed his skull and caused brain damage, wouldn't she have been constrained from doing it again and again? Was it her prerogative, moral or legal, to deprive him of the means to live a full life?"⁴⁰ The book stops just short of calling for jailing Native pregnant women who drink.

Louise Erdrich, in her introduction, said that she would stop fetal alcohol syndrome "any way I could" and argued in the language of law that Adam's birth mother "had no right to harm her, and our, son."⁴¹ This is the logic from which incarceration flowed. The book's case for fury at those who drink during pregnancy also included harrowing statistics about its pervasiveness. Dorris claimed that one in three Native children had fetal alcohol syndrome, though even the highest public health estimates put the rate between fifty and one hundred times lower.⁴² Lakota (Sioux) writer and feminist Elizabeth Cook-Lynn has suggested that the trope of the vanishing Indian was part of what people loved about the book, for "there seems to be no end to the interest that people have in declaring the Sioux dead or dying."⁴³

Although alcohol is a legal drug, one that, in fact, is used more frequently by white people with college degrees than by those who are not white or are less educated,⁴⁴ the moral panic around fetal alcohol syndrome contributed to the widespread criminalization of Native women. One effect was very much like that produced by the crack-baby crisis: the belief that there was a racialized underclass that was stunted from birth. Television and print media produced features that decried the child abuse and even "genocide" perpetrated by Native women (projection, much?), including a weeklong segment on NBC in 1989 entitled *Tragedy at Pine Ridge*. Pregnant alcoholic women, mostly Native American, were put in jail to "protect" their fetuses. Mothers who drank lost their children to the foster care system. American Indian children with developmental problems were overdiagnosed with fetal alcohol syndrome. A 1994 study on reservations in Arizona found that between half and two-thirds of the children diagnosed with FAS had Down's or some other genetic developmental issue that was entirely sufficient to account for the children's developmental delays. Instead of looking to obvious medical explanations like Down's, physicians turned to FAS as a catchall diagnosis for children with developmental issues on reservations.[45]

In the book itself and in the wider cultural conversation that it engendered, there seemed to be little compassion for the person who carried Adam, a teenager who died within a couple of years of his birth from alcohol poisoning. As Dorris and Erdrich did the rounds of media interviews and Congressional hearings, no one seemed to suggest that the birth mother herself might have been a hurting child deserving of compassion.[46]

Native women on reservations were particularly vulnerable to incarceration for drinking. Because the Major Crimes Act gives the federal government prosecutorial power over violent crimes on reservations—a legacy of colonialism and the absence of self-government—maternal drinking could be dealt with in federal court and as a felony. For example, Marie Big Pipe, a teenage, alcoholic mother of three, was sentenced to almost four years in the federal penitentiary in Lexington, Kentucky, for nursing her baby while under the influence of alcohol. She lost her parental rights and all three of her children were taken into foster care. She was never offered treatment for her drinking or even medical care, although after her arrest and the taking of her children, she was found having drunk herself nearly into a coma. Because her "crime" was tried under federal jurisdiction as a felony, it was, horribly, to the FBI that she tried to explain her depression, her efforts to refrain from nursing when she was drinking and the baby's refusal of the bottle, the fact that she had children because she was raped at home and at boarding school, and her inability to afford an abortion or find a way to travel several hours to Sioux Falls, to the only abortion clinic in the state. Rather than find in this troubled child's story a reason to get her help, the US attorney for South Dakota charged her with "assault with intent to commit serious bodily injury," as if she had hit the baby rather than tried to care for it.[47]

If there had been some hope that the Indian Child Welfare Act (ICWA) was going to ease the numbers of children taken off-reservation into foster care and adoptions, *The Broken Cord,* the alarm over fetal alcohol syndrome, and subsequent crises related to meth and opioids made this promise ever more remote. The number of Native children in out-of-home care declined for a time, until the serial alarms over drugs and alcohol, when it jumped to a higher rate than before.[48] The Marie Big Pipe case suggests why. With the lone exception of a four-part series of articles by Elizabeth Cook-Lynn about the case that ran in *Indian Country Today* under the title "The Criminalization of Alcoholism: A Native Feminist View," there was no outcry over this case. Marie Big Pipe's attorney, her relatives and friends, tribal social services, and, perhaps most poignantly, Marie herself, raised no ruckus, but treated the extended sentence in the federal penitentiary as an entirely reasonable outcome of nursing a baby as an alcoholic. In contrast to the 1960s and '70s, child taking was normalized. Because of ICWA, the South Dakota State Department of Social Services had to work with the tribal council to terminate her parental rights, but that turned out to be easy to do. Cook-Lynn wrote:

> The white man's law and the tribe's adoption of Anglo government have removed the traditional forms of punishment and control for

criminal acts. As tribal police, court systems, state social service agencies, and Christian conservatives replace traditional tribal ideas and systems of control, the legal focus on the young, child-bearing Indian woman as culprit and criminal has been of major concern to women's groups. If the Marie Big Pipe case is any indication of law enforcement and justice on the reservation, it is a sad portrayal of the failure of the system and the subsequent loss of a woman's human and civil rights, and obviously of her treaty rights as well. The complex issue of Indian sovereignty, that is, the "power of self-governance and the inherent right to control their internal affairs," is as much a subject of this discussion as is a woman's right to protection by the law.[49]

The interlocking problems of colonialism, sexual violence, Christian conservative evangelism on the reservation, misogyny, and racism put Marie Big Pipe and other Native women in jail, even federal prison, and took their children.

It bears pointing out that addressing poverty, inequality, and violence might have been much more effective in preventing fetal alcohol syndrome than criminalizing people who binge drink. Some studies have suggested that alcohol is damaging to the fetus only when the mother is malnourished, stressed, and exposed to environmental toxins and/or smoking. If one were to pick the best way to improve fetal outcomes from a public health perspective, it certainly would not be putting pregnant people in jail. Jailing and imprisoning people does not ensure healthy outcomes for pregnancies; it causes people to lose jobs and miscarry, stresses important relationships, and exposes people to collateral consequences after a conviction—from making it hard to rent an apartment to being excluded from jobs and careers. Those who engage in binge drinking (or crack use) during pregnancy are already in terrible pain and trouble in their lives; according to some studies, *most* of the mothers who lost infants affected by fetal alcohol syndrome were dead within a few years as a result of violence or alcoholism.[50]

"Reforming" Welfare

If the criminalization of drug use and drinking for pregnant women in the '80s and '90s was not enough, income supports were also withdrawn. In the mid-1990s, the combined efforts of two Southerners—President Bill Clinton of Arkansas and Speaker of the House Newt Gingrich of Georgia—accomplished what the region's state legislatures (as well as some in the North and West) had been attempting for decades with various kinds of rules about suitable homes and fit mothers: ending welfare. The legacy of the 1950s and '60s fights in the South cutting aid to Black mothers and taking their children to prevent school desegregation were written all over their efforts. Gingrich announced his intention to file such legislation by describing it as a measure to "take the children of welfare mothers and put them in orphanages." When the measure eliminating Aid to Families with Dependent Children (AFDC) and replacing it with Temporary Assistance for Needy Families (TANF, which ultimately covered only about a quarter as many people with far less money in benefits) was finally passed, its preamble was a long discourse on sexual morality, illegitimacy, and the virtues of men in the house and heterosexual marriage. It was the suitable-home debate all over again: an attack on those imagined to be Black women (the majority of recipients were white) and an effort to take their children.[51]

What was new in this struggle over welfare benefits was the absence of cross-class solidarity about the effects of poverty or a discourse that cutting government benefits would mean some people losing their children. They did, and still do—a Maine study from 2014 found almost one in four families cut from TANF lost their children. Other effects found by the study were similar to the cuts to welfare in Louisiana to uphold school desegregation—about one-third of those losing benefits were homeless for some period, half could not reliably find heat in the winter, most had their electricity cut off, and almost all experienced hunger. Even the places mothers (and less often, fathers) turned for help when they were cut off had not changed much: church-based soup kitchens and food pantries were still a key source of support.[52] The difference was that in the 1990s and thereafter, the loudest voices in the conversation failed to acknowledge the importance of welfare for keeping children fed and housed and protecting mothers from domestic violence. The strong economy in the '90s and rising incomes for some people made it possible to argue that if welfare recipients would just work harder, they would not be poor. That was not any truer in the '90s than it was in the '60s, but the belief that wealth was just around the corner for everyone had taken pernicious root.

Some did try to lead resistance to welfare reform, but the spark did not catch. The National Organization for Women (NOW) organized civil disobedience, a hunger strike, and lobbying against welfare reform; the American Association of University Women denounced the efforts to end welfare, and Black feminists and women's historians were particularly outspoken about the critical importance of supporting it. But the rank-and-file members of feminist organizations were not equally mobilized by the welfare reform debate. When the NOW Legal Defense and Education Fund did a direct-mail piece on welfare reform, not only did the campaign fail to raise money, but it sparked hate mail from some NOW members.

The "feminist" position in the debate seemed to be embodied by Congresswomen who voted for welfare reform and were particularly keen on making men pay child support and punishing them when they did not, which they saw as the remedy for women's poverty. The problems with this position were legion. It required aid recipients to answer questions from welfare officials about their intimate lives again (who they slept with, when, and for how long). It forced poor women to stay in financial and hence personal relationships with nonmarital partners, opening them to disputes over custody and, sometimes, physical abuse from men they had tried to leave. Finally, it assumed that men had money to give them. For impoverished men, the child-support requirement could lock them into a cycle of missed payments, imprisonment, and unemployment, followed by more missed payments (or worse: unarmed Black man Walter Scott was shot and killed by a white police officer in 2015 in North Charleston, South Carolina, when he ran from a traffic stop rather than risk jail when he was behind on his child support). The secular and religious gospel of wealth that reigned in the '90s resulted in more lost children and less solidarity.[53]

Take a Percocet, Lose Your Kids, Go to Jail?

Over the next several decades, these public policy fights—the wars on drugs, welfare, and abortion—waxed and waned in intensity, but continued. Pregnancy, if anything, became a more intense site of conflict. As prison abolitionists and other critics of mass incarceration became increasingly visible in the public conversation, so too did exceptionally harsh treatment of pregnant prisoners. Neglect and the pervasive shackling of people who were in labor or delivering—even in jurisdictions where it was formally counter to law or policy—made explicit incarceration's historic link to enslavement and the chain gang, as Black feminist critics like Angela Davis have pointed out. Some prisoners were not even offered medical care during labor and were forced to deliver alone in prison cells.[54]

New laws, or novel applications of old laws, increasingly criminalized drug taking during pregnancy through insistence on "fetal personhood," particularly in a handful of states that were anxious to criminalize abortion, including Alabama and Tennessee. In Mississippi, antiabortion activists tried and failed to pass a ballot proposition that would make the fetus a person. Arrests of women who were accused of taking drugs during pregnancy were particularly hard to track, because they were often plea bargained, but it was clear they were rising: in a 2013 study, Lynn Paltrow and Jeanne Flavin found that nationally, between 1973 and 2005, there had been at least 413 arrests or other state actions against women for using drugs while pregnant. In a November 2014 op-ed in the *New York Times,* Paltrow and Flavin wrote that they had identified an additional 380 cases involving pregnant women since 2005. Journalist Nina Martin identified nearly 500 cases in Alabama alone between 2006 and 2015.[55]

Addiction specialists are extremely critical of this kind of enforcement. "To simplify a complex medical and psychosocial issue into a criminal issue is really just like using a hammer to play the piano," said Dr. Deborah Frank, a pediatrician and director of Boston Medical Center's Grow Clinic for Children. In Alabama, physicians defied a judge's order and refused to return a pregnant woman to jail after she was sent to the University of Alabama/Birmingham hospital following an accident. While the judge sought to force her to stop using opioids, the addiction specialists in Birmingham pointed out that the medical consensus is that this endangers the fetus and that the best option is to prescribe substitutes like suboxone. "Opiate withdrawal in pregnancy can affect fetal blood flow causing harm during periods of fetal development," wrote Dr. Peter Lane, medical director of the Addiction Recovery Program at the hospital. Law enforcement, long hostile to opioid substitutes like methadone, is exceptionally bad at understanding the needs of fetuses and pregnant people struggling with addiction. Some of these cases involve exceptionally small amounts of drugs; one of the women whom journalist Nina Martin identified took, in total, a single Valium in two half doses. She was criminally prosecuted and lost custody of both her children.[56]

Growing numbers of the mothers prosecuted are white, suggesting that earlier decades' exceptionally racialized enforcement has given way to a wider selection of cases to pursue, but all the women caught in this dragnet are still extremely poor. The opioid epidemic is described as a problem affecting white people, in contrast to crack, and this seems to have softened the rhetoric—addiction is referred to as a disease more often, and as a crime less often—without making criminal prosecution any less harsh. (Indeed, there is a case to be made that the opioid epidemic, born out of medical prescriptions and Big Pharma lying about how addictive it was, largely spared African Americans because of the long-documented undertreatment of Black people's pain. Racism bites white people, too.)

This period saw the consolidation of the long arc of punishing communities of color for the rebellions of the mid-twentieth century by taking their children. We are no longer shocked by the operations of the foster care system, even though it was born in its current form only in the 1960s. The recent decades of taking the children of women in particular (though also men, trans folk, and nonbinary people) who go to jail or prison has normalized it. Growing disparities in wealth beginning in the 1980s broke apart the solidarities that had served as a defense against taking the children of impoverished people during the civil rights era. The 1980s also saw the beginnings of immigrant detention—particularly of Haitians and Central Americans—that led us to the crisis of separating the children of refugees and asylum seekers on the border in the Trump administration. The criminalization of families of color, and the widespread taking of their children into foster care for petty or imagined crimes, provided the template for taking children at the border. The effort to criminalize migrant parents simply for crossing—even if they did so legally—and claiming that they were neglectful, was a strategy that developed over decades of punishing Black, Latinx, and Native parents.

5 Taking the Children of Refugees

In July 2019, there was a dustup on Twitter between the House Oversight Committee and President Trump over the question of how exceptional the Trump administration's policy of taking the children of asylum seekers was. The House committee sought to publicize hearings about conditions faced by children in Border Patrol facilities in 2019. These detention camps, designed for the short-term processing of adults, were turned into long-term facilities for children, in apparent violation of the law. The Democratic leadership of the committee tweeted out a photo of children with silver emergency blankets at the McAllen Detention Center in Texas—from 2014. Republican members of the House as well as the president himself were quick to point out that these were minors detained by the Obama administration.[1] This, in turn, led to renewed efforts to sow confusion about what the Obama administration policies had been. Although the 2014 photos were of children who *arrived* unaccompanied, rather than of children who were *made* unaccompanied, critics had a point. The Obama administration—like the Clinton, Reagan, and both Bush administrations—had put children in detention camps. Those who found the Trump administration's sometimes quite explicit anti-immigrant racism and efforts to subvert the international asylum system utterly objectionable found themselves casting around: what, exactly, made Trump's policy different? To find the answer, it helps to look back over the century and a half that Texas and the rest of the Southwest have been part of the United States.

Producing the Border

The US-Mexico border has been there for long enough that it seems normal that this is where one country ends and the other begins, and even that it would be the subject of national enforcement. When white nationalists call for action to "defend the border," we know what they mean, whether we agree or not. Yet there is nothing natural about the border or the belief that the people beyond a certain limit don't belong in the United States, nor even that they might require a visa to move north of it. To paraphrase Gloria Anzaldúa, a lot of people did not so much cross the border as get crossed by it.

In 1848, the United States drew a line across Latin America beginning at the Rio Grande and called everything to its north the United States, taking possession from Mexico of the lands that were to become Texas, California, New Mexico, Arizona, Nevada, Utah, and parts of Wyoming and Colorado. Although in one sense this was the end point of a cycle of events that began with the secession of the Republic of Texas from Mexico in 1836 to protect the institution of slavery and then the Mexican-American War, in another sense it was just the beginning of a process of trying to occupy these lands and make them part of the United States.[2] The creation of the new border (which was modified almost immediately, in 1854, with the Gadsden Purchase of land that is now southern New Mexico and Arizona) also overlaid a new colonization process on indigenous peoples, replacing the violence of Spanish colonialism with the new wretchedness of US imperialism.[3]

The peoples who had called the region home when it was Mexico or New Spain (or one of many older, indigenous place names), including Latinx/Hispanic and Native peoples, have continued to live there and engage in migrations south and north. Sometimes the peoples of the Southwest and West have lived together relatively easily, intermarrying and sharing the governance of the place; more often, Native peoples but also Latinx folk have been subject to violence, massacres, lynching, and efforts to take their lands and water in that arid place. There were also armed uprisings by Native and Mexican peoples after 1848. While eliminating Natives and Mexicans from the Southwest was never literally possible—indigenous and Latinx populations have grown steadily in the twentieth and twenty-first centuries—an Anglo dream of it as a white and US American region remains, and it has grown more virulent the more it is thwarted. It is the place where, as Anzaldúa wrote, "the third world grates up against the First. And bleeds."[4]

White nationalists call Mexican migration to these borderlands the Reconquista—the Reconquest. But that claims entirely too much about how Anglo they ever were. Spanish is still a lingua franca even on the US side, whether on reservations or in border towns.[5] Until the middle of the twentieth century, there were only intermittent efforts by the US federal government to systematically control migration from the south, and all the way north to Washington State, the West's agriculture depended on seasonal, circular migrations of Mexicans and other Latin Americans who came to pick crops and then returned home. In the 1930s, tens of thousands of Mexicans and Mexican Americans—many of whom were US citizens—were driven south across the border by officials and mobs as the Depression inaugurated a wave of anti-immigrant sentiment; some lost everything as their homes and property were seized. In the 1950s, after a decade of recruitment by US growers in Mexico to fill labor shortages in California, Arizona, and Texas, US officials, with the cooperation of Mexico, launched Operation Wetback to once again drive Mexicans out of the country in that era of anti-Communist paranoia.[6]

In the twenty-first century—as in the nineteenth and twentieth—people walk or drive across the border daily for school, work, love, shopping, health care, family, and religious reasons, as well as just for fun. The current regime, which tries to account for and control all crossers coming north by militarizing the border, is quite recent, dating to the 1990s. In 1994, the Clinton administration inaugurated Operation Gatekeeper, which sought to halt the open but illegal traffic across the many cities and towns that the border crosses, driving all migrants either to official checkpoints or into Arizona's desert, a dangerous landscape for those who don't know it, where undocumented migrants have died by the thousands.[7]

The Tohono O'odham Nation, with a reservation the size of Connecticut along seventy-five miles of the Arizona-Sonoran border, has about 32,000 members on the US side. In 1854 with the Gadsden Purchase, the border crossed their traditional lands, leaving several villages—currently estimated at 2,000 members—on the Mexican side. The two halves of this Native nation used what were essentially cattle gates to cross back and forth for ceremonies, health care, and to consult with tribal leadership. Then in 2016, the last of these were welded shut, leaving members of the nation on the southern side cut off, suddenly three hours from a grocery store. While tribal members can legally cross at regular border checkpoints with only a tribal ID, many speak only O'odham and there have been reports of people stopped, arrested, and deported.[8]

Meanwhile, child taking once again became an urgent issue in the region. In Oklahoma—where eastern tribes were relocated in the 1830s, having been forced to walk across the country by the military in a march so lethal it became known as the Trail of Tears—courts took the child of a Cherokee Iraq War veteran and placed her with a Georgia couple that wanted to adopt her (with the consent of her Latina mother but not her Cherokee father). In 2018 in Texas, a judge was temporarily able to declare the Indian Child Welfare Act void and place a child eligible for enrollment in the Cherokee and Navajo Nations in an Anglo family, setting off a legal conflict designed to upend Native sovereignty and bring down more than two hundred years of Indian law jurisprudence.[9]

A Long History of Child Taking

Immigrants and asylum seekers have long been vulnerable to losing their children. While the waves of immigrants that came to the shores of the United States and provided the labor for its factories were not targeted for child removal per se, their right to their own children was certainly the subject of indifferent regulation. As abolitionists like Harriet Jacobs noted, the immigrants who fed the machine of industrialization may have owned themselves, which was something, but they were free only in a very limited sense. Until 1938, immigrant children worked while their whiter and wealthier counterparts went to school. The smallest children, though, were of no use to the great maw of industry that swallowed so many European, Chinese, and Latin American immigrants, and the question of how to care for children under 5 or 6 when every adult had to work to keep the wolf from the door was a sometimes desperate question. Some parents, almost always single mothers, left infants and small children with orphanages and other underfunded institutions, even though such places often had horrifying mortality rates.

From the 1850s through the 1920s, orphan trains took children from these threadbare East Coast institutions to the Midwest and West. While some of these children were genuine orphans whose parents had been lost to illness or accidents, many others had been dropped off at institutions by parents or other relatives who hoped to reclaim them when they sorted out problems of housing, ill health, unemployment, or poverty. Orphan trains were a tidy solution to the problem of the children of the unruly immigrant and impoverished classes—sometimes socialist, often criminalized. The disorderly classes of the urban East Coast were at best unimportant to and ignored by the wealthy reformers who sought an inexpensive way to dispense with the problem of child welfare institutions; at worst, they were a threat—the "mob" that was producing strikes and riots in what was very nearly industrial warfare in this period.[10]

After decades of relatively open immigration from Europe, the late nineteenth and early twentieth centuries saw an abrupt clamping down. It began in the late 1870s and early 1880s in California with a racist movement to exclude the Chinese first through claims they were immoral and then because they were supposedly taking white people's jobs. By 1924, after waves of deportations of immigration on both coasts—a combination of anti-Communism, anti-Semitism, racism, and arguments about whether they were draining public resources and taking white men's jobs—the US

Congress passed a rigid quota system that sharply curtailed immigration for several decades. In 1954, the McCarren-Walter Act slowly loosened the restrictions for some, although it still awarded 85 percent of the annual US visas quota essentially to white people—to those from Northern and Western Europe. As before, there was still essentially open immigration from Canada and the Americas. The 1954 act also opened a token number of visas to "Asiatics," who were still essentially banned under a racial quota law.

The 1965 Immigration and Nationality Act transformed immigration to the United States, imposing restrictions for the first time for Latin Americans who wanted to live in the United States and eliminating the racial quota system. It offered much more open immigration for those from Asia and prioritized family reunification for citizens living in the United States. Yet it set the terms for Southwest border militarization and interdiction, marking the beginning of the end of the freer system of circular migration across the Americas.

Central Americans

The 1980s, with its anti-Communist armed conflicts, saw the first big wave of Central American refugees and immigrants in the United States, with the majority going to California. They were treated quite differently from the anti-Communist refugees, prominently Cubans, who had been welcomed to the East Coast in earlier decades, and from the less welcome immigrants and asylum seekers, particularly Haitians, who had been detained at the Guantánamo Bay Naval Base in Cuba and the Krome detention center in Miami. Central Americans, especially the adults, were quite welcome from the point of view of local employers, if not the INS. First Mexico and secondarily Central America had come in the early twentieth century to function as a kind of labor reserve for the United States. Agribusiness, service industries, and the construction sector in the United States, alongside employers of housekeepers and nannies, relied on being able to access a labor force that—under the shadow of deportation—could be expected to work cheaply and outside the federal system of labor protections, like minimum wage. In times of labor oversupply, these workers could be pushed back to Latin America; in times of shortage, more could be recruited.

The arrival of large numbers of children signaled the death of this tacit bargain, however. The deal was essentially that workers would not stay in the United States, and employers and local communities would not pay the costs of reproducing the labor force. Children would stay in home countries to get educated, get their health care, and grow to an age when they could be of use as workers. When people became too old or disabled to work, they could also be forced back across the border. In this way, Latin America functioned like South Africa's homelands or Bantustans under apartheid, a reserve where women, children, and elders were expected to subsist off a worker's remittances or whatever subsistence farming they could scratch out.

In the 1980s, this system began to falter in Latin America, as region-wide anti-Communist wars forced many to flee their home countries. Women became a larger and larger group of migrants, often bringing children across the border as well. By the 1990s, with the Clinton-era militarization of the border, this system broke down even further, as workers could no longer return to home countries to birth or father children, renew relationships with children or partners, or visit elders as they were dying. By 2014, when Central American children started arriving unaccompanied, it was clear that the border militarization and deteriorating conditions of violence victimizing impoverished people in the region had destroyed the old system.

Unaccompanied children began filing asylum petitions in large numbers for the first time after 2000, claiming a right to safety as drug cartels, police violence and impunity, economic collapse, and gangs threatened their well-being. US social policy continued to try to keep the old labor agreement in place. Its collapse was why conservatives and white nationalists were in a dead panic about small children crossing the border.

Yet come they did. Even earlier, in the 1980s, many children and adults had fled from Central America. Some children left rather than be forced to fight in the war—the governments in El Salvador and Guatemala and the Contras in Nicaragua and Honduras forcibly conscripted child soldiers[11]—while others migrated to escape violence less explicitly targeting them or simply in hopes of something better. When they arrived in the United States, most sought to find relatives and disappear into the general population, which was becoming easier as Central American immigrant communities grew.

Nevertheless, as soon as there were significant numbers of Central Americans in the US Southwest, there were children in detention camps and separated from their parents. While many slipped across the border unnoticed, the unlucky ones were picked up by the INS—between 7,400 and 8,500 children a year between 1987 and 1993. They were strip-searched, detained, and then usually released to parents or guardians to await hearings on immigration charges.[12] There were also, for a time, large, sprawling Red

Cross camps on the Texas-Mexico border that housed Central American families.[13]

In 1985, Jenny Lisette Flores was part of a smaller group of children who were held for months or years—the immigration and refugee hearing system was slow by design—because under new INS rules, no guardian could claim them. If her mother picked her up, she would essentially be turning herself in as an undocumented immigrant and become subject to deportation. Jenny's father had been killed in El Salvador, and her mother was not willing to run that risk. For children like Jenny, there was no school, no special provisions for children at all. Her mother worked with Carlos Holguin, an attorney with the National Center for Immigrant Rights, to try to get Jenny released to a cousin, but the INS had in 1984 restricted the list of "close relatives" who could take custody of an unaccompanied minor, and cousins were among those excluded. This effort to turn every child into a member of a nuclear family would keep tens of thousands in immigration detention over the next three decades.

Holguin took the Reagan administration to court on immigrant child detention—the conditions under which children were held and the question of whether they should be detained at all. To him, it was a no-brainer that unless the cousin was a child molester, Jenny Flores was better off with him than in an old hotel that had been converted into an immigrant detention facility, sharing a room with three adult male strangers, strip-searched, and with no minimal standards in force for health, sanitation, or access to education or age-appropriate diversions. (She was also, he believed, being used as a kind of bait to get the mother to turn herself in.) Jenny Flores was, after all, being held on a civil charge, an immigration violation that hadn't even been heard by a judge yet. It was ridiculous for the INS to claim that they were refusing to release her because they were looking out for her best interests.

The courts and the INS proved much more willing to clean up the conditions of immigrant detention for children than to release them. The Flores case ultimately split into three: one on strip searches, one on whether refugee and immigrant children could be held in detention at all, and one, subsequently, on the conditions of that detention (*Flores v. Meese*). While the Reagan administration defended strip-searching teen girls like Jenny Flores—even though it could cite only one case where a strip search had found anything: a mirror, which it claimed was a weapon. California courts struck down strip searches, and the government did not appeal (although subsequent administrations also did strip searches, apparently illegally). In 1987, the Reagan administration tentatively agreed to safer and more humane conditions in detention, the *Flores v. Meese* Settlement Agreement.[14] The Flores Agreement stipulated that children would be held for only a few days in the "least restrictive setting"—a licensed, nonsecure facility—while it was determined whether they should be deported or reunited with relatives. Otherwise, they would be placed in a foster home or licensed facility with age-appropriate programs.

But the most important part of the Flores litigation was the Supreme Court case to determine whether children could be put in immigration detention at all. The Reagan and first Bush administrations aggressively defended the practice of holding about two thousand children a year. They sought to keep detaining children even after the Ninth Circuit ruled that they had to be released to relatives, appealing that ruling to the Supreme Court. In *Reno v. Flores,* the government's strategy was to defend detention by arguing that it was humane and homelike (pointing, in fact, to the results of a not-quite-concluded settlement demanding more humane conditions).[15] The Justice Department lawyer insisted:

> While [INS officials] retain legal custody until an appropriate guardian can be found, they have entered into a series of quite expensive agreements with private, state-licensed child welfare organizations to place the children in these homes, pending location of a family member or the appointment of a guardian. . . . Half of the care providers are . . . group homes and foster homes established by the Catholic Church. . . . They don't have barbed wire. The INS . . . retained legal custody of these children while they're in these homes . . . so that they can pay for it. They're not imposing substantial restraints on these children. . . . The directors of these child-care facilities are actually paid to help the children find family members. The whole objective is to find people that they can link up with and live with in a caring and supportive environment, and typically that is successful.[16]

Advocates for migrant children painted a much different picture, citing nine different child advocacy groups that testified to harsh conditions:

> A recent case of a twelve-year-old undocumented youth taken into immigration court in handcuffs and shackles reignited public interest in INS treatment of youth. . . . INS has no standards for children in detention and according to the children's own testimony, use of handcuffs is not uncommon in addition to arbitrary punishment, inadequate food, lack of access to counsel or phones. One youth who was subsequently sent to Juvenile Hall described the vast improvement over INS detention conditions.[17]

Another report found these conditions:

> The El Centro [youth detention] facility is a converted migrant farm workers' barracks which has been secured through the use of fences and barbed wire. . . . At [the San Diego] facility each barracks is secured through the use of fences, barbed wire, automatic locks, observation areas, etc. In addition, the entire residential complex is secured through the use of a high security fence (16–18′), barbed wire, and supervised by uniformed guards. . . . No facility had recreational or educational areas, equipment or materials meeting accepted standards for juvenile detention. In all four facilities, young children ate their meals with unrelated adults. The major activity at each facility is TV watching and lining up to make collect telephone calls.[18]

In 1993, by a 5–4 majority, the high court ruled in favor of keeping children in detention, with Justice Antonin Scalia writing for the majority that "where the conditions of Governmental custody are decent and humane such custody surely does not violate the Constitution." In his dissent, Justice John Paul Stevens insisted that on the contrary, jailing children for offenses that were only as legally weighty as a parking ticket was obscenely punitive.[19]

During the Clinton years, little changed. About 200 children were being held in long-term immigrant detention at any given time, or about 2,000 a year, some of whom (though not all) had requested asylum. ("Long-term" meant more than seventy-two hours, which was the maximum amount of time INS procedures allowed holding a child without record-keeping). In 1997, a Human Rights Watch report damned the practice of jailing children—particularly those who were lawfully present in the United States because they had applied for asylum. It called on the INS to release children to relatives or child welfare agencies, to inform them of their legal rights, and to provide education and books in detention centers.[20]

The report was embarrassing to the Clinton administration, and so it finally concluded the Flores Settlement Agreement begun under the Reagan administration. Both sides agreed to minimal standards for the humane treatment of child migrants, which promised—ironically as it seems now—that "the INS treats, and shall continue to treat, all minors in its custody with dignity, respect and special concern for their particular vulnerability as minors." The settlement ratified INS's close-relative rule, allowing children to be released only to a brother, sister, parent, grandparent, aunt, or uncle, and only if the administration determined that the child was not a flight risk or a danger to the community. If a child must be held, it would be under safe and sanitary conditions in a licensed child welfare facility, with access to food and water, medical care, adequate temperature control, and lawyers, and segregated from unrelated adults and child prisoners charged with crimes.[21]

The Flores Agreement was intended to be temporary; there was a clause calling for the agreement (and the judge's oversight of it) to end in five years, provided the INS put in place rules that codified the agreement. As I write this in 2020, neither the INS nor its successor, Customs and Border Protection, has ever put those administrative rules in place, nor has Congress ever legislated on the proper treatment of child migrants, and so the Flores Settlement (and the judge who oversees it, Dolly Gee) has continued to be the arbiter of the appropriate way to handle immigrant children whom the US government cannot or will not release to their parents.[22]

Unfortunately, the Flores Agreement has rarely been sufficient in itself to deter abuse by immigration officials. Indeed, the George W. Bush administration detained unaccompanied minors and small children with their parents under far harsher conditions than the Clinton administration or even Reagan did.

As we have seen, it was the George W. Bush administration that first separated children from their parents, notwithstanding the Trump administration's claim that it was Obama. It began after the September 11, 2001, terrorist attacks, when the Bush administration began a wholesale crackdown on immigrants and asylum seekers, including children. It started taking children from parents, as well as separating parents from each other. Instead of family detention, it—like the Trump administration subsequently—created a legal fiction that it was detaining "unaccompanied children" by separating them from their caregivers.[23]

An Amnesty International report in 2003 called attention to these conditions and found that the second Bush administration and Customs and Border Protection were essentially ignoring the Flores rules for child detention. According to Amnesty International, child migrants were spending years in detention without judicial review of their claims to stay in the United States; strip searches had been reinstituted; and they were housed with juveniles convicted of crimes, beaten by guards, and subject to solitary confinement for infractions like poor sportsmanship, swearing, or even grammatical mistakes.[24] Children as young as 7 were brought to immigration hearings in shackles, with belly chains and leg irons.[25] In 2005, the Congressional Appropriations Committee ordered the Bush administration to stop separating families, telling it to use the Intensive Supervised Appearance program (ankle monitors and case management) or, if absolutely necessary, "to use appropriate detention space to house [families] together."

Rather than release families, the Bush administration expanded family detention. Where the previous system had relied on a single small facility, the Berks Detention Center in Pennsylvania, for family detention, the administration opened a much larger one to hold more families, the T. Don Hutto Detention Center near Austin, Texas. It quickly became a symbol of the abusiveness of the system. A former medium security prison for men, with capacity for more than five hundred, it lacked the green space of Berks (a former nursing home that housed up to eighty-four people) and was characterized by cells on long hallways with bars on the windows. It was a dramatic change in the treatment of refugee families who were lawfully present in the United States; previously, they usually had been released into the community to await an asylum hearing. At Hutto, children of refugees awaiting hearings on asylum claims were denied schooling, trapped all day in cells with either unrelated adults or their parents and with no recreation facilities. They weren't even allowed crayons or pajamas. The ACLU and others filed a lawsuit to stop the separation of children and other practices that were prohibited under the Flores Agreement, resulting in a new settlement again promising to minimize family detention and the separation of children from parents.[26] (Under the Obama administration, the facility was converted to a women's immigration detention facility. When a guard was charged with sexually assaulting women on their way to deportation, immigration advocates suggested that this revealed a great deal about the long-standing climate of rampant violence in the facility, overseen by the private Corrections Corporation of America.[27])

Deporting Parents without Their Children

Under the George W. Bush and Obama administrations, children were also taken from their parents through detention and deportation of parents; the children who were left behind were put in the foster or adoption system. The Urban Institute, an immigrant rights group, suggested in two reports that hundreds of thousands of children may have been affected by federal immigrant deportations under the second Bush and Obama administrations, an unknown number of whom might also have been placed in foster care against their parents' wishes. In 2005, an estimated 4.5 million children in the United States had at least one undocumented parent.[28] In addition, between 2004 and 2008, an estimated 5,000 US citizens were deported for failing to produce the proper documents when they were questioned by ICE.[29]

Detaining and deporting parents without their children was not exactly an accident, and it is not too much to say that ICE, in effect, took children. During dramatic daytime workplace raids, children were left behind at school, at day care, or alone in their homes when single parents or both parents in a household were detained. ICE agents who dropped their own children off at school or daycare on their way to work had to know or suspect that this was exactly what they were doing. The locations of detainees' children were easily knowable facts that ICE simply chose not to inquire about, and preventing immigrants from using phones and accessing lawyers prevented them from making their own arrangements for their children. And, indeed, ICE officials tacitly acknowledged as much when the agency changed its practices in response to critics. Because children are not allowed to travel internationally on planes or get passports without the involvement of parents or guardians, deporting people without their children often meant they could not get their children back without extraordinary good luck or the involvement of activist lawyers. Especially when children were taken into foster care, state child welfare systems often refused to work across national borders, and foster parents who were seeking to adopt often had little motivation—or simply lacked the knowledge—to find small children's parents.[30]

The children left behind after workplace raids were some of the most visible symbols of the Bush administration's harshness toward immigrants. One whose photo became particularly famous was Baby Tomasa: a little girl, about 2, clutching her mother tightly, waiting to hear what would happen to her father, who was picked up in a raid and accused of being in the United States without proper papers. She is adorable with her pigtails, clutching a green Dora the Explorer blanket—a well-loved and well-cared for child, but she looks straight into the camera, eyes full of tears and wide with fear. This picture, taken by Peter Pereira, a photographer for the *New Bedford Standard-Times,* became a symbol of ICE workplace raids for those inside and outside the United States.[31] Migrants under the age of 18 who were working at the plant with Tomasa's father were taken into Massachusetts foster care.

George W. Bush happened to be visiting Guatemala when that particular raid took place, and Baby Tomasa's photo was published in the Guatemalan press. Protesters and state officials grilled him about the 240 children who had been left behind, as was reported in the local press.[32] In response to a question from President Oscar Berger about children being separated from families in the context of the raid, Bush denied it. "No es la verdad," he claimed. "That's not the way America operates. We're a decent, compassionate country. Those kinds of things we do not do. We believe in families, and we'll treat people with dignity."[33] It was the same American exceptionalism so many people produced about the Trump administration policy of separating children from their parents at the border: "This is America. We don't do that."

After workplace raids in 2007 and 2008, school officials in New Bedford, Massachusetts, and Postville, Iowa, unable to get from ICE lists of who had been detained, tried frantically to arrange backup caregivers for children they guessed might be affected so that no child would go home to an empty house to await parents who were not coming back. In Los Angeles, one US-citizen mother who had brought her young children with her to work, on her way to a parent-teacher conference, complained that her children were traumatized after being detained while ICE officials questioned employees and led some away in handcuffs.[34]

The aftermath of a raid is a lot like a natural disaster. Social services, churches, and community-based organizations rally and try to get people information, income supports, and housing, especially at first. Families left behind report disruption, post-traumatic stress symptoms, loss of income, loss of homes, moving in with relatives, and chronic hunger from increased poverty.[35]

Two examples suggest how, under the second Bush and Obama administrations, deportation and child welfare proceedings worked in concert to result in people losing children. Encarnación Bail Romero was one of 136 immigrants detained in a workplace raid of a poultry processing plant in Missouri in April 2007, and her parental rights to her six-month-old son were terminated as a result. Hers was among the first raids the Department of Homeland Security pursued as part of a campaign it called Operation Return to Sender, which promised to aggressively prosecute "crimes" related to false identification, to sentence and hold people on those crimes, to conduct workplace raids, and to deport people whose status was suspect. So Bail was charged with possessing a fake ID and served a year and a half in jail for that crime, waiting to be deported after she had served her sentence and planning to take her baby with her back to Guatemala.

However, a Missouri judge, calling her a criminal with a "lifestyle" that was bad for the child, sounding for all the world like he was judging an "unsuitable home" in the 1960s, took the child and placed him in an adoptive home. At first, her baby, Carlos, stayed with two aunts. But they were sharing a tiny apartment with six of their own children and had very little money. When a teacher's aide at one of their children's schools offered to find someone else to care for Carlos, they agreed. Three months later, the aide visited Bail in jail, saying a couple with land and a beautiful house wanted to adopt Carlos. She said no. A few weeks later, an adoption petition arrived at the jail, in English. Bail was not literate in Spanish, never mind English. Still, with the help of a Mexican cellmate, a guard, and a bilingual Guatemalan visitor, she prepared a response to the court: "I do not want my son to be adopted by anyone," she wrote on a piece of notebook paper. "I would prefer that he be placed in foster care until I am not in jail any longer. I would like to have visitation with my son."

Although she repeatedly asked judges and lawyers for help, it was a year before she found a lawyer who would take the case. By then, it was too late. The couple caring for Carlos complained that she had sent no money for his support and had not contacted him. A year and a half after she went to jail, a judge terminated her parental rights and permitted the other couple to adopt him. "Her lifestyle, that of smuggling herself into the country illegally and committing crimes in this country," Judge Dally wrote, referring to the false ID, "is not a lifestyle that can provide stability for a child. A child cannot be educated this way, always in hiding or on the run."[36]

Bail's case is unusual in that we know about it, because she testified before Congress about losing her baby. Yet it was hardly the only one in this period; arrests and deportations became more common after the INS was transformed into the Department of Homeland Security. In the first decade after 2000, hundreds of thousands of immigrants were deported by ICE because even seeking health care or social services for a child could ensnare people in immigration enforcement.

In another closely watched case, María Luis, a Guatemalan Maya-K'iche' woman in Grand Island, Nebraska (the site of another large workplace raid, although Luis had come to the attention of authorities earlier), had her parental rights terminated following her arrest for lying to the police and subsequent deportation. Luis had taken her 1-year-old daughter, Angelica, to the doctor for a respiratory infection. Although she was a K'iche' speaker, the doctors instructed her in Spanish about how to care for the child. When she failed to arrive for a follow-up appointment, social services went to her house with the police. When asked if she was her children's mother, María, frightened that she would be in trouble because of her immigration status, said she was the babysitter. The police arrested her on a criminal charge for falsely identifying herself, and she was deported.

Her children, Angelica and Daniel, 7, went to foster care, and state social services began proceedings to terminate her parental rights. Federal immigration officials gave her no opportunity to participate in those proceedings, and she lost the children. In April 2009, four years after the children had been sent to foster care, the

Nebraska Supreme Court restored her parental rights, saying that federal immigration officials had denied her due process rights in interfering with her ability to participate in the state proceedings. State officials had never provided her with an interpreter, never explained the process through which she could seek custody of the children, and never made any effort to reunify the family, largely because social service workers "thought the children would be better off staying in the United States."[37] In an echo of the fight over the Indian Child Welfare Act, people under federal jurisdiction—in this case, those suspected of immigration status violations—lost children to a state and, precisely because of the jurisdiction problem, were powerless to defend their children.

In another case, one redolent with the reminders of slavery, a woman accused of being out of status gave birth in shackles before losing her baby. In 2008, Alma Chacón, was picked up and accused of an immigration violation after a routine traffic stop; she went into labor two days later. Transported to the hospital in shackles, she gave birth tied to her bed with a twelve-foot chain. Her baby was removed as soon as she was born and was placed in foster care for seventy-two days. Chacón had been in the United States for eighteen years.

Although both the Arizona Department of Corrections and Federal policy forbid restraining a laboring woman, the Maricopa County Sheriff's Office believed it could make its own rules. "Let's assume someone is faking labor—that's a hypothetical—and she then chose to escape and hit or assault the hospital staff," said Jack McIntyre, a deputy sheriff in Maricopa County. "She could do that easily because it's an unsecured area."[38] A year later, that policy was still in force. Another detained immigrant, Miriam Mendiola-Martinez gave birth under the same conditions just before Christmas in 2009.[39]

The Cartels and Central American Children and Youth

Central America and Mexico were becoming brutally violent for impoverished people—including, not incidentally, children—in significant part because of the rise of criminal organizations. The violence was often blamed on children and youth themselves— gangs, or *maras*, and their forcible recruitment of other children. There can be little doubt that US policies of deporting "criminal aliens" established Los Angeles street gangs, Calle 18 and MS 13, in Central America, and that these maras work with cartels like the Zetas. Yet children and youth are also the victims of international traffic in arms, the circulation of capital through development programs and drugs, and the forced migration of people through deportations, especially from the United States, and labor, especially for US agribusiness and corporations. As scholar Deborah Levenson points out in *Adios Niño,* the maras could not possibly have as much influence as they are said to without the active collaboration of the police and military in Guatemala and elsewhere. Indeed, most observers concede that the maras are blamed for all sorts of extortion and killing that they could not have possibly done. In a perfectly circular chain of logic, the police are empowered by politicians to use violence with little accountability through strong-arm policing—the *mano duro* policies right-wing politicians get elected on. The gangs—and more importantly, the cartels—act with impunity because the police and the military are not their opponents. They are two parts of the same organizations.[40]

As we have seen, the growth of the cartels in Mexico and Central America began in the 1980s with the CIA's decision to look the other way (or worse, some charge, to offer encouragement) as drug traffickers paid for arms for the Contras with cocaine profits. Planes that flew guns to the Contras in Honduras did not return to California, Florida, or Mexico empty, but full of cocaine.[41] Small-scale drug operations up and down Mexico were unified as large cartels, becoming hugely profitable. In the 1990s, Mexican drug syndicates benefited immensely from the demise of the Colombian Cali and Medellín cartels and the US military action against Colombian drug traffickers with Plan Colombia beginning 2000, allowing Mexican groups to become the dominant players region-wide, from Central America to the US Southwest.[42]

The purpose of the cartels goes far beyond supplying drugs to the large consumer market in the United States. They are also involved in extortion (of businesses and migrants), kidnapping, massacres, and controlling those who distribute pirated or legitimate goods. The people they terrorize are primarily impoverished, and because the cartels are transnational, they are able to follow those who flee their violence as refugees from one country to another.[43]

In 2004, the cartels gained much more extensive access to military-style weapons as the assault-weapons ban in the United States ended, creating a region-wide secondary market.[44] And if that was not enough, under both the second Bush and Obama administrations, the Bureau of Alcohol, Tobacco, and Firearms deliberately allowed assault weapons to be sold from Arizona to Mexico, apparently in an effort to see if they wound up in the hands of the Sinaloa cartel.[45] That same organization benefited immensely from the Mexican drug war, in which its competitors came under sustained attack by the Mexican federal police and military under Presidents Felipe Calderón (2006–2012) and Enrique Peña Nieto (2012–2018). When he was finally captured for the second time and put on trial, Sinaloa leader El Chapo Guzmán testified that the two presidents' administrations had accepted hundreds of millions of dollars in bribes. That syndicate survived Mexico's drug war conspicuously intact.[46]

The violence in Mexico pushed criminal organizations to deepen existing ties to Central America, where it was easier to maneuver. This coincided with political efforts in the region, including on the left, to bypass federal governments for political and development initiatives, preferring instead to operate at the more democratic level of face to face communities. Major players like the Interamerican Development Bank (through which the World Bank funneled much of its aid), NGOs, and individual donor nations focused on the local level.[47]

As international aid and development funds increasingly bypassed the central state governments and flowed to municipalities, the money of government was pushed downward to ever smaller administrative units. As a result, corruption spread downward. In some places, crime syndicates took over political power in small towns and secondary cities, running cartel leadership and their family members for posts like mayor, enabling them to control police, taxation, and bribes while ensuring that aid money and even corporate aid to local governments went directly to the cartels. In others, corrupt actors directly incorporated themselves as NGOs. According to a forthcoming study, two NGOs linked to a cartel were supposed to be providing school uniforms for children and distributing beans. They did neither. But they did receive more than US$10 million. Another was supposed to be providing training programs for farmers affected by climate change. While it never ran a single session, between 2011 and 2013, it received US$12 million in government contracts.[48]

Regime Change

In 2009, the United States renewed its role as an agent of regime change in Central America. With the apparent support of Secretary of State Hillary Clinton and President Barack Obama, Manuel Zelaya was overthrown as president of Honduras in a military coup. Members of the military feared the consequences of killing him, so they put him on a plane in his pajamas. Many Latin American and US journalists and activists cried foul at the time, and later, pressed their case during Clinton's presidential campaign. While the evidence linking the United States to the coup itself is circumstantial—having to do with the speed with which the administration ratified its outcome—Clinton did admit in her autobiography *Hard Choices* that it was she as secretary of state who moved to produce an apparent consensus in the Americas to ensure that Zelaya would not be restored to power (even as other governments and human rights actors throughout the hemisphere were trying to accomplish just that): "In the subsequent days [after the coup] I spoke with my counterparts around the hemisphere, including Secretary [Patricia] Espinosa in Mexico," Clinton writes. "We strategized on a plan to restore order in Honduras and ensure that free and fair elections could be held quickly and legitimately, which would render the question of Zelaya moot."[49] These damning two sentences, however, can be found only in the hard-cover version of the book, published in 2014. It was scrubbed from the 2015 paperback edition after critics of Clinton's role in the coup—including indigenous environmentalist Berta Cáceres before her murder at the hands of Honduran security forces—began quoting this passage widely as evidence of Secretary Clinton's undemocratic and illegal participation in "rendering the question of Zelaya moot."

The new Honduran government waged war on the opposition, starting a wave of killings that immediately doubled the homicide rate—already the highest in the world—and signaled to many the return of death squads. Members of Congress—under pressure from activists—sent two letters to Secretary Clinton calling, unsuccessfully, for an end to US aid (as required by US law following a military coup).[50] The coup opened the door to "violence and anarchy," as historian Dana Frank wrote in *Foreign Affairs*.[51] Opposition activists—peasants, labor leaders, LGBT movement figures, lawyers, judges, journalists—were murdered. "At the same time," writes Frank, "they let the police run wild. It is well documented that the police are tied to organized crime, drug traffickers, gangs, and extortionists; a member of the government's own police cleanup commission recently estimated that only 30 percent of the police are 'rescuable.'"[52] The US-backed coup in Honduras started what became the second mass wave of refugees of the decade: children from Central America.

A "Surge" in Unaccompanied Minors

In 2014, about 68,000 refugee children came from Central America to the United States unaccompanied by an adult, and that many again came with a parent—generally infants and toddlers with their mothers.[53] They walked across the border, often having endured a grueling journey of being smuggled in cars, avoiding attention on buses, and a few older ones on tops of trains—all risking robbery, kidnapping, accidents, and extortion. Some of the worst dangers of the journey involved the risk of falling into the hands of the police in southern Mexico. For instance, the San Fernando massacre of 2010, in which seventy-two Central American migrants were murdered by the Zetas and buried in a mass grave, began when the police pulled them off intercity buses and turned them over to the cartel.[54] (Although the Zetas are now a criminal organization, their history underscores how interlocked they are with the military: they broke off from special forces groups in Mexico and Guatemala.) Central American families paid as much as $7,000 for a *pollito,* a smuggler, to take them to the border of the United States, mostly to pay off authorities and the Zetas. There—in a carefully scripted series of events—children and youth crossed the border, sought out a Border Patrol enforcement official, and asked to be taken into custody to be considered for refugee status.[55]

The number of Central American child migrants in 2014 was double the number in 2013. US conservatives called this a "surge" and made it a signature issue, claiming that it had been caused by the "loose" immigration policies of the Obama administration (though they did not complain about its participation in the Honduran coup, which might have been more to the point). Republican party operatives even organized antichild demonstrations in California and Arizona.[56] Democrats also called for policies to "crack down" on child migrants, but they blamed a "culture of violence" in Central America—gangs and domestic violence—for the influx and called for more money for police and militaries (despite ample evidence that these entities were a significant cause of the violence). The Obama administration was at the rightward edge of the Democratic response, planning for expedited hearings to deport child migrants without determining if they were eligible for asylum—which is to say, without asking if they would likely be killed if they returned, as at least some them, in fact, were.[57]

As a deterrent to future asylum seekers, the administration put children and mothers in detention, saying that Judge Dolly Gee's insistence that the Flores Agreement meant that children could be held for only twenty days before they were transferred to a refugee shelter would prevent Homeland Security from "protecting the public safety and enforcing U.S. immigration laws." The administration argued that having a child with you was basically a free pass to get out of detention. It reinstituted the Bush administration's policy of expanded family detention, opening new centers in Artesia, New Mexico; Karnes, Texas; and Dilley, Texas. Having learned from the Bush administration that housing families near population centers like Austin, Texas, with significant immigrant rights communities invited litigation, the Obama administration put them in isolated desert towns. In a precursor to what would become the Trump administration policy, it also used charges of neglect to separate mothers from their children.[58]

The Obama administration's efforts to stem the crisis of children seeking asylum turned on family detention and deportation initially, but subsequently, Vice President Joe Biden also called for an "alliance for prosperity" that would step up support for tourism, free trade zones, and privatization that benefitted elites. They also gave massive amounts of aid to the police and the military on the presumption—the fiction—that the function of Central American security forces was to protect women and children from domestic violence and youth-on-youth crime from gangs, the maras. Instead, they were often giving money to close allies of the cartels. Biden and the Obama administration also pressured Mexico to do the dirty work of criminalizing, jailing, and deporting Central American migrants who may have been headed for the United States as soon as they crossed the border into Mexico through Plan Frontera Sur (Southern Border Plan). [59] Although the situation in Central America was hardly entirely of the United States' making, and Central American politicians, military officials, and *narcos* have a great deal to answer for, it is also true that the United States was deeply involved.

Proimmigrant groups like Ni Uno Más/#Not1More [deportation], signaling their feminist roots by taking up a slogan and hashtag coined by activists against *feminicidio* (the state-complicit killing of women), defended the children and women targeted by the Obama administration for deportation. They called attention to the heavily armed Border Patrol, the cartels and paramilitary groups that were blurring the line between criminals (those outside the law) and officials (those who make the law), and a carceral system in the United States that, conspicuously in the case of Central American migrants, has generally made no distinction between refugees, migrants, and those accused of or convicted of a crime. They argued against the belief the police and militaries should be understood as opposed to, rather than complicit in, the violence that was forcing Central Americans to migrate, making home "the mouth of a shark," in the words of Somali refugee poet Warsan Shire. You couldn't argue for support for the police as an answer to domestic violence. The police and the military were killing women, too.[60]

DACA

The other significant resistance to the Obama administration–era criminalization and deportation of immigrants was the fight for DACA (Deferred Action for Childhood Arrivals), which was reincarnated as a fight for an executive order from the president after the DREAM (Development, Relief, and Education for Alien Minors) Act failed in Congress. Although there was considerable debate among activists over whether it made sense to engage in activism for "good" immigrants: the "innocents" who were unaware of being brought to the country while out of status, who did well and went to school, college, or the military. Among young people themselves, however, there was also an urgent desire to come out of the shadows. This was especially true of those who were queer, who had witnessed the political effects of a coming-out strategy and experienced the personal freedom of no longer hiding their sexual identity. Civil disobedience in Chicago and Tucson, blowing up the protocols of hiding and instead calling on local and federal authorities to either deport them or grant them protected status, marked the new radicalism of so-called Dreamers (for the never-passed DREAM Act) and ultimately resulted in the Obama executive order for DACA. This renewed activism was also met by right-wing blowback, as the Republican-led states of Alabama, Georgia, and Arizona tried to accuse undocumented immigrants of "stealing" a public college education and banned undocumented students from state colleges and universities.[61]

President Obama always worked both sides when it came to immigration politics. He saw white anti-immigrant forces as both a major threat to his presidency and a constituency he needed to placate, at the same time that his administration understood itself as responsive to claims for Latinx racial justice. So DACA was, from one perspective, a fig leaf to hide the immigrant child detention centers. Never was this more evident than during the nationally televised speech granting the executive order on DACA in 2012. At the exact same time, his administration was moving mothers and infants from the detention camp in Dilley, Texas, to hide them from immigration lawyers who were winning cases to get them free, working out of a nearby trailer that they had turned into an impromptu law office. Following the Bush administration's defeat and negative publicity in response to its detention camp, T. Don Hutto near Austin, the Obama administration had sited its camps far from urban centers where there might be lawyers and activists who could draw attention to them. Taking advantage of the DACA speech, it moved mothers, infants, and toddlers—some of whom were scheduled to be released the next day—far from even the lonely trailer that had been set up to protect them.[62]

Zero Tolerance

Now we come to the Trump administration's separation of children from parents, relatives, and other caregivers who brought them to the United States in a pilgrimage to seek refugee status. In spring 2017, Trump's attorney general Jeff Sessions and homeland security secretary Kirstjen Nielson announced and implemented a policy directed at asylum-seeking families with children who presented themselves at the border requesting asylum. For a year, the administration secretly piloted a policy of taking children from immigrants and placing them in detention and criminally prosecuting asylum seekers. Before negative press put the administration on the defensive, senior White House officials made the new policy into a photo op. They touted the policy as "zero tolerance." In May 2018, Sessions, Nielsen, and Vice President Mike Pence made a series of appearances at the Southwest border to celebrate the success of the new policy. Sessions explained to a law enforcement conference in Arizona, albeit not quite in these words, that they were circumventing the laws on refugees' right to resettlement by stopping those they suspected of being asylum seekers at the regular ports of entry, telling them the United States was "full."

They forced many of them to cross elsewhere and then claimed that presenting themselves at other points on the border constituted "illegal entry" and that they were "smuggling" their children. These 2018 announcements by senior administration officials were treated as a series of high fives: victory celebrations for the administration in its communications with law enforcement, the right wing, and Trump's base.

For those in the administration like Stephen Miller, who spoke for white nationalists, child separation was designed to be a spectacle, with parts of Trump's political base actively cheering. A critic from within the Republican Party, operative Rick Wilson, told a reporter: "Their core supporters want anybody who's darker than a latte deported. They're not happy about immigration of any kind. They don't believe in the asylum process. They want to take and separate these families as a matter of deterrence and as a sort of theater of cruelty." In other words, Wilson suggested that they wanted the images of breastfeeding babies torn from their mothers' arms on television; they wanted the sounds of wailing children who had lost their parents on the radio waves. While Australia's island concentration camps for migrants or Algeria's policy of marching immigrants into the Sahara without water were arguably crueler, their policies were enacted with less fanfare and international media. Routine practices in US immigrant detention—rapes and beatings, disappearing people's belongings, and threatening or placing citizen children in foster care or adoptions—are done behind closed doors. They are not, in short, telegenic spectacles to incite the venom of those who violently hate immigrants.[63]

For others, accustomed to the dog-whistle politics of the Republican Party, where racism was supposed to be simultaneously trumpeted and deniable, the family-separation policy was meant to be hidden. "The expectation was that the kids would go to the Office of Refugee Resettlement, the parents would get deported, and that no one would care," a Trump administration official admitted to Jonathan Blitzer of the *New Yorker*.[64]

Immigrant advocates made sure he was wrong. On May 8, 2018, when Secretary Nielsen testified before the Senate for a budget hearing, a group of immigration and women's rights activists stood up with their children in their arms and walked out to protest the policy. The demonstration made the nightly news, and activists told reporters that they wanted mothers who had lost their children to stop being invisible to Congress: "Our government, the United States of America, is separating families who are coming to our borders seeking protection, and when I say that, I mean literally ripping children out of their parents' arms because they've come here asking for help," said Michelle Brané, director of the migrant rights and justice program at the Women's Refugee Commission.[65]

In the weeks that followed, journalists and activists continued to amplify that message. Vox and ProPublica obtained audio of children crying for "Mami" and "Papi" while ICE officials mocked them, and activists played it at demonstrations against child separation around the country. The daily drumbeat of photos in the press documenting immigrant children crying, living in makeshift shelters, receiving psychotropic medications in shelters, and being flown all over the country to shelters and foster homes created a crisis for state policy.

Members of the Trump administration, never inclined to apologize for anything, began saying that the spectacle of child separation was deliberate. Stephen Miller told the *Washington Post* that the goal was to upset Democratic members of Congress, to hold the children hostage until Democrats agreed to fund a border wall. Others described it as a strategy to get migrants to drop their asylum claims and agree to be deported back home in exchange for the return of their children. Kellyanne Conway told NBC that "as a mother, as a Catholic, as a person with a conscience" she was horrified by the policy, suggesting that she understands with great clarity that the administration had stepped into the trap that slavery abolitionists had set almost two centuries before. You can't tear children from the arms of their parents in this country without invoking slavery.

Indeed, despite the fact that evangelicals remained unshaken in their support of Trump throughout the whole Stormy Daniels scandal, Christian churches across the political spectrum began speaking out against the policy, reprising their role in the movement to abolish slavery. Abolitionists were suddenly everywhere, as journalists on Twitter began reminding us of the antislavery movement's denunciation of children being ripped from their mothers' arms. Even Trump was compelled to say, "I hate the children being taken away."[66] An image from outside an Episcopal church in Tucson, Arizona—a place that had briefly been part of the Confederate States of America—is particularly interesting. A journalist's photo of a child being taken by a Border Patrol officer was captioned "Jesus Doesn't Want Children to Be in Cages." The use of the word *cages* is borrowed from the lexicon of prison abolitionists, who have consciously evoked the movement to abolish slavery to talk about prisons.

The crisis of the policy—although not the policy itself—was put to rest in late June 2018 by a judge who insisted that children and parents had to be reunited. The explicitness of the child separation policy and the abolitionist response accomplished what many had thought was impossible: it made immigrants sympathetic to a large swathe of the US American public.

There were also white nationalists on the political right who were absolutely thrilled about the images of children being separated from their parents. They were all over the comments section of newspaper articles about child separation. White nationalists are a part of Trump's base, and they celebrated this news. These are the people who gathered at Charlottesville in 2018 as the "alt-right"; they are the people who shitposted and exchanged memes and declared Trump their leader both before, but especially after, Hillary Clinton wound them up with her "basket of deplorables" speech in 2016; and they are the Pepe the Frog and incel crowd who dream of—and sometimes do—kill Black folks, immigrants, and women in defense of the white ethnostate. They were the audience for all the claims that immigrants are criminals and "rapists," and they are the ones who have called for "zero tolerance" of immigrants at all costs.

White House senior policy advisor Stephen Miller was apparently the architect of "zero tolerance." Like Steve Bannon before him, his job was to be the voice of the racist right in the administration. As a number of journalists noted, the outrage over the policy was exactly what Miller hoped for. A critic from within the Republican Party, characterized by *Vanity Fair* as "an outside White House adviser," said, "Stephen actually enjoys seeing those pictures at the border. He's a twisted guy. . . . There's always been a way he's gone about this. He's Waffen-SS."[67] While Miller is not actually a member of any white pride or Nazi parties as far as we know, he is a college friend of Richard Spencer's, the white nationalist leader who coined the term *alt-right,* and the two worked together at Duke University to organize an anti-immigrant event.[68]

Miller's vision for the United States, and one might suspect Donald Trump's as well, seems to be a racial one, in which the law of the land is Indian genocide, racial slavery or some near-equivalent in mass incarceration and convict labor, and zero tolerance for immigrants.

The point is *not* that Stephen Miller and Trump's supporters on the far right are racists. That's not interesting. Lots of people are racist; the United States has a long history of racism. Rather, the issue is that their political philosophy is about racial nationalism, and that is what motivates their genocidal desire to create a white country. In Europe and the Americas, the political history of the nations has alternated between racial nationalism, the desire for a white ethnostate, which is associated with fascism and other hard-right formations, and a civic nationalism, which, while often racist, nevertheless imagines the nation as composed of different racial groups.[69]

Child separation policy is a product of racial nationalism, the genocidal impulse to annihilate the nation's outsiders by interrupting their reproduction. This is why the 1948 Convention on Genocide identifies one of the elements of the crime of genocide as "forcibly transferring children of the group to another group." The delight in sobbing brown children being separated from their parents is about driving out Central American and other immigrant or refugee parents and raising their children in institutions or in white families, reproducing boarding school policy. The Trump administration sought to enact a new kind of immigration policy, one grounded firmly in the political philosophy of the hard right, a new racial nationalism that maintained only the barest veneer of adherence to democratic institutions.

Events in 2019, however, revealed the weakness of the strategy of the immigration policy's opponents as well as their historical memory. Critics of foster care and mass incarceration like Black feminist scholar Dorothy Roberts pointed out early on that the failure to recognize the parallels between the policy targeting refugees and policies affecting the impoverished within the United States made its critics much less effective. When the administration began to claim that it was separating parents from their children because they were "a danger" to their children—either because they had criminal records or, on the flimsiest of evidence, were neglecting their children—the response was far more muted. The Trump administration also argued that it did not need to provide soap, toothbrushes, towels, blankets, opportunities to sleep, or temperatures much above freezing to be in compliance with the Flores Agreement's requirements of "safe and sanitary" conditions in immigrant detention for children.[70] Yet even when children taken from their parents were crowded into squalid Border Patrol camps in blatant disregard of the Flores Agreement and died from influenza and other diseases, the policy's critics failed to regain their momentum.[71]

Racism—and the gaps in historical memory—made it far more difficult to mobilize around a policy that claimed that asylum seekers were bad parents. Supporters of separating children at the border invoked countermemories of mass incarceration and criminalization built during the crack epidemic and the fetal alcohol syndrome crisis: we do this all the time; we have always separated children from their criminal parents. The long history of racist claims about Black and Native women's inadequacy as parents and lack of maternal feelings was deployed in these charges that refugees were dangerous or neglectful parents. We are haunted by our collective inability to think of those who lose their children to foster care or face criminal charges as having claims to their kids that deserve to be taken seriously. Above all, the relative silence by 2019 was a failure of remembrance of taking children as part of the arsenal of state terrorism against unruly or rebellious communities.

Conclusion

Taking Children Back—Resistance

What can people do to stop children from being taken from their parents, kin, and caregivers? Dissent and protest, as generations have done before, persistently and in many diverse forms. Abolitionists built a grassroots movement through their urgent work in churches and in the sermons of itinerant preachers, Black and white, and by founding anti-slavery societies, organizing walk-outs at colleges and universities, and speaking and writing for every imaginable kind of gathering, large and small. They made the stories of babies and children separated from their weeping mothers inescapable by filling books (even children's primers), their own newspapers, street corners, and lecture halls with them. The Association on American Indian Affairs helped impoverished mothers and grandmothers who had never travelled across their home state before to testify before Congress, to tell the Overseas Press Club about their lost children, and to go to court and demand them back. Central Americans asked their priests for help, testified in international courts, and reached for solidarity from Europe, the United States, and up and down Latin America. ACLU lawyers filed suit on behalf of parents deported without their children in 2017 and 2018 and demanded their readmission to the United States to reclaim them.[1] All sorts of actions, organizing, and images have been important. The more we know about the history of child taking and the resistance to it, the more effective protest can be.

It is less clear, however, that it has mattered who the president is, even though calls for voting for one or another candidate in national elections have become a favored form of protest in early twenty-first century social media. There is a "Trump exceptionalist" position that insists that children were put in detention camps because he became president. Indeed, he ran on an anti-immigrant platform and formed an administration that prominently included white nationalists and sympathizers. Still, it is entirely possible that a different president would have put children in immigrant detention under the circumstances the Trump administration faced, including rising numbers of applicants for asylum, which had prompted both the second Bush administration and the Obama administration to open new detention centers. It is also not clear that Trump's administration could have or would have taken children from their refugee parents and put them in camps if that path had not already been well-established through the long history of child taking and the decades-long history of separating asylum-seeking children at the Southwest border. The George W. Bush administration, as we have seen, established the policies of separating migrant children, even though he had run, at least initially, against the xenophobic wing of the Republican Party in his primary campaign against Pat Buchanan. After September 11, 2001, his White House bowed to nationalist and xenophobic elements in both parties and took children from their families and put them, alone, in large-scale detention centers. The Obama administration was more likely to keep mothers and small children who arrived together in "family" detention centers, although that period saw the beginning of the use of "neglect" as a political strategy to separate mothers from their children. The Obama administration also detained large numbers of unaccompanied children, many in the same facilities that the Trump administration would later use. Trump and his critics simply made child separation much more explicit than it had been in the Bush or Obama administrations. Reforming US immigration policy and halting the separation of children from their parents as a political tactic against immigrant and refugee communities will require more than a change in president.

Sometimes presidents *have* been important to stopping the use of child taking as a tactic of fear and intimidation, but only because of the political movements that have defined these presidencies. The election of Abraham Lincoln certainly mattered to the ending of slavery and its separation of parents and children. Still, he never would have signed the Emancipation Proclamation without an abolitionist movement; Lincoln himself admitted that slavery had been a "minor question" in his mind until 1854, and even during the Civil War he had to be pushed by the tremendous passion of the abolitionist cause.[2] The creation of day schools as alternatives to Indian boarding schools owed a debt to the election of Franklin Delano Roosevelt in 1932 and his appointment of the activist John Collier as head of the Bureau of Indian Affairs. Just as the New Deal owed a powerful debt to the socialist movement that Roosevelt tried to both ride to power and stay to the right of, the Indian New Deal could never have happened without the substantial opposition to assimilation, land grabs, and the colonial efforts to obliterate traditional cultural practices in Indian country. On the other hand, Collier's high-handedness in forcing tribal nations to adopt specific forms of governance generated substantial opposition during his tenure, pushing the final resolution of the question of authority over the fate of children forward in time to the much more grassroots campaign for the Indian Child Welfare Act between 1968 and 1978. Roosevelt had also been responsible for the internment of Japanese and Japanese American people in wartime detention centers from 1942 to 1945. It had clearly been the anti-boarding-school movement, not the man, who opposed detention.

Solidarities mattered at least as much as asking for relief in the halls of power. When tens of thousands of children in New Orleans lost their welfare benefits and were at risk of going to foster care in 1960, Black churchgoers cooked for them, and civic groups and community newspapers solicited and coordinated national and international donations of food and money. They enlisted the help of the ACLU in getting the Social Security Administration to change its policies. They petitioned the president, threatened to go to the United Nations, and called on European organizations to give material aid and moral support. Civil rights groups also provided what only movements can, which is the ability to change consciousness, or what we might also call the framework that a community uses to understand what is happening. Activists in the Urban League—often thought of as at the most conservative end of the range of civil rights groups, the least militant, and most invested in respectability—refused the narrative of unfit, sexually promiscuous mothers who were too lazy to work and so were on welfare. Powerfully, they insisted instead that it was the state and federal governments that were acting immorally, allowing Black babies to starve in order to defend segregated schools.

Similarly, when the Red Power movement began promoting its vision of self-determination for poor and working-class Native people in the 1960s and '70s through its push for tribal sovereignty, it gave shape and broader meaning to mothers' and foster mothers' resistance to state welfare workers. Where welfare workers tried to shame them for their poverty, their pregnancies, their unemployment, and the condition of their housing, Red Power connected them to a narrative about tradition and resistance that ultimately made the ability to control whether children were taken off reservations by the state one of the keystones of tribal autonomy.

Concern and care matter. Poet Marge Piercy once wrote, "Attention is love, what we must give / children, mothers, fathers, pets, / our friends, the news, the woes of others."[3] Paying attention to the pain of others and raising objections when people are criminalized by the state and then lose their children for what had once been considered minor infractions has made a difference. Welfare workers who refused to encourage mothers cut off public assistance to "voluntarily" relinquish their children, forcing the state to do it through the juvenile justice system instead, introduced friction into the machine of taking Black children and slowed it. As a result, fewer children lost their mothers, and fewer mothers, their children. People who filed lawsuits or wrote opinion pieces against the criminalization of pregnant women of color in the 1980s made it more difficult for prosecutors to criminalize them. That there were people marching and facing down tear gas after the police shot Mike Brown and left his body lying in the street all day in Ferguson, Missouri, meant that those who argued that stealing cigarillos (if, in fact, he did) justified his death did not have the last word, and the people who marched started a movement (not for the first time) against police killing of unarmed youth.[4] Those who have held speak-outs and introduced city council resolutions demanding attention to the epidemic of missing and murdered indigenous women have refused to let it be made invisible. The killing of Native and Black daughters and sons has been kept from vanishing over these four long centuries by the protest and public grieving of African American and indigenous communities. Telling the stories and calling attention to what happened keeps the loss and even death of children from assuming the force of inevitability.

The reverse is also true. Silence allows children to be separated from their parents, and what we fail to pay attention to has consequences. In contrast to the activism of the Urban League in 1960, in the mid-1990s activists, policy makers, and journalists did not make the point that so-called welfare reform would cause struggling parents to lose their children, as it in fact did. Indeed, this is exactly what it was designed to do; Speaker of the House Newt Gingrich, drawing on the earlier legislative legacy in the South, announced this intention explicitly. The collective failure of people of conscience to object to the taking of welfare-eligible children has allowed it to continue for more than thirty years.

The feminist and queer insistence that children do not have to be raised in nuclear families is important. Indigenous people struggled with Anglo social workers about elders, single mothers, and other kin caring for children as part of the effort to get ICWA passed. White segregationists targeted Black single mothers and cut off their support in the fight to keep school children separate and unequal. Black single, lesbian, and bisexual mothers are still, in 2020, particularly likely to be scrutinized by child protective services and to lose their children to foster care.[5] Those who have struggled to support all those who are reputedly "bad" parents because of who they are—people who are unmarried, queer, trans, undocumented, who have criminal records, who have too often used alcohol or drugs, or who made their living in unrespectable or illegal ways—have helped children stay with their parents.

Grappling with what religious communities believe and support matters. Jewish groups organizing under the rubric of "Never Again Is Now" have born witness and offered a narrative linking US immigrant children's detention camps to Nazi concentration camps. In defiance of new regimes of deportation, mainline Protestant and Catholic churches have turned their basements into sanctuaries for immigrants, allowing children and parents to continue to live in the same country and community. Struggles over whether and how to support church, mosque, and synagogue members who have criminal records, who wrestle with drinking, or who may have used drugs during pregnancy can make the difference between their children going to—or staying in—foster care or not. The abolition of slavery led to virtually a holy war in the United States, with denominations and congregations splitting over it. The prison abolition movement, which, alongside the decriminalization of drugs and mental-health episodes, has the potential to do more than almost anything to keep parents and children together, and it has put down roots in religious congregations, as well as flourishing in civic groups like Critical Resistance and Students Against Mass Incarceration.

Activists are most effective when there are multiple kinds of protest and levels of action. Family members of the disappeared in Latin America demanded justice for their murdered and disappeared children through street demonstrations and court cases, in reports to truth commissions and the Inter-American Court of Human Rights, and asking for and sometimes getting help from up and down the Catholic Church hierarchy, from the pope to bishops to priests and nuns to lay catechists. These family members pulled in grassroots international solidarity movements and fought for prosecutions of police, military, and presidents. They passed around photos through informal networks, worked with mental health practitioners, and supported the development of laboratory tests and databases. They published books and worked with left activists. Above all, they were tenacious and relentless, devoting decades to finding children who had been taken by the state. They were also able to continually renew their activism as conditions changed, whether standing against the transnational adoption of kidnapped children from Guatemala in 2008 or building a national movement across Mexico to demand justice for the disappeared teacher-training students from Ayotzinapa, Mexico, and the hundreds of thousands of other children and youth killed or lost through the combined forces of small-town political power, the drug cartels, the police, and the military.

Social movement solidarities matter. In the 1980s, feminists mobilized against religious fundamentalist claims about reproduction and good mothers and were profoundly suspicious of claims about fetal personhood, "crack babies," and fetal alcohol syndrome. Lawyers like Lynn Paltrow of the ACLU Reproductive Freedom Project challenged the legal basis of cocaine testing in labor and delivery, insisting that even those struggling with drugs had a right to due process and to be free from differential treatment because of race or poverty. Physician and public health scholar Wendy Chavkin made sure that doctors and the general public heard about the lack of scientific consensus about the damage supposedly afflicting "crack babies." INCITE! Women of Color Against Violence stood against the incarceration of people who were drinking or using drugs during their pregnancy, insisting that they were entitled to treatment, support, and healing from sexual violence, rather than the cages and the moral opprobrium that led to despair and, often, early death, not only for parents but for their children as well. In July 2019 in Oklahoma, a range of social movements worked together to stop Fort Sill from being turned into an immigrant detention camp for children. They included Tsuru for Solidarity, a Japanese American activist group; Oklahoma: AIM Indian Territory; DREAM Action Oklahoma; Black Lives Matter Oklahoma City; and the Indigenous Environmental Network. This coalition not only brought together local racial justice groups but incarnated a vision for a movement that remembered Japanese internment, Indian boarding schools, Latinx youth deportation, climate justice, and the killing of Black youth by vigilantes and state forces.[6]

One of the imperfectly realized promises of activism has been the development of a fully articulated solidarity movement linking Central American asylum seekers, Mexican activists for the disappeared, and US racial justice activists. The silence around the transnational organization of cartel and police violence allowed the Trump administration to press its case that asylum seekers could be sent to Mexico, Guatemala, and Honduras, as "safe third countries." In the 1980s, there was an extensive anti-Contra-war campaign and Central American solidarity movement in the United States that included religious communities providing sanctuary to refugees in churches; tens of thousands of members of "peace brigades" that went to Nicaragua and El Salvador; sister city projects; and other left, religious, feminist, gay, and peace networks that constituted an extensive civil society resistance to Reagan's wars in Central America.[7] They may not have stopped the state's child taking, but they produced transnational political mobilizations that insisted that everyday citizens could shape US foreign policy and demanded an accounting of its violence. They worked together with left political movements of the era in recognizing the intensifying crises of communities of color in the United States: incarceration, stagnating wages, rising unemployment, uncertain housing, food insecurity, decreasing access to health care, and rising differentials in Black and white infant and maternal mortality. Not unlike the Trump era, it was a time of massive resistance.

The panoply of groups and movements brought together by the Fort Sill protests—Black Lives Matter, DREAMers, AIM, Japanese anti-internment activists—could be even more formidable in combination with the decentered leadership of the Central American refugees and caravan organizers. Central Americans have long political experience operating with the language of human rights, which seems strangely absent from the US discourse of the treatment of asylum seekers, a category itself born in and through human rights legal structures. They also have extensive political experience in challenging regimes of terror that operate through child taking, and they have a powerful account of state and police violence.

Feminist, women's, and LGBT groups, who have strong networks and often can get a hearing on a national stage, have been less involved in movements against child taking than they could be. Reproductive justice feminists and trans and queer activists have been everywhere at street demonstrations against child separation and detention centers, but organizationally they have not been a visible part of the opposition. The significant exception has been the Women's Refugee Commission, which together with the Lutheran Immigration and Refugee Service, has been stalwart in calling attention to child separation and detention. Although a policy-oriented research and advocacy group in New York and Washington, not a grassroots political group, it is one of very few groups that has kept the focus on child separation policies through the Bush, Obama, and Trump administrations. It was one of the first organizations to sound the alarm about the Trump administration policy, which at that point had been going on for nearly a year, when they protested at the 2018 Congressional budget hearing, bringing babies and small children to the gallery to confront Kirstjen Nielsen as she requested additional funding for Homeland Security.

Some have argued that to focus on children is deradicalizing, that it is much easier to build sympathy for adorable children than, say, fighting for the admissibility of *chicas trans,* trans women, another group of people who died in alarming numbers in ICE detention in 2018 and 2019.[8] Probably building sympathy for children is easier, but that does not make it unimportant. Children are not just the ultimate "good" immigrants; they are also a symbol that Central Americans are here to stay—not just a cheap labor force that can be made available to US agribusiness and the service industry through the historical process of anti-Communist civil wars waged with massive assistance from US institutions, which strengthened central states by offering training and assistance to their military, intelligence, and bureaucratic infrastructure. The newer crisis is of the work that NGOs and international development aid has done to disable central states, allowing them to be partially supplanted by criminal syndicates that have built sturdy alliances with municipal police and militaries, this time with the United States providing the market for a multibillion-dollar drug enterprise and selling them the arms to enable them to hold power through violence. When Hondurans and then other Central Americans organized caravans for safe passage to the US border, it was part of a deliberate strategy to contest the terms of the old circular labor migration, to come as refugees to demand human rights through the international asylum process.[9] This wave of children, accompanied and unaccompanied, came *not* as part of a labor migration, but as asylum seekers. They came here to stay, to refuse any longer to just be the bodies that do hard, dirty jobs for starvation wages.

As Christina Sharpe writes in her moving meditation on Black survival in the afterlives of slavery, *In the Wake,* the grief of communities of color demands a reckoning,[10] and clearly the loss of children is part of that calculus. Although some have said that circulating images of children has had only the limited effect of sacralizing the innocent children while leaving intact the stereotypes of criminalized, reviled adults, in light of the long history of child taking, it seems more useful to say that there was actually a fight over whether children of color can ever be innocent and unthreatening, whether they can engender the kind of solicitude that (not-poor) white children are expected to get. Just as the image of enslaved mothers and babies worked to overturn the whole institution of slavery and pass the Thirteenth Amendment, holding up the images of immigrant and refugee children has worked to defend the United States, however imperfectly, from an unqualified victory for a white nationalist immigration policy or a new and uncontested chapter in the long history of taking children as a tactic of terror to put down insurgent communities.

Acknowledgments

I want to thank all those who helped make this book possible. I had the generous help and support of friends and colleagues at every turn, much more than anyone has a right to expect. The University of Massachusetts provided a sabbatical that provided the material support and time to write the book. Niels Hooper at University of California Press is the kind of old-school editor that everyone deserves and so few people are lucky enough to find. He nudged this book into existence at every turn, from encouraging me to write it in the first place to patiently helping me frame it, write it, revise it, and push it out in a timely way.

Audiences at a University of Minnesota Immigration History Research Center symposium and the Duke University History Department asked fabulous questions and helped move an early version of this project forward in particularly helpful ways. Thanks especially to Jocelyn Olcott and Kelly Condit-Shrestha, who provided the opportunity for these talks, and to Bianet Castellanos, who encouraged me to develop this project further for a blog post for the Gender Policy Report.

The Tepoztlán Institute for Transnational History and the Centroamérica study group at the University of Massachusetts Amherst provided spaces for thinking through some of the material in this book. I am particularly indebted to Martha Balaguera, the study group's convener and someone who pushed my thinking in so many ways. I am grateful also to Kevin Young, Diana Becerra, Jacob Carter, and Eric Sippert, who never betrayed my belief that Central Americanists are some of the best political thinkers there are.

The Five College Women's Studies Research Center seminar provided an incredibly supportive and provocative transnational feminist community that helped bring this book into existence. In these difficult times of scarcity in academe, it also sometimes provided a structure that kept exceedingly brilliant people in scholarly conversation from all over the world who, by choice or unfortunate circumstance, do not have a firm foothold in a university or college. I am indebted to them all. Individually and collectively, they provided intellectual labor that shaped this book: Frances Davey, Ynestra King, Patricia Montoya, Mary Njeri Kinyanjui, Amy Cox Hall, Crystal Hayes, Susanne Kranz, Charlotte Karam, Shagufta Nasreen, Neelofer Qadir, Chriss Sneed, Anagha Tambe, Susana Loza, and our fearless leader, Jennifer Hamilton. Nayiree Roubinian provided quietly competent material support to all our labors.

Jason Ruiz, Claire Daniel, and Martha Nichols gave this book generous and thoughtful readings that were tremendous help in keeping it engaging and in helping me figure out how to not let these horrifying stories become too discouraging to endure. Dorothy Roberts's early encouragement shaped it powerfully, as did Margaret Jacobs's. Robert Meredith performed miracles with the notes and the bibliography, and Barbara Armentrout was a superb copyeditor.

Of necessity, this book came together quickly, and more than ever in my work as a scholar I needed the friends and queer family who read and supported this book at every stage. J. T. Way read the entire manuscript, some of it twice, and provided brilliant feedback at every turn. He was also a crucial steadying presence in Monday morning email check-ins. Jen Jack Gieseking offered enthusiastic support and wonderfully thoughtful reading. Jennifer L. Nye not only did heroic amounts of social reproductive labor to support this book but also read and edited drafts. Lorgia Garcia Peña was spectacular at the last minute when I got pneumonia and needed editing help instantly.

Notes

Introduction

1. Haag, "'Womp Womp.'"
2. Bursztynsky, "Flu Vaccines." Ultimately, there were also statements about how "nobody likes" seeing children separated from their parents. See Cranley, "Kellyanne Conway." But in May 2018, Mike Pence, Kirstjen Nielsen, and Jeff Sessions all made photo-op appearances at the southwest border to celebrate the policy, and Sessions gave a speech to Texas law enforcement. See US Justice Department, "Attorney General Sessions Delivers Remarks Discussing the Immigration Enforcement Actions of the Trump Administration," Justice News, May 7, 2018, https://www.justice.gov/opa/speech/attorney-general-sessions-delivers-remarks-discussing-immigration-enforcement-actions.
3. See Blackhawk, "Federal Indian Law"; Big Boss (@escapedmatrix), "Don't act like America just started separating children from their loving parents," Twitter, July 3, 2018, 6:22 p.m., https://twitter.com/escapedmatrix/status/1146590044376973312; Brown, "'Barbaric'"; Hunter, "Child-Snatching"; Long, "70 Catholics Arrested"; and Miller, "Plan Halted."
4. Hillary Clinton (@HillaryClinton), "There's nothing American about tearing families apart," Twitter, June 20, 2018, 9:45 am, https://twitter.com/hillaryclinton/status/1009434414986747906?lang=en.
5. Schriro, "Weeping"; Gonzales, "Derechos en Crisis"; Johnson, "Department of (in) Justice." Dora Schriro, an attorney, was hired by the Obama Department of Homeland Security to reform family detention in the aftermath

of the Bush administration. Her article is a thoroughgoing assessment of the law, practices, and history.

6. Schriro, "Weeping."

7. Briggs, *Somebody's Children.*

8. Vidal, "State of the Union."

9. Vogt, *Lives in Transit,* 60.

10. Way, *Agrotropolis;* Nazario, "Pay or Die"; Nazario, "'Someone.'"; Balaguera, "Trans-migrations."

11. At the same time, transient male workers also made their own communities, not necessarily seeking nuclear families. See Shah, *Contagious Divides;* and Shah, *Stranger Intimacy.*

12. *Genocide* is defined by the UN General Assembly, Convention on the Prevention and Punishment of the Crime of Genocide. See Article 2, esp. section e.

13. See Alexandria Ocasio-Cortez (@AOC), "This administration has established concentration camps on the southern border of the United States for immigrants, where they are being brutalized with dehumanizing conditions and dying," Twitter, June 18, 2019, 6:03 a.m., https://twitter.com/aoc /status/1140968240073662466. See also Holmes, "Concentration Camps."

14. Faulkner, *Requiem for a Nun.*

15. Woodhouse and Gilger, "Tracing the Migrant Journey."

16. Thomas, "Cuban Refugees"; Petón, "Thousands of Cubans"; Mitchell, "Haitian Boat People."

17. Magaña-Salgado, "Fair Treatment Denied."

18. Benjamin, "Concept of History."

19. Feminist Newswire, "Protestors Demand Justice "; African American Policy Forum, "#SayHerName."

1. Taking Black Children

1. *Congressional Globe,* 28th Congress, 1st Session 1439 (1864), cited in Witte and Mero, "Removing Classrooms from the Battlefield," 391n64.

2. Hartman, *Lose Your Mother.*

3. Jones offered expert testimony on the separation of children for political purposes for a lawsuit against the Trump Administration by the State of

Washington and seventeen other states; see Exhibit 49, "Declaration of Martha S. Jones," State of Washington v. Donald J. Trump, 181-221, https://agportal-s3bucket.s3.amazonaws.com/uploadedfiles/Another/News/Press_Releases/motion%20declarations%2034-66.pdf.

4. Du Bois, *Negro American Family*, 21.

5. Higginbotham, *Matter of Color*; Morgan, "*Partus Sequitur Ventrum.*"

6. Gilbert, Titus, and Susan B. Anthony Collection, *Sojourner Truth*, 134.

7. Douglass, *Narrative*, 3.

8. Hartman, *Scenes of Subjection*.

9. *Flesh* invokes the crucial theorizing of reproduction in the Americas; see Spillers, "Mama's Baby."

10. See Hartman, *Scenes of Subjection*, 102-22; and McKittrick, *Demonic Grounds*.

11. Jacobs, *Incidents in the Life*, 11.

12. Quoted in Du Bois, *Negro American Family*, 25.

13. On the wide circulation of rape stories, see Yellin, *Women and Sisters*.

14. Quoted in Kristof, "Trump."

15. Calhoun, *Speeches*, p. 225.

16. Billingsley and Giovannoni, *Children of the Storm*, 29.

17. *Congressional Globe*, 38th Congress, 1st Session 1324 (1864), cited in Witte and Mero, "Removing Classrooms from the Battlefield," 391n64.

18. Circular posted on Maryland's Eastern Shore by a Union general, December 6, 1864, and letter from Andrew Stafford, November 4, 1864, cited in Berlin and Rowland, *Families and Freedom*, 211-13, 220-21. See also Edwards, *Gendered Strife*, 42-44, 47-54.

19. Lucy Lee to Lt. Col. W. E. W. Ross, January 10, 1865; and Charles L. Hooper to Wager Swayne, cited in Mitchell, *Raising Freedom's Child*, 154, 279. See also Foner, *Reconstruction*, 201.

20. Schwalm, *Hard Fight*, 250-51.

21. For stunning oral histories of this experience, see Orleck, *Storming Caesars Palace*. See also Foley, *White Scourge*; and Kelley, *Hammer and Hoe*.

22. U.S. Department of Labor statistics, cited in Bell, *Aid to Dependent Children*, 9-10.

23. Larabee, "Unmarried Parenthood," 449.

24. Bell, *Aid to Dependent Children*, 63.

25. Other Black legal scholars like Derrick Bell (*Silent Covenants*) are no fans of *Brown,* arguing that it relied on a strategy that portrayed Black children as damaged by schools that were often sources of strength and resistance, that it failed to enact—or even require—equality in public schools, and that it whipped up a powerful backlash. These are all important critiques. My point is not to praise *Brown* but to note the ways it put children at the forefront of a strategy to end segregation in public accommodations.

26. Mink and Solinger, *Welfare,* 217–22.

27. Kelley, *Race Rebels,* 95.

28. Arsenault, *Freedom Riders,* 154.

29. For children so violently turned into symbols, it matters to say their names: Addie Mae Collins (14), Cynthia Wesley (14), Carole Robertson (14), and Carol Denise McNair (11).

30. Davis, *An Autobiography;* Eskew, "'Bombingham.'"

31. Bell, *Aid to Dependent Children,* 96–100.

32. Mink and Solinger, *Welfare;* Solinger, *Wake Up Little Susie.*

33. Quoted in Bell, *Aid to Dependent Children,* 103.

34. Quoted in Bell, *Aid to Dependent Children,* 103.

35. Paul, "Punitive Sterilization," 89; Student Nonviolent Coordinating Committee, "Genocide in Mississippi."

36. Quoted in Student Nonviolent Coordinating Committee, "Genocide in Mississippi," 4.

37. Bell, *Aid to Dependent Children,* 107.

38. Bureau of Public Assistance, "Illegitimacy," 177. For a more extensive account of the obstacles to place Black children in adoptions in the 1950s and '60s, see Briggs, *Somebody's Children,* 49–55. It was a truism in this period that Black families didn't stigmatize out-of-wedlock pregnancies the way white families did, and they kept those children with them. While this may have been true, they also didn't have a choice.

39. Florida Department of Public Welfare, *Suitable Home Law, Preliminary Report,* 1960, cited in Bell, *Aid to Dependent Children,* 124–33.

40. Gale Durham and Millie Charles interviews by Taryn Lindhorst and Leslie Leighninger, quoted in Lindhorst and Leighninger "Ending Welfare," 568. See also Mink and Solinger, *Welfare,* 195; and Levenstein, "From Innocent Children."

41. Millie Charles interview by Taryn Lindhorst, New Orleans, June 9, 2000, quoted in Lindhorst and Leighninger "Ending Welfare," 572.

42. Marcus Neustadter, "Charges Gov. Davis Welfare Aid Remarks 'Irresponsible,'" *Louisiana Weekly*, October 1, 1960, 1, cited in Lindhorst and Leighninger, "Ending Welfare," 570, 583.

43. Reading the local Black press, especially the *Louisiana Weekly*, and talking to community people in 2000, Lindhorst and Leighninger did important work in calling attention to these local efforts by the Urban League and New Orleans activists and community organizations, in contrast to other historians of the Louisiana incident who noted only the attention-grabbing international stunt of British women sending aid. International attention did not happen without tremendous local groundwork.

44. "Kids 'Cry for Food' in New Orleans," *Chicago Defender*, September 3, 1960.

45. Levenstein, "From Innocent Children."

46. Honoré-Collins, "African American Incarceration"; Lawrence-Webb, "African American Children"; Mink and Solinger, *Welfare*.

47. Bell, *Silent Covenants*, 150.

48. Lawrence-Webb, "African American Children"; Babb, *Ethics in American Adoption;* Murray and Gesiriech, "Brief Legislative History." See also *King v. Smith*, 392 U.S. 309 (1968).

49. Thom Blair, "The Newburgh Story," *New York Amsterdam News*, July 22, 1961, 1, 26, 30, reprinted in Mink and Solinger, *Welfare*, 206-11; and Grant, *Politicization of Foster Care*, 31.

50. This was the year the Flemming rule was made law and Congress authorized funding for the program known as ADC foster care, which provided matching funds to states to place children in out-of-home care. Because the cost in the South of supporting a child on ADC was around $27.50, in foster care about $50, and in an orphanage or boarding school about $95, Washington policy makers had trouble believing that state officials would maliciously pull children when the economic costs were so high and the very small state coffers in the South made it so difficult to do. Even if federal matching funds made foster care affordable, if officials pulled enough children, they would have to put some in institutional care. See Alstein and McRoy, *Family Preservation*, 6-7; Schene, "Child Protective Services."

51. Brissett-Chapman and Isaacs-Schockley, *Children in Social Peril*, 49.

52. Brissett-Chapman and Isaacs-Schockley, *Children in Social Peril*, 88.

53. Bureau of Public Assistance, "Illegitimacy," 188.

54. Roberts, *Shattered Bonds*.

55. Kornbluh, *Battle for Welfare Rights*; Nadasen, *Welfare Warriors*; Orleck, *Storming Caesars Palace*.

56. Morgan, *Laboring Women*.

2. Taking Native Children

1. Blackhawk, "Federal Indian Law"; Blackhawk. "Indian Law That Helps"; Whitman, *Hitler's American Model*; Krieger, "Principles of the Indian Law," 307.

2. Prucha, *Documents*, 107; Matthiessen, *Spirit of Crazy Horse*. For a thoroughgoing history of the railroads as an agent of the colonial project, see Karuka, *Empire's Tracks*.

3. Olson, *Red Cloud*; Miller, *Ghost Dance*; Pratt, *Battlefield and Classroom*, 163, 202, 220, 227.

4. Witmer, *Indian Industrial School*, 31.

5. Pratt, *Battlefield and Classroom*.

6. Mauro, *Art of Americanization*.

7. Theodore Fischbacher, *A Study of the Role of the Federal Government in the Education of the American Indian* (San Francisco: R and E Research Associates, 1974), cited in Adams, "Fundamental Considerations."

8. Lomawaima, "Domesticity," 229.

9. Philp, *John Collier's Crusade*, 81.

10. "I have heard too many stories of cowboys running down children and bringing them hogtied to town to think it is all an accident. . . . They are transferred from school to school, given white people's names, forbidden to speak their own tongue, and when sent to distant schools are not taken home for three years." Coolidge, "'Kid Catching,'" 18–21.

11. *In re Lelah-Puc-Ka-Chee* 98 F. 429 (N.D. Iowa 1899).

12. Nabokov, *Native American Testimony*, 220.

13. See *Indian Family Defense*, "Historic School Victory," December 1976.

14. Child, "Runaway Boys, Resistant Girls."

15. Archuleta, Child, and Lomawaima, *Away from Home*.

16. Archuleta, Child, and Lomawaima, *Away from Home.*

17. Smith, *Conquest.*

18. Evans-Campbell et al., "Indian Boarding School Experience."

19. Quoted in Marshall, Zak, and Metz, "Doctor Compares Conditions."

20. See Collier, "American Congo"; Collier, "America's Treatment"; Philp, *John Collier's Crusade;* Institute for Government Research, *Problem of Indian Administration,* 348, 15.

21. The fundamental goal of allotment, the taking of Native land, was helped considerably by a group with very different interests: white homesteaders who saw in this reform the opportunity to remove all that "unproductive" reservation land and give it to "productive" white settlers. Native peoples were redefined en bloc as farmers, even or especially those who got their livelihood from hunting, fishing, or forest products. This resulted in two particularly useful outcomes for those who sought white control of reservation land: American Indians needed a smaller land base, and there was leftover land to sell to white homesteaders and the railroads at bargain prices. Oil was discovered in Oklahoma, and the "Five Civilized Tribes"—having suffered the Trail of Tears and Jackson's policy of removal from Georgia on the promise that in Oklahoma, at least, they would be undisturbed by Anglo settlers—were beset with hosts of oilmen, shady business dealers, and even the members of organized crime syndicates, who robbed and cheated them out of their land, people who made their living "grafting off the Indians," as the practice was popularly known. From the Southeast to Kansas to the Southwest, it is estimated that the land base of Indian country was depleted from 138 million acres of treaty land in 1887 to a mere 48 million acres when allotment was finally halted in 1934; 20 million acres of that land was desert or semidesert. See Canby, *American Indian Law.*

22. Philp, *John Collier's Crusade.*

23. Evans-Campbell et al., "Indian Boarding School Experience," 421.

24. Charlotte Kelley (Assiniboine) interview, n.d., Montana Tribes Digital Archives, https://montanatribes.org/charlotte-kelley/.

25. See Adams, *Education for Extinction;* Child, *Boarding School Seasons;* Horne and McBeth, *Essie's Story;* Hyer, *One House, One Voice;* Lomawaima, *Prairie Light.*

26. *Indian Family Defense,* "Devil's Lake Sioux Resistance," Winter 1974; Jacobs, *A Generation Removed,* 100.

27. *Indian Family Defense,* "The Destruction of Indian Families," Winter 1974, 1–2.

28. *Indian Affairs,* "AAIA and Devils Lake Sioux Protest Child Welfare Abuses," June–August 1968.

29. Bertram Hirsch, interview with Margaret Jacobs, September 30, 2011, quoted in Jacobs, *A Generation Removed,* 103.

30. Byler, Deloria, and Gurwitt, "Another Chapter."

31. *Indian Family Defense,* "Devil's Lake Sioux Resistance," Winter 1974, 6.

32. US Census Bureau, *Statistical Abstract* 1961.

33. Estes, *Our History;* Cook-Lynn, *From the River's Edge.*

34. Quoted in Estes, *Our History,* 133.

35. Berrick, *Faces of Poverty,* 169.

36. Cohen, "Public Assistance Provisions," 8–10; see also Deanna Lyter, "No Citizenship, No Welfare: American Indians and Arizona's Aid to Dependent Children Program," paper presented at the annual meeting of the American Sociological Association, Atlanta Hilton Hotel, Atlanta, August 16, 2003.

37. Children were placed in adoptions by the Indian Adoption Project (IAP) and its successor, the Adoption Resource Exchange of North America (ARENA), which deliberately sought white homes for Native children both in the United States and Canada. While many inside and outside the Child Welfare League of America (which administered the contracts for both programs in the United States) have condemned these programs, and certainly they shared the same logic of elimination of Indianness, evidenced particularly by the fact that they rebuffed efforts to find Indian homes for children, I don't discuss these programs for "hard to place children" here because they were not organized as *child-taking* programs. For more on both, see Briggs, *Somebody's Children,* ch. 2; Ellen Herman's Adoption History Project website, https:// pages.uoregon.edu/adoption/topics/IAP.html; and contemporary and historical documents in Native media, such as these in *Akwesasne Notes:* "Latest in the 'Social Genocide' Field: Adoption of Indian Children by White Families," Late Autumn 1972; "An Editorial Comment on Indian Children Who Need Homes," January–February 1972; "'Far from the Reservation': Title of Study of Indian/ White Adoptions," January–February 1972; "Saskatchewan Native People Ask for Control of Adoption and Group Care of Indian, Metis Children," January– February 1972; "Rift in N.W.T. Council over Native Adoption Practices and Pri-

orities," January–February 1972; "We Cannot Be Critical Unless We Ourselves Are Willing to Take Action," May 1972; "Michigan Indian Groups Searching for Homes to Avoid Losing Children," May 1972.

38. *Indian Family Defense,* "Senate Probes Child Welfare Crisis," May 1974, 2.

39. *Indian Family Defense,* "Serena Case," May 1974, 2.

40. The concept of jumping scales from the local to the national and transnational is Maylei Blackwell's; see Blackwell, *"Translenguas."*

41. *Indian Affairs,* "AAIA and Devils Lake Sioux Protest Child Welfare Abuses," June–August 1968.

42. *Indian Affairs,* "HEW to Study Child Welfare Abuses," September–November 1968; Hirsch, "Keynote Address."

43. Landry, "Native History."

44. *Indian Affairs,* "The Destruction of Indian Families," January 1973.

45. *Indian Affairs,* "Court Actions," Winter 1974.

46. Personal communication, Frederick M. Van Hecke, March 16, 2005.

47. *Indian Affairs,* "The Destruction of Indian Families," January 1973.

48. *Indian Affairs,* "The Abduction of Benita Rowland," Winter 1974.

49. For the Leonard Peltier story, see Matthiessen, *Spirit of Crazy Horse;* and Apted, *Incident at Oglala.*

50. US Congress, *Revolutionary Activities.*

51. Apted, *Incident at Oglala.*

52. US Congress, "Indian Child Welfare."

53. US Congress, "Indian Child Welfare."

54. Maine Wabanaki–State Child Welfare, *Report.*

55. See David Southerland, writer, prod., dir., *Kind Hearted Woman,* WGBH/Frontline and Independent Television Service, 2013, https://www.pbs .org/wgbh/frontline/film/kind-hearted-woman/. The story at the center is Robin Poor Bear's brilliant and painful #MeToo kind of effort to get the Spirit Lake Sioux and other tribal nations and rural communities to acknowledge and fight sexual and domestic violence.

56. The Flemming rule was promulgated in 1961, the year it launched the taking of 150,000 Black children. The emergency medicine paper, Kempe et al., "Battered Child Syndrome," was published in 1962. It certainly made waves in policy circles, resulting in the establishment of child abuse hotlines across the

country, beginning in 1973. Kempe's paper put violence against children at home on our conceptual and social maps in important ways. But in pointing to the earlier Flemming rule and school desegregation history, my point is to insist that two historical trajectories are entwined in foster care, but nevertheless separable: In one, foster care was meant to be a racialized punishment for women in insurgent communities whose sexual and reproductive behavior was taken to be shameful (or shameable). The other is this class- and race-mixed history of child violence, which in some ways provided cover for the bias against Black and brown women of some welfare systems. In the United States, we still take vastly more children for "neglect"—which may or may not be a proxy for poverty— than for abuse. For histories that cite Kempe's paper, see Nelson, *Making an Issue;* Gordon, *Heroes;* Sealander, *Failed Century;* Pleck, *Domestic Tyranny.* The Flemming rule was an administrative rule, subsequently enacted as law by Congress as P.L. 87-31 and the 1962 Public Service Amendments.

57. Roberts, *Shattered Bonds.*

3. Taking Children in Latin America

1. Solis and Corchado, "Asylum Seekers."

2. Human Rights Watch, "Argentina."

3. Osorio, "Stolen Babies."

4. Marchak, *God's Assassins;* Hodges, *Argentina's "Dirty War";* Taylor, *Disappearing Acts.*

5. Guest, *Behind the Disappearances;* Portnoy, *Little School.*

6. Arditti, *Searching for Life,* 109-11.

7. Arditti, *Searching for Life,* 70-71.

8. Arditti, *Searching for Life,* 70-71.

9. Arditti, *Searching for Life,* 7.

10. Comisión Nacional sobre la Desaparición de Personas (CONADEP), *Nunca Más,* 286.

11. Arditti, *Searching for Life,* 57.

12. On the Argentine rulers' anti-Semitism, see Timmerman, *Prisoner Without a Name.*

13. See Norma Blandon Castro, "Democratization of Education in El Salvador: Examining the Participation of Women," paper for the 1998 Meeting of

the Latin American Studies Association, Chicago, Illinois, September 24–26, 1998. See also Williams and Walter, *Militarization and Demilitarization*, 90.

14. Grandin, *Last Colonial Massacre*, 4; Shenk and Armstrong, *El Salvador*, 163; Stanley, *Protection Racket State*.

15. In 1976, Carter campaigned on a promise to withdraw support from dictatorships that routinely violated human rights, but by 1979, facing a tough (and ultimately unsuccessful) reelection bid, he caved. With a Sandinista victory imminent in Nicaragua, Carter broke his own policy in order to begin providing the El Salvadoran military with arms and money. Under Reagan, full-scale support for the right-wing Salvadoran state began again.

16. Danner, *Massacre at El Mozote*; Wood, *Insurgent Collective Action*.

17. Sprenkels, *El dia más esperada*, 21.

18. Asociación Pro-Búsqueda, *La paz en construcción*, 15.

19. Asociación Pro-Búsqueda, "La desaparición forzada de niños y niñas en El Salvador durante el conflicto armado," http://www.probusqueda.org.sv /quienes-somos/resena-historica/la-desaparicion-forzada-de-ninos-y-ninas-en-el-salvador-durante-el-conflicto-armado/. See also Sprenkels, *El dia más esperada;* and Asociación Pro-Búsqueda, *Historias para tener presente,* 56–57.

20. Unfinished Sentences, "Still Searching."

21. See *Serrano Cruz Sisters v. El Salvador,* Inter-American Court of Human Rights, Merits, Reparations and Costs, March 1, 2005, 2; details at https://iachr .lls.edu/cases/serrano-cruz-sisters-v-el-salvador.

22. See Inter-American Court of Human Rights, "El Salvador es responsible por la desparición forzada de una niña y cuatro niños durante el conflict armado; "*Caso Rochac Hernández y otros v. El Salvador,*" press release, November 27, 2014.

23. Sprenkels, *El dia más esperada,* 39.

24. Rozov, "Serrano-Cruz Sisters."

25. Krauss, "How US Actions Helped."

26. See *Serrano Cruz Sisters v. El Salvador,* Inter-American Court of Human Rights, Merits, Reparations and Costs, March 1, 2005, https://iachr.lls.edu /cases/serrano-cruz-sisters-v-el-salvador. Lea Marren (*Salvador's Children*) reported on her dealings with the embassy and her suspicions that the staff knew that children were being taken. For children in military barracks, see Sprenkels, *Stories Never to Be Forgotten*.

27. Weiner and Dillon, "Shadowy Alliance."

28. Weiner and Dillon, "Shadowy Alliance," 12.

29. Green, *Fear as a Way.*

30. Liga Guatemalteca, *Corazones en fiesta,* 71.

31. Comisión para el Esclarecimiento, *Guatemala.*

32. Comisión para el Esclarecimiento, *Guatemala,* 46.

33. Comisión para el Esclarecimiento, *Guatemala,* 66.

34. Beltrán, *Hidden Powers.*

35. Proyecto Interdiocesano de Recuperación, *Guatemala;* Oficina de Derechos Humanos, *Hasta encontrarte.*

36. ITVS, *Discovering Dominga.*

37. Briggs, *Somebody's Children,* 197–222.

38. See Casa Alianza Foundation and Myrna Mack Survivors Foundation, *Adoptions in Guatemala;* reports in Spanish and English (translation) are available via an archived list at https://www.brandeis.edu/investigate/adoption /guatemala-sources.html#MyrnaMack.

39. Casa Alianza Foundation and Myrna Mack Survivors Foundation, *Adoptions in Guatemala.*

40. Goicoechea, *Report of a Fact-Finding Mission.*

41. Americas Watch Committee, "Human Rights in Nicaragua," 24.

42. Kornbluh and Byrne, *Iran-Contra Scandal.*

43. A Congressional commission chaired by John Kerry confirmed that some CIA-employed operatives were involved in cocaine trafficking but was unable to establish that the CIA knew about the trafficking or that it was extensive or to link it to the flooding of US cities with crack. The Kerry Commission did, however, hear from the Drug Enforcement Agency's Thomas Zapeda, who testified that his agency was forced to close its office in Honduras when he began to uncover extensive evidence that the Honduran military was involved in the drug trade from Columbia, threatening the CIA's working relationship with Honduran officers in their anti-Contra operations. The CIA's own report was more candid, but it was also classified. In 1982, the second volume of the CIA's Hitz Report revealed that the CIA had, at the start of the Contra operation in 1982, concluded a memorandum of understanding with US Attorney General William French Smith, exempting the agency from reporting drug trafficking by its nonemployees, meaning its "assets, pilots who ferried sup-

plies to the contras, as well as contra officials and others." The CIA did, at least, admit to suppressing drug-enforcement operations limiting transshipment of cocaine through Honduras and agreeing to look the other way if its pilots were flying planes full of coke. During this same period, the drug cartels in Mexico also became involved in shipping cocaine (not just marijuana) and consolidated their operations. Prosecutions of the syndicates in the United States were also interrupted by the CIA. Reporters and other investigators pointed out that these charges were identical to how the CIA had allegedly operated in Laos in the 1970s, recruiting the Hmong to fight the North Vietnamese and then looking the other way as they expanded their heroin operations first to US troops in Vietnam, then to the US mainland. See Hernandez, *Narcoland;* McCoy, *Politics of Heroin;* Webb, *Dark Alliance.*

44. Romo, "Chile's 'Children of Silence'"; Adler, "Spain's Stolen Babies."

45. Clearly there was also a French rightist influence here as well. When the United States refused to sell arms to Argentina under the Carter administration, France provided arms and military training. Sexualized torture and the extensive use of rape that resulted in many pregnancies in detention was a particularly French innovation in the global use of torture, as we learned in the case of Djamila Bupatcha, an Algeria militant who was raped by a French soldier. The case, championed by Simone de Beauvoir, became a cause célèbre when she and her lawyer attempted, unsuccessfully, to try the soldier in a French court; see CIA, President's Daily Brief, "Argentina: New Foreign Policy Directions," July 19, 1978 National Security Archive, approved for public release December 8, 2016, https://nsarchive2.gwu.edu//dc.html?doc=3238659-3-CIA-President-s-Daily-Brief-Argentina-New.

46. Goldman, *Art of Political Murder.*

47. Danner, *Massacre at El Mozote.*

48. Cowan, *Securing Sex.*

49. Gill, *School of the Americas.*

50. National Security Archive, Electronic Briefing Book no. 122, "Prisoner Abuse: Patterns from the Past," updated February 25, 2014, https://nsarchive2.gwu.edu//NSAEBB/NSAEBB122/index.htm.

51. See National Security Archive Electronic Briefing Book no. 73—Part I, "New Documents Describe Key Death Squad under Former Army Chief Galtieri," attachment to press release, https://nsarchive2.gwu.edu/NSAEBB/NSAEBB73/.

52. Marren, *Salvador's Children;* Marcetic, "Negroponte's Crimes"; Corn, "Unfit to Lead"; LeMoyne, "Testifying to Torture."

4. Criminalizing Families of Color

1. Webb, *Dark Alliance;* Parry, *Lost History;* Parry, "America's Debt"; and Devereaux, "How the CIA Watched."
2. Paquette, "One in Nine Black Children."
3. Burnett, "Transcript."
4. Reuters, "Trump Rule."
5. Briggs, *How All Politics.*
6. Marable, *Race, Reform, and Rebellion;* Duggan, *Twilight of Equality?*
7. Ward, *Men We Reaped,* 198–99.
8. del Olmo, "Hidden Face of Drugs."
9. Baum, "Legalize It All."
10. Morash, Haarr, and Rucker, "Comparison of Programming."
11. Murakawa, *First Civil Right.*
12. Alexander, *New Jim Crow.*
13. Gilmore, *Golden Gulag.*
14. Roberts, *Shattered Bonds.*
15. Centers for Disease Control, "Infant Mortality."
16. Centers for Disease Control, "Infant Mortality"; Mathews, MacDorman, and Thoma, "Infant Mortality Statistics."
17. Brody, "Cocaine."
18. Neuspiel, "Let's Not Call," A18.
19. Jackson, "America's Shameful Little Secret" A20; Krauthammer, "Crack Babies"; Krauthammer, "Put Cocaine Babies."
20. Hinds, "Instincts of Parenthood," 8.
21. Blakeslee, "Crack's Toll among Babies," 1.
22. Siegel, "In the Name."
23. Lewin, "Drug Use in Pregnancy," A14; Blakeslee, "Child-Rearing Is Stormy," B5; " Chira, "Children of Crack," 1.
24. Humphries, *Crack Mothers,* 21, 42–47.
25. Chavkin, "Cocaine and Pregnancy," 1626–27.
26. Wright, 12 *Million Black Voices,* 109. For more on Wright, see Lisa Young, "The Persistent Afterlife of the Racial Restrictive Covenant," paper

presented at the American Studies Association annual meeting, Atlanta, GA, November 8–11, 2018.

27. On race differentials in infant mortality, see Briggs, *How All Politics,* 133; Jackson, "America's Shameful Little Secret," A20.

28. Quoted in Twohey, "Crack-Baby Myth," 3340–41.

29. Chavkin, "Cocaine and Pregnancy," 1626–27.

30. Armstrong, *Conceiving Risk, Bearing Responsibility,* 173; Humphries, *Crack Mothers,* 44–45; Duke, "D.C. Revises"; Fullilove, Lown, and Fullilove, "Crack 'Hos and Skeezers."

31. Feminist activists have been making these arguments about the Violence Against Women Act for years, but see also Goodmark, *Troubled Marriage,* 18–22; Gottschalk, *Prison and the Gallows,* 139–64, esp. 150–55.

32. Humphries, *Crack Mothers.*

33. Kaufman, "Foster Children at Risk"; Anderson, "Race Tilt"; Paltrow, Cohen, and Carey, "Year 2000 Overview"; Humphries, *Crack Mothers.*

34. *Boston Globe,* "More U.S. Children."

35. Ocen, "Pregnant While Black."

36. After Dorris's death by suicide following allegations of sexual abuse by his daughters, a high-profile *New York* magazine story repeated the charge sometimes levelled at him that he was not really Indian. A *Washington Post* piece followed, charging that the *New York* article included a large number of errors, including mistaking his parentage. According to the *Post* rebuttal, the man his mother married, Dorris, was not Michael's father. In this version, no genealogy is possible because we don't know the name of the man by whom she became pregnant. All of this is beside the point if we follow "Indian-ness" through tribal enrollment. Dorris was not enrolled in any tribe and grew up with his Anglo mother in a moneyed part of Louisville, KY. At a time when many Native kids were still attending Indian boarding schools in the late '50s and early '60s, Dorris attended a private, white, Catholic all-male high school. He was raised with a family story about an Indian, or part Indian, father who had died serving in World War II. (The father, it turned out, actually committed suicide; it is hard to know what to do with the two-father story of the *Post.*)

Of course, using tribal enrollment as the only standard for Indianness is complicated: not all tribes are federally recognized, and not all fathers acknowledge their children. If, as Joanne Barker (*Native Acts*) argues, the standard should be not who you claim, but who claims you, the answer is still unclear.

According to one account, Dorris may have spent summers with his father's relations on reservations in Montana and Washington. His master's thesis at Yale was on the effect of offshore drilling on Alaskan Native communities. Dorris, especially after his marriage to Louise Erdrich (Turtle Mountain Band of Chippewa) and his adoption of two other Native kids, belonged as an adult to an Indian family and lived a life committed to the building of an extraordinarily good Native studies program at Dartmouth and to Native issues more broadly. See Konigsberg, "Michael Dorris's Troubled Sleep"; Sharp, "Michael Dorris."

37. Golden, *Message in a Bottle,* 64.

38. Dorris, *Broken Cord,* 262.

39. Dorris, *Broken Cord,* 193.

40. Dorris, *Broken Cord,* 165.

41. Dorris, *Broken Cord,* xviii.

42. Armstrong, *Conceiving Risk, Bearing Responsibility,* 5; Golden, *Message in a Bottle,* 64.

43. Cook-Lynn, "Review," 42–45.

44. Armstrong, *Conceiving Risk, Bearing Responsibility,* 173.

45. Erikson, "Doctors Mislabel Defects"; H. E. Hoyme, L. Hauck, and D. J. Meyer, "Accuracy of Diagnosis of Alcohol Related Birth Defects by Non-Medical Professionals in a Native American Population," paper presented at the David W. Smith Morphogenesis and Malformations Workshop, Mont-Tremblant, Québec, Canada, 1994.

46. Dorris, *Broken Cord;* The one luminous exception is Cook-Lynn, "Review," 42–45.

47. In 1993, Elizabeth Cook-Lynn and Dianne Zephier-Bird wrote a four-part newspaper series for *Indian Country Today* entitled "Criminalization of Alcoholism: A Native Feminist View," republished as Cook-Lynn, "Big Pipe Case." Cook-Lynn made the decision to use a pseudonym, Marie Big Pipe, when she wrote about this case, feeling that publishing and amplifying her story in a small community would be shaming. I have followed her lead here.

48. Plantz, *Indian Child Welfare.*

49. *Indian Country Today* series republished subsequently as Cook-Lynn, "Big Pipe Case," 82.

50. Armstrong, *Conceiving Risk, Bearing Responsibility,* 7, 82.

51. Adler, "Disability"; Van Biema, "Storm over Orphanages."

52. Butler, *TANF Time Limits.*

53. Robles and Dewan, "Skip Child Support"; Mink, "Introduction to Disdained Mothers," Kornbluh and Mink, *Ensuring Poverty*.

54. Angela Davis writes from the image of a Black woman prisoner, ignored and laboring alone, to understand the state of reproductive politics in the 1990s. Davis, "Outcast Mothers and Surrogates." Priscilla Ocen, similarly, argues that the pervasive shackling of laboring women at all levels of the penal system is indicative of the history that links enslavement, the chain gang, and the contemporary penal system. Ocen, "Punishing Pregnancy."

55. Paltrow, "*Roe v. Wade*"; Ocen, "Birthing Injustice"; Paltrow and Flavin, "Pregnant, and No Civil Rights"; Martin, "Take a Valium."

56. Frank quoted in Calhoun, "Criminalization of Bad Mothers"; Lane quoted in Yurkanin, "Pregnant Addict Tests Limits"; Martin, "Take a Valium."

5. Taking the Children of Refugees

1. Holmes, "Democrats."

2. Wolfe, "Settler Colonialism."

3. See Blackhawk, *Violence over the Land;* and Saldaña-Portillo, *Indian Given*.

4. Anzaldúa, *Borderlands/La Frontera*, 3.

5. Guidotti-Hernández, *Unspeakable Violence;* Dunn, *Militarization;* Anzaldúa, *Borderlands/La Frontera*. For an example of the racist uses of the Reconquista (a term borrowed from the Iberian context), see Huntington, "Hispanic Challenge."

6. Sánchez, *Becoming Mexican American;* Hernández, *Migra!;* Dunn, *Militarization*.

7. There were many waves of anti-immigrant sentiment and efforts at interdiction throughout the twentieth century, from the Bisbee deportation of striking mine workers in 1917, the hundreds or thousands of Mexicans killed by Texas Rangers before 1920 (see Muñoz Martínez, *Injustice Never Leaves You*), and riots and immigration raids that drove out Mexican Americans in the 1930s (see Sánchez, *Becoming Mexican American;* De Leon, *Land of Open Graves*).

8. Mendoza, "Border Crossed Us"; Wiles, "Closed Border Gate"; Woods, "Tohono O'odham Brothers' Arrest."

9. Briggs, "Why Feminist Should Care."

10. Rivlin and Manzo, "Homeless Children"; Fitzgerald, *Habits of Compassion;* Gordon, *Great Arizona Orphan Abduction.*

11. Gates and Reich, "Think Again." A well-known feature film on child soldiers in El Salvador is Luis Mandoki's *Voces Inocentes* (Lionsgate, 2004).

12. Flores v. Meese, 681 F. Supp. 665 (C.D. Cal. 1988).

13. Schriro, "Weeping in the Playtime," 453.

14. *Flores,* 681 F. Supp. at 665.

15. Although the case was argued by the Reagan and Bush justice departments, it was ultimately decided just after the Clinton administration came into office and so was somewhat misleadingly given the name of Clinton's attorney general on decision.

16. Barr v. Flores, 1992 WL 687875 (U.S.), 7–9 (U.S. Oral Arg., 1992).

17. Barr v. Flores, 1992 WL 511956 (U.S.), 10 (U.S. Cal. Resp. Brief, 1992).

18. *Barr,* 1992 WL 511956 (U.S.), 10.

19. *Flores,* 681 F. Supp. 665 (C.D. Cal. 1988); Reno v. Flores, 507 U.S. 292 (1993).

20. Human Rights Watch, *Slipping through the Cracks.*

21. *Flores v. Reno* Settlement Agreement (C.D. Cal. 1997).

22. Cornish and Kelly, "Flores Settlement"; Melley, "Judge Puts Blame."

23. Women's Commission, "Locking Up Family Values."

24. Bernstein, "U.S. to Overhaul Detention Policy"; Swarms, "Government Has Improperly Detained."

25. Swarms, "Government Has Improperly Detained," 18.

26. In re Hutto Family Detention Ctr. Settlement Agreement (W.D. Tex., August 26, 2007), ECF No. 92–1.

27. Talbot, "Lost Children"; Heartland Alliance, "Reports of Sexual Assault at Hutto Detention Center Latest Evidence of Need for Immediate Reform," press release, June 1, 2010, https://www.immigrantjustice.org/index .php/press_releases/reports-sexual-assault-hutto-detention-center-latest-evidence-need-immediate-reform.

28. Chaudry et al., "Facing Our Future Children"; Capps et al., "Paying the Price."

29. Stevens, "Thin ICE."

30. See Michelle LaPointe, "Resisting Anti-Immigrant Backlash: Feminists Respond to HB 87 and Beyond," presentation to the National Women's Studies Association annual meeting, Atlanta, GA, November 11, 2011.

31. Montgomery, "Poster Child."

32. Reynoso and González Arrecis, "240 niños sin padres."

33. Rutenberg and Lacey, "Bush Meets Anger."

34. Bazar, "Citizens Sue."

35. Chaudry et al., "Facing Our Future Children."

36. Thompson, "After Losing Freedom"; Butera, "Children of Immigrants."

37. Thompson, "Court Rules for Deportee."

38. Fernández, "Pregnant Latina."

39. Fernández, "Pregnant and Shackled."

40. Levenson, *Adiós Niño*.

41. Cockburn and Cockburn, "Guns, Drugs"; Hernandez, *Narcoland*.

42. Boullosa and Wallace, *Narco History*.

43. Gibler, *To Die in Mexico*; Paley, *Drug War Capitalism*.

44. Lemon, "Mexico's Gun Violence"; *New York Times*, "Hypocrisy, Locked and Loaded."

45. Horwitz, "Earlier ATF Gun Operation"; *New York Times*, "Gun Walking."

46. Hamilton, "Felipe Calderón"; Burnett, Peñaloza, and Benincasa, "Mexico Seems to Favor."

47. Way, *Agrotropolis* (manuscript courtesy of the author).

48. Nazario, "Pay or Die."

49. Quoted in Frank, "Hopeless in Honduras?"

50. Emmons, "Death Squads Are Back."

51. Frank, "Hopeless in Honduras?"

52. Frank, "Hopeless in Honduras?"

53. U.S. Customs and Border Protection, "Southwest Border Unaccompanied Alien Children FY 2014," last modified November 24, 2015, https://www.cbp.gov/newsroom/stats/southwest-border-unaccompanied-children/fy-2014.

54. Associated Press, "Mexican Police"; Evans, "Mexico."

55. Martinez, "Los niños"; Restrepo and Garcia, "Surge of Unaccompanied Children."

56. Martinez, Yan, and Shoichet, "Growing Protests."

57. Gonzalez, "Expedited Hearings"; Human Rights Watch, "US: Surge in Detention."

58. Women's Commission, "Locking Up Family Values."

59. Biden, "Plan for Central America"; Goodfriend, "Alliance for Insecurity."

60. "No one leaves home unless / home is the mouth of a shark. You only run for the border / when you see the whole city / running as well." Warsan Shire, "Home," available at SeekersGuidance Global Islamic Seminary, https:// seekersguidance.org/articles/social-issues/home-warsan-shire/.

61. DasGupta, "Queering Immigration"; Cisneros, "Undocuqueer."

62. Megan Kludt, personal communication, October 2012.

63. BBC News, "Australia's Asylum Policy"; Falcón, "'National Security'"; Al Jazeera, "Walk or Die."

64. Blitzer, "Will Anyone."

65. Quoted in Silva, "Advocates Walk Out."

66. Scherer and Dawsey, "Trump Cites."

67. Sherman, "'Stephen Actually Enjoys.'"

68. Harkinson, "Trump's Newest Senior Adviser."

69. See Stern, *Proud Boys*.

70. Christophi, "Feds Tell 9th Circuit."

71. Badger and Miller, "Americans Love Families"; Dewan, "Family Separation"; Sacchetti, "ACLU."

Conclusion: Taking Children Back—Resistance

1. Davis, "San Diego Judge Orders."

2. Foner, *Fiery Trial*.

3. Piercy, "Art of Blessing," 5.

4. Taylor, *From #BlackLivesMatter*, 2.

5. Harp and Oser, "Factors."

6. Maruyama, "On Common Ground"; INCITE!, *Color of Violence*; Kolata, "Bias Seen."

7. Peace, "Anti-Contra-War Campaign"; Battista, "Unions and Cold War"; Smith, *Resisting Reagan*; Hobson, *Lavender and Red*.

8. Two of the twenty-four people who died between January 21, 2018, and June 1, 2019, were trans women. See Levin, "Trans Woman Who Died."

9. Balaguera, "Citizenship in Transit."

10. Sharpe, *In the Wake*.

Bibliography

Adams, David Wallace. *Education for Extinction: American Indians and the Boarding School Experience, 1875–1928.* Lawrence: University Press of Kansas, 1995.

———. "Fundamental Considerations: The Deep Meaning of Native American Schooling, 1880–1900." *Harvard Educational Review* 58, no. 1 (1988): 1–28.

Adler, Katya. "Spain's Stolen Babies and the Families Who Lived a Lie." BBC News, October 18, 2011.

Adler, Michele. "Disability among Women on AFDC: An Issue Revisited." Washington, DC: Office of the Assistant Secretary for Planning and Evaluation, US Department of Health and Human Services, January 1, 1993.

African American Policy Forum. "#SayHerName: Resisting Police Brutality against Black Women." July 16, 2015. http://aapf.org/sayhernamereport.

Al Jazeera. "Walk or Die: Algeria Abandons 13,000 Refugees in the Sahara." June 25, 2018.

Alexander, Michelle. *The New Jim Crow: Mass Incarceration in the Age of Colorblindness.* New York: New Press, 2012.

Altstein, Howard, and Ruth G. McRoy. *Does Family Preservation Serve a Child's Best Interests?* Washington, DC: Georgetown University Press, 2002.

Americas Watch Committee. "Human Rights in Nicaragua 1986." February 1987.

Anderson, Troy. "Race Tilt in Foster Care Hit; Hospital Staff More Likely to Screen Minority Mothers." *L.A. Daily News,* June 30, 2008.

Anzaldúa, Gloria. *Borderlands/La Frontera: The New Mestiza.* 4th ed. San Francisco: Aunt Lute Books, 2012.

Apted, Michael, dir. *Incident at Oglala.* Spanish Fork Motion Picture Company, Carolco International, and Seven Arts, prod., 1991.

Archuleta, Margaret L., Brenda J. Child, and K. Tsianina Lomawaima, eds. *Away from Home: American Indian Boarding School Experiences, 1879–2000.* Phoenix; Heard Museum, 2000.

Arditti, Rita. *Searching for Life: The Grandmothers of the Plaza de Mayo and the Disappeared Children of Argentina.* Berkeley: University of California Press, 1999.

Armstrong, Elizabeth M. *Conceiving Risk, Bearing Responsibility: Fetal Alcohol Syndrome and the Diagnosis of Moral Disorder.* Baltimore: Johns Hopkins University Press, 2003.

Arsenault, Raymond. *Freedom Riders: 1961 and the Struggle for Racial Justice.* New York: Oxford University Press, 2006.

Asociación Pro-Búsqueda. *Historias para tener presente.* San Salvador: UCA Editores, 2001.

———. La paz en construcción: Un studio sobre la problemática de la niñez desaparecida por el conflict armado en El Salvador. San Salvador: Asociación Pro-Búsqueda de Niñas y Niños Desaparecidos, 2000.

Associated Press. "Mexican Police Helped Cartel Massacre 193 Migrants, Documents Show." NPR, December 22, 2014.

Babb, L. Ann. *Ethics in American Adoption.* Westport, CT: Bergin and Garvey, 1999.

Badger, Emily, and Claire Cain Miller. "Americans Love Families. American Policies Don't." *New York Times,* June 24, 2018.

Balaguera, Martha. "Citizenship in Transit: Perils and Promises of Crossing Mexico." PhD diss., University of Massachusetts, 2019.

———. "Trans-migrations: Agency and Confinement at the Limits of Sovereignty." *Signs: Journal of Women in Culture and Society* 43, no. 3 (2018): 641–64.

Barker, Joanne. *Native Acts: Law, Recognition, and Cultural Authenticity.* Durham, NC: Duke University Press, 2011.

Battista, Andrew. "Unions and Cold War Foreign Policy in the 1980s: The National Labor Committee, the AFL-CIO, and Central America." *Diplomatic History* 26, no. 3 (Summer 2002): 419–51.

Baum, Dan. "Legalize It All." *Harper's Magazine,* April 2016.

Bazar, Emily. "Citizens Sue after Being Detained in Workplace: An Inconvenience or a Violation of Rights?" *USA Today,* June 25, 2008.

BBC News. "Australia's Asylum Policy 'Cruel', UN Says." November 18, 2016.

Bell, Derrick. *Silent Covenants: Brown v. Board of Education and the Unfulfilled Hopes for Racial Reform.* New York: Oxford University Press, 2005.

Bell, Winifred. *Aid to Dependent Children.* New York: Columbia University Press, 1965.

Beltrán, Adriana. *Hidden Powers in Post-Conflict Guatemala.* Washington, DC: Washington Office on Latin America, 2003. https://www.wola.org.

Benjamin, Walter. "On the Concept of History [Theses on the Philosophy of History]." 1940; English trans. Accessed July 30, 2019. https://www.sfu.ca/~andrewf/CONCEPT2.html.

Berlin, Ira, and Leslie S. Rowland. *Families and Freedom: A Documentary History of African-American Kinship in the Civil War Era.* New York: New Press, 1997.

Bernstein, Nina. "U.S. to Overhaul Detention Policy for Immigrants." *New York Times,* August 6, 2009.

Berrick, Jill Duerr. *Faces of Poverty: Portraits of Women and Children on Welfare.* New York: Oxford University Press, 1995.

Biden, Joseph R., Jr. "Joe Biden: A Plan for Central America." Opinion, *New York Times,* January 29, 2015.

Billingsley, Andrew, and Jeanne M. Giovannoni. *Children of the Storm: Black Children and American Child Welfare.* New York: Harcourt, Brace, Jovanovich, 1972.

Blackhawk, Maggie. "Federal Indian Law as Paradigm within Public Law." *Harvard Law Review* 132, no. 7 (May 2019): 1791–1877.

———. "The Indian Law That Helps Build Walls." *New York Times,* May 26, 2019.

Blackhawk, Ned. *Violence over the Land: Indians and Empires in the Early American West.* Cambridge: Harvard University Press, 2006.

Blackwell, Maylei. "*Translenguas:* Mapping the Possibilities and Challenges of Transnational Women's Organizing across Geographies of Difference." In *Translocalities/Translocalidades: Feminist Politics of Translation in the Latina Américas,* edited by Sonia E. Alvarez, Claudia de Lima Costa, Veronica Feliu, Rebecca Hester, Norma Klahn, and Millie Thayer, 290–320. Durham, NC: Duke University Press, 2014.

Blakeslee, Sandra. "Child-Rearing Is Stormy When Drugs Cloud Birth: Adopting Drug Babies." *New York Times,* May 19, 1990.

———. "Crack's Toll among Babies: A Joyless View, Even of Toys." *New York Times,* September 17, 1989.

Blitzer, Jonathan. "Will Anyone in the Trump Administration Ever Be Held Accountable for the Zero-Tolerance Immigration Policy?" *New Yorker,* August 22, 2018.

Boston Globe. "More U.S. Children Using Foster Care." December 12, 1989.

Boullosa, Carmen, and Mike Wallace. *A Narco History: How the United States and Mexico Jointly Created the "Mexican Drug War."* New York: OR Books, 2016; first printing 2015.

Briggs, Laura. *How All Politics Became Reproductive Politics: From Welfare Reform to Foreclosure to Trump.* Oakland: University of California Press, 2016.

———. *Somebody's Children: The Politics of Transracial and Transnational Adoption.* Durham, NC: Duke University Press, 2012.

———. "Why Feminists Should Care about the Baby Veronica Case." *Indian Country Today,* Indian Country Media Network. August 16, 2013. https://newsmaven.io/indiancountrytoday/archive/why-feminists-should-care-about-the-baby-veronica-case-vRp4N7Q3MoeWjsfmHlG7vg/.

Brissett-Chapman, Sheryl, and Mareasa Issacs-Shockley, eds. *Children in Social Peril: A Community Vision for Preserving Family Care of African American Children and Youths.* Washington, DC: Child Welfare League of America Press, 1997.

Brody, Jane. "Cocaine: Litany of Fetal Risks Grows." *New York Times,* September 6, 1988.

Brown, DeNeen L. "'Barbaric': America's Cruel History of Separating Children from Their Parents." *Washington Post,* May 31, 2018.

Bureau of Public Assistance. "Illegitimacy and Its Impact on the Aid to Dependent Children Program." In *Welfare: A Documentary History of Politics and Policy,* edited by Gwendolyn Mink and Rickie Solinger, 174–90. New York: NYU Press, 2003.

Burnett, John. "Transcript: Homeland Security Secretary Kirstjen Nielsen's Full Interview with NPR." NPR, May 10, 2018.

Burnett, John, Marisa Peñaloza, and Robert Benincasa. "Mexico Seems to Favor Sinaloa Cartel in Drug War." NPR, May 19, 2010.

Bursztynsky, Jessica. "The US Won't Provide Flu Vaccines to Migrant Families at Border Detention Camps." CNBC, August 20, 2019.

Butera, Emily. "Are the Children of Immigrants Becoming Needless Statistics in the Child Welfare System?" Restore Fairness, November 16, 2009. https://www.colorlines.com/articles/are-children-immigrants-becoming-needless-statistics-welfare-system.

Butler, Sandra. *TANF Time Limits and Maine Families: Consequences of Withdrawing the Safety Net.* Report for Maine Equal Justice Partners, March 2013. https://www.mejp.org/sites/default/files/TANF-Study-SButler-Feb2013.pdf.

Byler, William, Sam P. Deloria, and A. Gurwitt. "Another Chapter in the Destruction of American Indian Families." Yale Reports (radio program), no. 654, 1973.

Calhoun, Ada. "The Criminalization of Bad Mothers." *New York Times,* April 25, 2012.

Calhoun, John Caldwell. *The Speech of John C. Calhoun: Delivered in the Congress of the United from 1811 to the Present Time.* New York: Harper & Brothers, 1843.

Canby, William C., Jr. *American Indian Law in a Nutshell.* 4th ed. St. Paul, MN: West, 2004.

Capps, Randy, Rosa Maria Castañeda, Ajay Chaudry, and Robert Santos. "Paying the Price: The Impact of Immigration Raids on America's Children." Washington, DC: Urban Institute for the National Council of La Raza, 2007. https://www.urban.org.

Casa Alianza Foundation and Myrna Mack Survivors Foundation. *Adoptions in Guatemala: Protection or Business?* With support from the Social Movement for the Rights of Children and Adolescents, Human Rights Office of the Archbishop of Guatemala, and Guatemalan Social Welfare Secretariat. Translation by UNICEF. Guatemala City: Guatemala, 2007. https://www.brandeis.edu/investigate/adoption/guatemala-sources.html#MyrnaMack.

Centers for Disease Control. "Infant Mortality and Low Birth Weight among Black and White Infants—United States, 1980–2000." *Morbidity and Mortality Weekly Report* 51, no. 27 (July 12, 2002): 589–92.

Chaudry, Ajay, Randy Capps, Juan Manuel Pedroza, Rosa Maria Castañeda, Robert Santos, and Molly M. Scott. "Facing Our Future: Children in the

Aftermath of Immigration Enforcement." Washington, DC: Urban Institute, 2010. https://www.urban.org.

Chavkin, Wendy. "Cocaine and Pregnancy—Time to Look at the Evidence." *Journal of the American Medical Association* 285, no. 12 (2001): 1626-27.

Child, Brenda J. *Boarding School Seasons: American Indian Families, 1900–1940.* Lincoln: University of Nebraska Press, 2000.

———. "Runaway Boys, Resistant Girls: Rebellion at Flandreau and Haskell, 1900–1940." *Journal of American Indian Education* 35, no. 3 (Spring 1996): 49-57.

Chira, Susan. "Children of Crack: Are The Schools Ready? A Special Report: Crack Babies Turn 5, and Schools Brace." *New York Times,* May 25, 1990, 1.

Christophi, Helen. "Feds Tell 9th Circuit: Detained Kids 'Safe and Sanitary' without Soap." Courthouse News Service, June 18, 2019. https://www.courthousenews.com.

Cisneros, Jesus. "Working with the Complexity and Refusing to Simplify: Undocuqueer Meaning Making at the Intersection of LGBTQ and Immigrant Rights Discourses." *Journal of Homosexuality* 65, no. 11 (September 19, 2018): 1415-34.

Clinton, Hillary. *Hard Choices: A Memoir.* New York: Simon & Schuster, 2014.

Cockburn, Andrew, and Leslie Cockburn. "Guns, Drugs, and the CIA." *PBS Frontline,* May 17, 1988.

Cohen, Wilbur J. "Public Assistance Provisions for Navajo and Hopi Indians: Public Law 474." *Social Security Bulletin* (June 1950): 8-10.

Collier, John. "American Congo." *Survey,* August 1, 1923.

———. "America's Treatment of Her Indians." *Current History* (August 1923): 771-78.

Comisión Nacional sobre la Desaparición de Personas (CONADEP). *Nunca Más: Informe de la Comisión Nacional Sobre la Desaparición de Personas.* Buenos Aires: EUDEBA, 1984.

Comisión para el Esclarecimiento Histórico. *Guatemala, memoria del silencio = Tz'inil Na'tab'al.* Vol 12. Guatemala City: CEH, 1998.

Conlon, Deirdre, and Nancy Hiemstra, eds. *Intimate Economies of Immigration Detention: Critical Perspectives.* New York: Routledge, 2016.

Cook-Lynn, Elizabeth. "The Big Pipe Case." In *Reading Native American Women: Critical/Creative Representations,* edited by Inés Hernández-Avila, 77-92. Lanham, MD: Altamira Press, 2005.

———. *From the River's Edge.* 2nd ed. St. Paul, MN: Living Justice Press, 2012.

———. "Review of *The Broken Cord.*" *Wicazo Sa Review* 5, no. 2 (1989): 42–45.

Coolidge, Dane. "'Kid Catching' on the Navajo Reservation: 1930." In *The Destruction of American Indian Families,* edited by Steven Unger, 18–21. New York: Association on American Indian Affairs, 1977.

Corn, David. "Unfit to Lead." *Nation,* March 14, 2005.

Cornish, Audie, and Mary Louise Kelly, hosts. "The History of the Flores Settlement and Its Effects on Immigration." *All Things Considered.* NPR, June 22, 2018.

Cowan, Benjamin. *Securing Sex: Morality and Repression in the Making of Cold War Brazil.* Chapel Hill: University of North Carolina Press, 2016.

Cranley, Ellen. "Kellyanne Conway: 'Nobody Likes' Policy Separating Families at the Border." *Business Insider,* June 17, 2018.

Danner, Mark. *The Massacre at El Mozote.* New York: Vintage Books, 1993.

DasGupta, Debanuj. "Queering Immigration: Perspectives on Cross-Movement Organizing." *Scholar & Feminist Online,* no. 10.1–10.2 (Fall 2011–Spring 2012). https://sfonline.barnard.edu/a-new-queer-agenda /queering-immigration-perspectives-on-cross-movement-organizing/.

Davis, Angela Y. *Angela Davis: An Autobiography.* New York: International Publishers Co, 2013.

———. "Outcast Mothers and Surrogates: Racism and Reproductive Politics in the Nineties." In *American Feminist Thought at Century's End: A Reader,* edited by Linda S. Kauffman. Cambridge: Blackwell, 1993.

Davis, Kristina. "San Diego Judge Orders 11 Separated Parents Can Return to U.S. to Pursue Asylum." *San Diego Union-Tribune,* September 5, 2019.

De Leon, Jason. *The Land of Open Graves: Living and Dying on the Migrant Trail.* Oakland: University of California Press, 2015.

del Olmo, Rosa. "The Hidden Face of Drugs." *Social Justice* 18, no. 4 (1991): 11–47.

Devereaux, Ryan. "How the CIA Watched Over the Destruction of Gary Webb." *Intercept,* September 25, 2014. https://theintercept.com.

Dewan, Shaila. "Family Separation: It's a Problem for U.S. Citizens, Too." *New York Times,* June 22, 2018.

Dorris, Michael. *The Broken Cord.* New York: Harper & Row, 1989.

Douglass, Frederick. *Narrative of the Life of Frederick Douglass, An American Slave, Written by Himself.* 2nd ed. Dublin: Webb and Chapman, 1846.

Du Bois, W. E. B. *The Negro American Family*. Atlanta: Atlanta University, 1908.

Duke, Lynn. "D.C. Revises Infant Death Figures; Rate for 6 Months Remains More Than Twice National Average." *Washington Post,* December 16, 1989.

Duggan, Lisa. *The Twilight of Equality? Neoliberalism, Cultural Politics, and the Attack on Democracy*. Boston: Beacon Press, 2004.

Dunn, Timothy J. *The Militarization of the US-Mexico Border 1978-1992: Low-Intensity Conflict Doctrine Comes Home*. Austin: CMAS Books, 1996.

Edwards, Laura F. *Gendered Strife and Confusion: The Political Culture of Reconstruction*. Urbana: University of Illinois Press, 1997.

Emmons, Alex. "Death Squads Are Back in Honduras, Activists Tell Congress." *Intercept,* April 12, 2016. https://theintercept.com.

Erikson, Jane. "Doctors Mislabel Defects: Fetal Alcohol Misdiagnosed." *Arizona Daily Star,* November 27, 1995.

Eskew, Glenn T. "'Bombingham': Black Protest in Postwar Birmingham, Alabama." *The Historian* 59, no. 2 (1997): 371-90.

Estes, Nick. *Our History Is the Future: Standing Rock versus the Dakota Access Pipeline, and the Long Tradition of Indigenous Resistance*. New York: Verso, 2019.

Evans, Michael, ed. "Mexico: Los Zetas Drug Cartel Linked San Fernando Police to Migrant Massacres." *National Security Archive,* December 22, 2014. http://www2.gwu.edu/~nsarchiv/NSAEBB/NSAEBB499/.

Evans-Campbell, Teresa, Karina L. Walters, Cynthia R. Pearson, and Christopher D. Campbell. "Indian Boarding School Experience, Substance Use, and Mental Health among Urban Two-Spirit American Indian/Alaska Natives." *American Journal of Drug and Alcohol Abuse* 38, no. 5 (September 2012): 421-27.

Falcón, Sylvanna. "'National Security' and the Violation of Women: Militarized Border Rape at the US-Mexico Border." In *Color of Violence,* edited by INCITE! Women of Color Against Violence, 119-29. Durham, NC: Duke University Press, 2016.

Faulkner, William. *Requiem for a Nun*. 2nd ed. New York: Vintage, 1975.

Feminist Newswire. "Protestors Demand Justice after Denver Police Fatally Shoot Queer Latina Teen." January 30, 2015. https://feminist.org.

Fernández, Valeria. "Pregnant and Shackled: Hard Labor for Arizona's Immigrants." *New American Media,* January 26, 2010. http://news .newamericamedia.org.

———. "Pregnant Latina Says She Was Forced to Give Birth in Shackles after One of Arpaio's Deputies Racially Profiled Her." *Phoenix New Times,* October 20, 2009. http://www.phoenixnewtimes.com.

Fitzgerald, Maureen. *Habits of Compassion: Irish Catholic Nuns and the Origins of New York's Welfare System,* 1830–1920. Urbana: University of Illinois Press, 2006.

Foley, Neil. *The White Scourge: Mexicans, Blacks, and Poor Whites in Texas Cotton Culture.* Berkeley: University of California Press, 1997.

Foner, Eric. *The Fiery Trial: Abraham Lincoln and American Slavery.* New York: W.W. Norton, 2010.

———. *Reconstruction: America's Unfinished Revolution.* New York: Harper and Row, 1989.

Frank, Dana. "Hopeless in Honduras?" *Foreign Affairs,* November 22, 2013.

Fullilove, Mindy Thompson, Anne Lown, and Robert Fullilove. "Crack 'Hos and Skeezers: Traumatic Experiences of Women Crack Users." *Journal of Sex Research* 29, no. 2 (1992): 275–87.

Gates, Scott, and Simon Reich. "Think Again: Child Soldiers." NPR, May 27, 2009.

Gibler, John. *To Die in Mexico: Dispatches from Inside the Drug War.* San Francisco: City Lights, 2011.

Gilbert, Olive, Frances W. Titus, and Susan B. Anthony Collection. *Narrative of Sojourner Truth: A Bondswoman of Olden Time, Emancipated by the New York Legislature in the Early Part of the Present Century; with a History of Her Labors and Correspondence Drawn from Her "Book of Life."* Battle Creek, MI: Published for the Author, 1878. https://catalog .hathitrust.org/Record/009602620.

Gill, Lesley. *The School of the Americas: Military Training and Political Violence in the Americas.* Durham, NC: Duke University Press, 2004.

Gilmore, Ruth Wilson. *Golden Gulag: Prisons, Surplus, Crisis, and Opposition in Globalizing California.* Berkeley: University of California Press, 2007.

Goicoechea, Ignacio. *Report of a Fact-Finding Mission to Guatemala in Relation to Intercountry Adoption.* The Hague: Hague Conference on

Private International Law, 2007. http://findingfernanda.com/category
/reports-2/.

Golden, Janet. *Message in a Bottle: The Making of Fetal Alcohol Syndrome.*
Cambridge, MA: Harvard University Press, 2005.

Goldman, Francisco. *The Art of Political Murder: Who Killed the Bishop?* New
York: Grove Press, 2007.

Gonzales, Alfonso. "Derechos en Crisis: Central American Asylum Claims in
the Age of Authoritarian Neoliberalism." *Politics, Groups, and Identities,*
May 20, 2018, 1–19.

Gonzalez, Richard. "Expedited Hearings for Migrant Children Raise
Concerns." NPR, August 1, 2014.

Goodfriend, Hillary. "An Alliance for Insecurity?" *NACLA Report on the
Americas,* June 14, 2017.

Goodmark, Leigh. *A Troubled Marriage: Domestic Violence & the Legal System.*
New York: NYU Press, 2011.

Gordon, Linda. *The Great Arizona Orphan Abduction.* Cambridge: Harvard
University Press, 1999.

———. *Heroes of Their Own Lives: The Politics and History of Family Violence.*
New York: Viking, 1988.

Gosztola, Kevin, and Brian Solestein. "Let's Not Rewrite History to Defend
Joe Biden's Record of Cynical Dog-Whistle Politics," *Shadowproof,* May 5,
2019. https://shadowproof.com.

Gottschalk, Marie. *The Prison and the Gallows: The Politics of Mass Incarceration in America.* Cambridge: Cambridge University Press, 2006.

Grandin, Greg. *The Last Colonial Massacre: Latin America in the Cold War.*
Chicago: University of Chicago Press, 2004.

Grant, L. Trevor. *The Politicization of Foster Care in New York City.* Jamaica,
NY: Yacos Press, 1996.

Green, Linda. *Fear as a Way of Life: Mayan Widows in Rural Guatemala.* New
York: Columbia University Press, 1999.

Guest, Iain. *Behind the Disappearances: Argentina's Dirty War against Human
Rights and the United Nations.* Philadelphia: University of Pennsylvania
Press, 1990.

Guidotti-Hernández, Nicole M. *Unspeakable Violence: Remapping U.S. and
Mexican National Imaginaries.* Durham, NC: Duke University Press, 2011.

Gutiérrez, Elena R. *Fertile Matters: The Politics of Mexican-Origin Women's Reproduction*. Austin: University of Texas Press, 2009.

Haag, Matthew. "'Womp': Corey Lewandowski Mocks Child with Down Syndrome Separated from Mother." *New York Times*, June 20, 2018.

Hamilton, Keegan. "Felipe Calderón Has No Regrets about His Bloody War against Mexico's Cartels." *Vice*, November 21, 2018. https://www.vice.com.

Harkinson, Josh. "Trump's Newest Senior Adviser Seen as a White Nationalist Ally." *Mother Jones*, December 14, 2016.

Harp, Kathi L. H., and Carrie B. Oser. "Factors Associated with Two Types of Child Custody Loss Among a Sample of African American Mothers: A Novel Approach." *Social Science Research* 60 (November 2016): 283–96.

Hartman, Saidiya. *Lose Your Mother: A Journey along the North Atlantic Slave Route*. New York: Farrar, Straus, and Giroux, 2008.

———. *Scenes of Subjection: Terror, Slavery, and Self-Making in Nineteenth-Century America*. New York: Oxford University Press, 1997.

Hernandez, Anabel. *Narcoland: The Mexican Drug Lords and Their Godfathers*. Translated by Iain Bruce and Lorna Scott Fox. New York: Verso, 2014.

Hernández, Kelly Lytle. *Migra! A History of the U.S. Border Patrol*. Berkeley: University of California Press, 2010.

Hernández-Nieto, Rosana, and Marcus C. Gutiérrez; and Francisco Moreno-Fernández, dir. *Hispanic Map of the United States*. Cambridge: Instituto Cervantes, Harvard University, 2017. doi: 10.15427/OR035-11/2017EN.

Higginbotham, A. Leon. *In the Matter of Color: Race and the American Legal Process; The Colonial Period*. New York: Oxford University Press, 1978.

Hinds, Michael DeCourcy. "The Instincts of Parenthood Become Part of Crack's Toll." *New York Times*, March 17, 1990.

Hirsch, Bertram. "Keynote Address." In *The Indian Child Welfare Act—The Next Ten Years: Indian Homes for Indian Children*, edited by Troy R. Johnson, 18–26. Los Angeles: UCLA American Indian Studies Center, 1990.

Hobson, Emily K. *Lavender and Red: Liberation and Solidarity in the Gay and Lesbian Left*. Oakland: University of California Press, 2016.

Hodges, Donald C. *Argentina's "Dirty War": An Intellectual Biography*. Austin: University of Texas Press, 1991.

Holguin, Carlos. "The History of the Flores Settlement and Its Effects on Immigration." Interview by Audie Cornish and Mary Louise Kelly. *All Things Considered*, NPR, June 22, 2018.

Holmes, Jack. "Democrats Just Jumped into the Trump Atrocity Trap." *Esquire*, July 11, 2019.

———. "An Expert on Concentration Camps Says That's Exactly What the U.S. Is Running at the Border." *Esquire*, June 13, 2019.

Honoré-Collins, Cynthia P. "The Impact of African American Incarceration on African American Children in the Child Welfare System." *Race, Gender and Class* 12, no. 3/4 (2005): 107–18.

Horne, Esther Burnett, and Sally McBeth. *Essie's Story: The Life and Legacy of a Shoshone Teacher*. Lincoln, NE: Bison Books, 1999.

Horwitz, Sari. "Earlier ATF Gun Operation 'Wide Receiver' Used Same Tactics as 'Fast and Furious.'" *Washington Post*, October 6, 2011.

Human Rights Watch. "Argentina: Amnesty Laws Struck Down." June 16, 2005. https://www.hrw.org.

———. *Slipping through the Cracks: Unaccompanied Children Detained by the U.S. Immigration and Naturalization Service*. New York: Human Rights Watch, 1997.

———. "US: Surge in Detention of Child Migrants." June 25, 2014. http://www.hrw.org.

Humphries, Drew. *Crack Mothers: Pregnancy, Drugs, and the Media*. Columbus: Ohio State University Press, 1999.

Hunter, Tera W. "The Long History of Child-Snatching." Editorial, *New York Times*, June 3, 2018.

Huntington, Samuel P. "The Hispanic Challenge." *Foreign Policy*, October 28, 2009.

Hyer, Sally. *One House, One Voice, One Heart: Native American Education at the Santa Fe Indian School*. Santa Fe: Museum of New Mexico Press, 1990.

INCITE!, ed. *Color of Violence: The INCITE! Anthology*. Durham, NC: Duke University Press, 2016. First published 2006 by South End Press (Boston).

Institute for Government Research. *The Problem of Indian Administration; Report of a Survey Made at the Request of Honorable Hubert Work, Secretary of the Interior, and Submitted to Him, February 21, 1928*. Washington: Brookings Institute, 1928.

ITVS. *Discovering Dominga*. Documentary film, July 8, 2003. https://itvs.org
/films/discovering-dominga.

Jackson, Derrick Z. "America's Shameful Little Secret." *Boston Globe,*
December 24, 1989.

Jacobs, Harriet. *Incidents in the Life of a Slave Girl*. New York: Open Road
Media, 2016.

Jacobs, Margaret. *A Generation Removed: The Fostering and Adoption of Indigenous
Children in the Postwar World*. Lincoln: University of Nebraska, 2014.

Johnson, Bryan. "Department of (in) Justice: We Can Lock Up Children in
Solitary Confinement." Blog post. Amoachi & Johnson, Attorneys at Law,
PLLC, May 9, 2015. https://amjolaw.com.

Karuka, Manu. *Empire's Tracks: Indigenous Nations, Chinese Workers, and the
Transcontinental Railroad*. Oakland: University of California Press, 2019.

Kaufman, Leslie. "Foster Children at Risk, and an Opportunity Lost." *New
York Times,* November 5, 2007.

Kelley, Robin D. G. *Hammer and Hoe: Alabama Communists during the Great
Depression*. Chapel Hill: University of North Carolina Press, 1990.

———. *Race Rebels: Culture, Politics, and the Black Working Class*. New York:
Free Press, 1994.

Kempe, C. Henry, Frederic N. Silverman, Brandt F. Steele, William Droegem-
ueller, and Henry K. Silver. "The Battered-Child Syndrome." *Journal of the
American Medical Association* 181, no. 1 (July 7, 1962): 17–24.

Kolata, Gina. "Bias Seen against Pregnant Addicts." *New York Times,* July 20,
1990.

Konigsberg, Eric. "Michael Dorris's Troubled Sleep." *New York,* June 16, 1997.

Kornbluh, Felicia. *The Battle for Welfare Rights: Politics and Poverty in Modern
America*. Philadelphia: University of Pennsylvania Press, 2007.

Kornbluh, Felicia, and Gwendolyn Mink, *Ensuring Poverty: Welfare Reform in
Feminist Perspective*. Philadelphia: University of Pennsylvania Press, 2019.

Kornbluh, Peter, and Malcolm Byrne. *The Iran-Contra Scandal: The Declassified History*. New York: New Press, 1993.

Krauss, Clifford. "How US Actions Helped Hide Salvadoran Human Rights
Abuses." *New York Times,* March 21, 1993.

Krauthammer, Charles. "Crack Babies Forming Biological Underclass." *St.
Louis Post-Dispatch,* July 30, 1989.

———. "Put Cocaine Babies in Protective Custody." *St. Louis Post-Dispatch,*
August 6, 1989.

Krieger, Heinrich. "Principles of the Indian Law and the Act of June 18, 1934."
George Washington Law Review, no. 3 (1935): 279–308.

Kristof, Nicholas. "Trump Wasn't First to Separate Families, but Policy Was
Still Evil." *New York Times,* June 20, 2018.

Landry, Alyssa. "Native History: AIM Occupation of Wounded Knee
Begins." *Indian Country Today,* February 27, 2017. https://newsmaven.io
/indiancountrytoday/.

Larabee, Mary S. "Unmarried Parenthood Under the Social Security Act." In
Proceeding of the National Conference of Social Work, 1939. New York:
Columbia University Press, 1939.

Lawrence-Webb, Claudia. "African American Children in the Modern Child
Welfare System: A Legacy of the Flemming Rule." In *Serving African
American Children: Child Welfare Perspectives,* edited by Sondra Jackson
and Sheryl Brissett-Chapman, 9–30. New York: Transaction Publishers,
1998.

Lemon, Jason. "Nearly All of Mexico's Gun Violence Is Committed by Illegal
Firearms Coming from the U.S, Officials Say." *Newsweek,* August 11, 2019.

LeMoyne, James. "Testifying to Torture." *New York Times Magazine,* June 5,
1988.

Levenson, Deborah T. *Adiós Niño: The Gangs of Guatemala City and the Politics
of Death.* Durham, NC: Duke University Press, 2013.

Levenstein, Lisa. "From Innocent Children to Unwanted Migrants and Unwed
Moms: Two Chapters in the Public Discourse on Welfare in the United
States, 1960–1961." *Journal of Women's History* 11, no. 4 (2000): 10–33.

Levin, Sam. "Trans Woman Who Died after Illness in US Custody Had Asked
to Be Deported, Family Says." *Guardian,* June 13, 2019.

Lewin, Tamar. "Drug Use in Pregnancy: New Issue for the Courts." *New York
Times,* February 5, 1990.

Liga Guatemalteca de Higiéne Mental. *Corazones en fiesta: Historias de
familias reunidas después del conflicto armado.* Guatemala City: Magna
Terra Editoriales, 2005.

Lindhorst, Taryn, and Leslie Leighninger. "Ending Welfare as We Know It" in
1960: Louisiana's Suitable Home Law." *Social Service Review* 77, no. 4
(2003): 564–84.

Lomawaima, K. Tsianina. "Domesticity in the Federal Indian Schools: The Power of Authority of Mind and Body." *American Ethnologist* 20, no. 2 (1993) 227–240.

———. *They Called It Prairie Light: The Story of Chilocco Indian School.* Lincoln: University of Nebraska Press, 1995.

Long, Marissa J. "70 Catholics Arrested in D.C. Protest over Trump Immigration Policies." *Washington Post,* July 18, 2019.

Magaña-Salgado, Jose. *Fair Treatment Denied: The Trump Administration's Troubling Attempt to Expand "Fast-Track" Deportations.* San Francisco: Immigrant Legal Resource Center. 2017. https://www.ilrc.org.

Maine Wabanaki–State Child Welfare Truth and Reconciliation Commission. *Report of the Maine Wabanaki-State Child Welfare Truth and Reconciliation Commission: Continuing the Conversation.* Online ver. July 2015. http://www.mainewabanakireach.org/maine_wabanaki_state_child_welfare_truth_and_reconciliation_commission.

Marable, Manning, *Race, Reform and Rebellion: The Second Reconstruction and Beyond in Black America, 1945-2006.* Jackson: University Press of Mississippi, 2007.

Marcetic, Branko "Negroponte's Crimes." *Jacobin,* August 2016. https://www.jacobinmag.com.

Marchak, Patricia. *God's Assassins: State Terrorism in Argentina in the 1970s.* Kingston, ON: McGill-Queen's University Press, 1999.

Marren, Lea. *Salvador's Children: Song for Survival.* Columbus: Ohio State University Press, 1992.

Marshall, Serena, Lana Zak, and Jennifer Metz. "Doctor Compares Conditions at Immigrant Holding Centers to 'Torture Facilities.'" ABC News, June 23, 2019.

Martin, Nina. "Take a Valium, Lose Your Kid, Go to Jail." ProPublica, September 23, 2015. https://www.propublica.org.

Martinez, Michael, Holly Yan, and Catherine Shoichet. "Growing Protests over Where to Shelter Immigrant Children Hits Arizona." CNN, July 16, 2014.

Martinez, Oscar. "Los niños no se van: Se los llevan." *El Faro,* July 13, 2014. http://www.elfaro.net/es/201407/noticias/15683/.

Maruyama, Hana C. "On Common Ground: Concentration Camps in the 'Home of the Free' at the Southwest Border and in History." *Abusable Past*

no. 3.3 (September 10, 2019). https://www.radicalhistoryreview.org
/abusablepast.

Mathews, T. J., Marian F. MacDorman, and Marie E. Thoma. "Infant
Mortality Statistics from the 2005 Period Linked Birth/Infant Death Data
Set." *National Vital Statistics Reports* 57, no. 2 (July 30, 2008): 1–32.

Matthiessen, Peter. *In the Spirit of Crazy Horse: The Story of Leonard Peltier and
the FBI's War on the American Indian Movement.* New York: Viking, 1983.

Mauro, Hayes Peter. *The Art of Americanization at the Carlisle Indian School.*
Albuquerque: University of New Mexico Press, 2011.

McCoy, Alfred W. *The Politics of Heroin: CIA Complicity in the Global Drug
Trade.* 2nd rev. ed. Chicago: Chicago Review Press, 2003.

McFadden, Robert. "Dennis Banks, American Indian Civil-Rights Leader,
Dies at 80." *Seattle Times,* October 30, 2017.

McKittrick, Katherine. *Demonic Grounds: Black Women and the Cartographies
of Struggle.* Minneapolis: University of Minnesota Press, 2006.

Melley, Brian. "Judge Puts Blame on Trump, Congress for Immigration
Crisis." AP News, July 10, 2018.

Mendoza, Jennifer. "The Border Crossed Us: The Tohono O'odham Nation's
Divide." *Medium,* May 15, 2018. https://medium.com.

Miller, David Humphreys. *Ghost Dance.* Lincoln: University of Nebraska
Press, 1985.

Miller, Ken. "Plan Halted to House Migrant Kids at Oklahoma's Fort Sill."
Army Times, July 28, 2019. https://www.armytimes.com.

Mink, Gwendolyn. "Introduction to Disdained Mothers and Despised Others:
The Politics and Impact of Welfare Reform," *Social Justice* 25, no. 1 (1998).

Mink, Gwendolyn, and Rickie Solinger, eds. *Welfare: A Documentary History
of Politics and Policy.* New York: NYU Press, 2003.

Mitchell, Christopher. "US Policy Toward Haitian Boat People, 1972–93."
Annals of the American Academy of Political and Social Science 534, no. 1
(1994): 69–80.

Mitchell, Mary Niall. *Raising Freedom's Child: Black Children and Visions of the
Future After Slavery.* New York: NYU Press, 2008.

Montgomery, David. "Poster Child." *Washington Post,* May 20, 2007.

Morash, Merry, Robin N. Haarr, and Lila Rucker. "A Comparison of Programming for Women and Men in US Prisons in the 1980s." *Crime and
Delinquency* 40, no. 2 (1994): 197–221.

Morgan, Jennifer L. *Laboring Women: Reproduction and Gender in New World Slavery.* Philadelphia: University of Pennsylvania Press, 2011.

Morgan, Jennifer L. "*Partus Sequitur Ventrum*: Law, Race, and Reproduction in Colonial Slavery." *Small Axe* 22, no. 1 (2018): 1–17.

Muñoz Martínez, Monica. *The Injustice Never Leaves You: Anti-Mexican Violence in Texas.* Cambridge, MA: Harvard University Press, 2018.

Murakawa, Naomi. *The First Civil Right: How Liberals Built Prison America.* Studies in Postwar American Political Development. New York: Oxford University Press, 2014.

Murray, Kasia O'Neill, and Sarah Gesiriech. *A Brief Legislative History of the Child Welfare System.* Washington, DC: Pew Commission on Children in Foster Care, 2004. https://www.pewtrusts.org/en/projects/archived-projects/commission-on-children-in-foster-care.

Nabokov, Peter. *Native American Testimony.* New York: Penguin Books, 1999.

Nadasen, Premilla. *Welfare Warriors.* New York: Routledge, 2004.

Nazario, Sonia. "Pay or Die." *New York Times,* July 26, 2019.

———. "'Someone Is Always Trying to Kill You.'" *New York Times,* April 5, 2019.

Nelson, Barbara J. *Making an Issue of Child Abuse: Political Agenda Setting for Social Problems.* Chicago: University of Chicago Press, 1986.

Neuspiel, Daniel. "Let's Not Call Cocaine-Exposed Children 'Crack Babies.'" Letter to the editor. *New York Times,* March 9, 1993.

New York Times. "Gun Walking the Mexican Border." Editorial. November 6, 2011.

———. "Hypocrisy, Locked and Loaded." Editorial. June 20, 2011.

Ocen, Priscilla A. "Birthing Injustice: Pregnancy as a Status Offense." *George Washington Law Review* 85, no. 4 (2017): 1163–223.

———. "Pregnant While Black: The Story of *Ferguson v. City of Charleston.*" In *Reproductive Rights and Justice Stories,* edited by Melissa Murray, Katherine Shaw, and Reva B. Siegel. St. Paul, MN: Foundation Press, 2019.

———. "Punishing Pregnancy: Race, Incarceration, and the Shackling of Pregnant Prisoners." *California Law Review* 100 (2012): 1239–311.

Oficina de Derechos Humanos de Arzobispado de Guatemala. *Hasta encontrarte: Niñez desaparecida por el conflicto armado interno en Guatemala.* 3rd ed. Guatemala City: ODHAG, 2005.

Olson, James C. *Red Cloud and the Sioux Problem.* Lincoln: University of Nebraska Press, 1968.

Orleck, Annelise. *Storming Caesars Palace: How Black Mothers Fought Their Own War on Poverty.* Boston: Beacon Press, 2005.

Osorio, Carlos. *Stolen Babies: Argentina Convicts Two Military Dictators.* National Security Archives Electronic Briefing Book, no. 383. July 5, 2012. https://nsarchive2.gwu.edu/NSAEBB/NSAEBB383/.

Paley, Dawn. *Drug War Capitalism.* Oakland: AK Press, 2014.

Paltrow, Lynn. "Roe v. Wade and the New Jane Crow: Reproductive Rights in the Age of Mass Incarceration." *American Journal of Public Health* 103, no. 1 (January 2013): 17–21.

Paltrow, Lynn, D. Cohen, and C. A. Carey. *Year 2000 Overview: Governmental Responses to Pregnant Women Who Use Alcohol or Other Drugs.* Philadelphia: National Advocates for Pregnant Women of the Women's Law Project, 2000.

Paltrow, Lynn M., and Jeanne Flavin. "Pregnant, and No Civil Rights." *New York Times,* November 7, 2014.

Paquette, Danielle. "One in Nine Black Children Has Had a Parent in Prison." *Washington Post,* October 27, 2015.

Parry, Robert. "America's Debt to Gary Webb." FAIR, March 1, 2005. https://fair.org.

———. *Lost History: Contras, Cocaine, the Press, and "Project Truth."* Arlington, VA: Media Consortium, 1997.

Paul, Julius. "The Return of Punitive Sterilization Proposals: Current Attacks on Illegitimacy and the AFDC Program." *Law and Society Review* 3, no. 1 (August 1968): 77–106.

Peace, Roger. "The Anti-Contra-War Campaign: Organizational Dynamics of a Decentralized Movement." *International Journal of Peace Studies* 13, no. 1 (Spring/Summer 2008): 63–83.

Petón, Mario J. "Thousands of Cubans Try to Enter the U.S. at a Border Now Practically Closed Off to Them." *Miami Herald,* August 20, 2019.

Philp, Kenneth R. *John Collier's Crusade for Indian Reform, 1920–1954.* Tucson: University of Arizona Press, 1977.

Piercy, Marge. "The Art of Blessing the Day." In *The Art of Blessing the Day: Poems with a Jewish Theme.* New York: Knopf, 2000.

Plantz, Margaret. *Indian Child Welfare: A Status Report; Final Report of the Survey of Indian Child Welfare and Implementation of the Indian Child*

Welfare Act and Section 428 of the Adoption Assistance and Child Welfare Act of 1980. Washington, DC: U.S. Department of the Interior, 1988.

Pleck, Elizabeth Hafkin. *Domestic Tyranny: The Making of American Social Policy against Family Violence from Colonial Times to the Present.* New York: Oxford University Press, 1987.

Portnoy, Alicia. *The Little School: Tales of Disappearance and Survival.* San Francisco: Cleis Press, 1998.

Pratt, Richard Henry. *Battlefield and Classroom: Four Decades with the American Indian,* 1867–1904. Edited and with an introduction by Robert Marshall Utley. New Haven, CT: Yale University Press, 1964.

Proyecto Interdiocesano de Recuperación de la Memoria Histórica (REMHI). *Guatemala: Nunca más.* 12 vols. Guatemala City: Gako, 1998. http://www.fundacionpdh.org/lesahumanidad/informes/guatemala/informeR-EMHI.htm.

Prucha, Francis Paul, ed. *Documents of United States Indian Policy.* 2nd ed. Lincoln: University of Nebraska Press, 1990.

Restrepo, Dan, and Ann Garcia. "The Surge of Unaccompanied Children from Central America." Center for American Progress, July 24, 2014. https://www.americanprogress.org.

Reynoso, Conié, and Francisco González Arrecis. "Redada deja a 240 niños sin padres." *Prensa Libre,* March 9, 2007.

Rivlin, Leanne G., and Lynne C. Manzo. "Homeless Children in New York City: A View from the 19th Century." *Children's Environments Quarterly* 5, no. 1 (1988): 26–33.

Roberts, Dorothy. *Shattered Bonds: The Color of Child Welfare.* New York: Basic Books, 2002.

Robles, Frances, and Shaila Dewan. "Skip Child Support. Go to Jail. Lose Job. Repeat." *New York Times,* April 19, 2015.

Romo, Rafael. "Chile's 'Children of Silence' Seek Truth." CNN, October 31, 2014.

Rozov, Maya. "The Serrano-Cruz Sisters v. El Salvador." *Loyola of Los Angeles International and Comparative Law Review* 36, no. 5 (2014): 2071–87.

Rutenberg, Jim, and Marc Lacey. "Bush Meets Anger over Immigration Issues as He Promotes Free Trade in Guatemala." *New York Times,* March 12, 2009.

Sacchetti, Maria. "ACLU: U.S. Has Taken Nearly 1,000 Child Migrants from Their Parents since Judge Ordered Stop to Border Separations." *Washington Post,* July 30, 2019.

Saldaña-Portillo, María Josefina. *Indian Given: Racial Geographies across Mexico and the United States.* Durham, NC: Duke University Press, 2016.

Sánchez, George J. *Becoming Mexican American: Ethnicity, Culture and Identity in Chicano Los Angeles, 1900–1945.* New York: Oxford University Press, 1993.

Sasser, Jade S. *On Infertile Ground: Population Control and Women's Rights in the Era of Climate Change.* New York: NYU Press, 2018.

Schene, P.A. "Past, Present, and Future Roles of Child Protective Services." *Future of Children* 8, no. 1 (Spring 1998): 23–38.

Scherer, Michael, and Josh Dawsey. "Trump Cites as a Negotiating Tool His Policy for Separating Immigrant Children from Their Parents." *Washington Post,* June 15, 2018.

Schriro, Dora. "Weeping in the Playtime of Others: The Obama Administration's Failed Reform of ICE Family Detention Practices." *Journal on Migration and Human Security* 5, no. 2 (2012): 452–80.

Schwalm, Leslie A. *A Hard Fight for We: Women's Transition from Slavery to Freedom in South Carolina.* Urbana: University of Illinois Press, 1997.

Sealander, Judith. *The Failed Century of the Child: Governing America's Young in the Twentieth Century.* Cambridge, UK: Cambridge University Press, 2003.

Shah, Nayan. *Contagious Divides: Epidemics and Race in San Francisco's Chinatown.* Berkeley: University of California Press, 2001.

———. *Stranger Intimacy: Contesting Race, Sexuality and the Law in the North American West.* Berkeley: University of California Press, 2012.

Sharp, Michael D. "Michael Dorris." In *Popular Contemporary Writers.* New York: Marshall Cavendish, 2006.

Sharpe, Christina. *In the Wake: On Blackness and Being.* Durham, NC: Duke University Press, 2016.

Shenk, Jan, and Robert Armstrong. *El Salvador: The Face of Revolution.* Boston: South End Press, 1982.

Sherman, Gabriel. "'Stephen Actually Enjoys Seeing Those Pictures at the Border': The West Wing Is Fracturing over Trump's Callous Migrant-Family Policy." *Vanity Fair,* June 20, 2018.

Siegel, Barry, "In the Name of the Children: Get Treatment or Go to Jail, One South Carolina Hospital Tells Drug-Abusing Pregnant Women. Now It Faces a Lawsuit and a Civil-Rights Investigation." *Los Angeles Times,* August 7, 1994.

Silva, Danielle. "Advocates Walk Out of Hearing to Protest Plan to Separate Migrant Families." NBC News, May 8, 2018.

Smith, Andrea. *Conquest: Sexual Violence and American Indian Genocide.* Boston: South End Press, 2005.

Smith, Christian. *Resisting Reagan: The U.S. Central America Peace Movement.* Chicago: University of Chicago Press, 1996.

Solinger, Rickie. *Wake Up Little Susie: Single Pregnancy and Race before* Roe v. Wade. New York: Routledge, 1992.

Solis, Dianne, and Alfredo Corchado. "Asylum Seekers Reportedly Denied Entry at Border as Trump Tightens 'Zero Tolerance' Immigration Policies." *Dallas Morning News,* June 6, 2018.

Spillers, Hortense J. "Mama's Baby, Papa's Maybe: An American Grammar Book." *Diacritics* 17, no. 2 (1987): 65-81.

Sprenkels, Ralph. *El dia más esperada: Buscando a los niños desaparecidos de El Salvador.* San Salvador: UCA Editores, 2001.

———. *Stories Never to Be Forgotten: Eyewitness Accounts from the Salvadoran Civil War.* Tempe, Arizona Bilingual Press/Editorial Bilingüe, 2015.

Stanley, William. *The Protection Racket State: Elite Politics, Military Extortion, and Civil War in El Salvador.* Philadelphia: Temple University Press, 1996.

Stern, Alexandra Minna. *Proud Boys and the White Ethnostate: How the Alt-Right is Warping the American Imagination.* Boston: Beacon Press, 2019.

Stevens, Jacqueline. "Thin ICE." *Nation,* June 5, 2008.

Streitfeld, David. "Sad Story." *Washington Post,* July 13, 1997.

Student Nonviolent Coordinating Committee. "Genocide in Mississippi." Pamphlet. Atlanta, GA: Student Nonviolent Coordinating Committee, n.d. (c. 1965). http://civilrights.woodson.virginia.edu/items/show/9.

Swarms, Rachel. "Study Says Government Has Improperly Detained Foreign Children." *New York Times,* June 19, 2009.

Talbot, Margaret. "The Lost Children: What Do Tougher Detention Policies Mean for Illegal Immigrant Families?" *New Yorker,* March 3, 2008.

Taylor, Diana. *Disappearing Acts: Spectacles of Gender and Nationalism in Argentina's "Dirty War."* Durham, NC: Duke University Press, 1997.

Taylor, Keeanga-Yamahtta. *From #BlackLivesMatter to Black Liberation.* Chicago: Haymarket Books, 2016.

Thomas, John F. "Cuban Refugees in the United States." *International Migration Digest* 1, no. 2 (1967): 46–57.

Thompson, Ginger. "After Losing Freedom, Some Immigrants Face Loss of Custody of Their Children." *New York Times,* April 23, 2009.

———. "Court Rules for Deportee on Custody." *New York Times,* June 28, 2009.

Timmerman, Jacobo. *Prisoner Without a Name, Cell Without a Number.* New York: Knopf 1981.

"Trump Rule Restricting Asylum Seekers Struck Down by Court." Reuters, August 2, 2019.

Twohey, Meagan. "The Crack-Baby Myth." *National Journal* 31, no. 46 (November 13, 1999): 3340–41.

Unfinished Sentences. "Still Searching: The Disappeared Children of the Quesera Massacre, El Salvador." YouTube, March 26, 2015. https://youtube/LoKPAey2Xbk.

UN General Assembly. Convention on the Prevention and Punishment of the Crime of Genocide. United Nations, Treaty Series, vol. 78. December 9, 1948. https://www.refworld.org/docid/3ae6b3ac0.html

US Census Bureau. *Statistical Abstract of the United States:* 1961. 82nd ed. June 1961. https://www.census.gov/library/publications/1961/compendia/statab/82ed.html.

US Congress. Senate Judiciary Committee. *Revolutionary Activities within the United States: The American Indian Movement; Report of the Subcommittee to Investigate the Administration of the Internal Security Act and Other Internal Security Laws.* Washington, DC: U.S. Government Printing Office, 1976.

———. Senate Select Committee on Indian Affairs. "Indian Child Welfare Statistical Survey, July 1976, Appendix G." *Indian Child Welfare Act of* 1977: First Session on S. 1214, To establish standards for the placement of Indian children in foster or adoptive homes, to prevent the breakup of Indian families, and for other purposes, August 4, 1977. Washington, DC: U.S. Government Printing Office, 1977.

Van Biema, David. "The Storm over Orphanages." *Time,* December 12, 1994.

Vidal, Gore. "The State of the Union." *Nation,* September 13, 2004.

Vogt, Wendy. *Lives in Transit: Violence and Intimacy on the Migrant Journey.* Oakland: University of California Press, 2018.

Ward, Jesmyn. *Men We Reaped: A Memoir.* New York: Bloomsbury, 2013.

Way, John T. *Agrotropolis: Urban Space and Youth Culture in Contemporary Guatemala.* Oakland: University of California Press, forthcoming.

Webb, Gary. *Dark Alliance: The CIA, the Contras, and the Crack Cocaine Explosion.* New York: Seven Stories Press, 1999.

Weiner, Tim, and Sam Dillon. "Shadowy Alliance—A Special Report: In Guatemala's Dark Heart, C.I.A. Lent Succor to Death." *New York Times,* April 2, 1995.

Whitman, James Q. *Hitler's American Model: The United States and the Making of Nazi Race Law.* Princeton, NJ: Princeton University Press, 2017.

Wiles, Tay. "A Closed Border Gate Has Cut Off Three Tohono O'odham Villages from Their Closest Food Supply." *Pacific Standard,* February 7, 2019. https://psmag.com.

Williams, Philip J., and Knut Walter. *Militarization and Demilitarization in El Salvador's Transition to Democracy.* Pittsburgh: University of Pittsburgh Press, 1997.

Witmer, Linda F. *The Indian Industrial School, Carlisle, Pennsylvania, 1879–1918.* Carlisle, PA: Cumberland County Historical Society, 1993.

Witte, Daniel, and Paul Mero. "Removing Classrooms from the Battlefield: Liberty, Paternalism, and the Redemptive Promise of Educational Choice." *BYU Law Review* 2008, no. 2 (May 1, 2008): 377–414.

Wolfe, Patrick. "Settler Colonialism and the Elimination of the Native." *Journal of Genocide Research* 8 no. 4 (December 2006): 387–409.

Women's Commission for Refugee Women and Children and Lutheran Immigration and Refugee Service. "Locking Up Family Values: The Detention of Immigrant Families." New York: Women's Commission for Refugee Women and Children, 2007. https://www.womensrefugeecommission.org.

Wood, Elisabeth J. *Insurgent Collective Action and Civil War in El Salvador.* Cambridge, UK: Cambridge University Press, 2003.

Woodhouse, Murphy, and Lauren Gilger. "Tracing the Migrant Journey: On the Ground in San Luis Rio Colorado, Mexico." *Fronteras,* KJZZ (NPR affiliate), August 19, 2019. https://fronterasdesk.org.

Woods, Alden. "Story Spreads of Tohono O'odham Brothers' Arrest, Deportation after Using Tribal Border Gate." *Arizona Republic,* August 2, 2018.

Wright, Richard. 12 *Million Black Voices: A Folk History of the Negro in the United States.* New York: Viking, 1941.

Yellin, Jean Fagan. *Women and Sisters: The Anti-Slavery Feminists in American Culture.* New Haven, CT: Yale University Press, 1992.

Yurkanin, Amy. "Pregnant Addict Tests Limits of Alabama's Harsh Drug Laws." AL.com, October 2, 2016. https://www.al.com.

Index

abolitionists: Black children and, 25, 27–28, 167, 178; prison abolition and, 124–25, 173; religious communities and, 173; taking children and, 17–19, 162–63

abortion rights, 110–12, 125–26

Abuelas (Grandmothers) de Plaza de Mayo, 80–81

Adios Niño (Levenson), 150

adoption: Black children and, 37, 184n38; citizenship and, 160; of Native children, 27, 188n37; organizing against, 95–97; placement of Black children and, 184n38; white people and, 37, 184n38, 188n37. *See also* foster care system

Adoption Resource Exchange of North America (ARENA), 188n37

Adoptions in Guatemala (Casa Alianza Foundation and Myrna Mack Survivors Foundation), 95–96

Aid to Families with Dependent Children (AFDC), 44, 122

Alabama, 20, 28, 33, 44, 125–26, 158

alcohol use: criminalization of, 106–10, 116–22, 171; fetal alcohol syndrome, 104, 116–22. *See also* drug use; fetal protection

Alexander, Michelle, 108

Algeria, 160, 193

American Association of University Women (AAUW), 123

American Civil Liberties Union (ACLU): family detention and, 143; lawsuit against T. Don Hutto Center, 4; New Orleans case, 170; Reproductive Freedom Project, 115–16, 174

American Indian Movement (AIM), 60, 68

anti-Communist conflicts, 4, 6, 14, 76–78, 134–36. *See also* Latin America

Anzaldúa, Gloria, 130

Apache Nation, 51–53

Argentina, 77–78, 79–83, 101, 193n45

Arizona, 129–31, 131–32, 150–53, 155, 158

welfare reform and, 30–37. *See also* enslavement of Black people

Blitzer, Jonathan, 161

Boland Amendment, 97–98

Bolivia, 80

Border Patrol, 1–2, 104, 128–29, 155, 157, 162, 165

Brané, Michelle, 161

Brazil, 80

The Broken Cord (Dorris), 116–19

Brown, DeNeen L., 2

Brown, Linda, 32–33

Brown, Mike, 171

Brown v. Board of Education, 32, 33–34, 184n25

Bupatcha, Djamila, 193n45

Bureau of Indian Affairs (BIA), 54, 58, 63, 66, 75, 169–70

Bush (George W.) administration: arms trafficking and, 151–52; asylum seekers and, 142–43, 168; child separation/detention policy, 142, 144–49, 176–77; deportation of parents without their children, 144–49; detention centers, 4, 46, 143, 156, 159, 168; expedited review and removal under, 10; family detention, 142–43, 156; unaccompanied minors and, 128–29, 142; workplace raids and, 145–46

Bush (George H. W.) administration: El Salvador and, 89; Flores Settlement Agreement and, 137–43, 156, 165, 198n15; Haitian refugees and, 10; immigrant child detention and, 138–39; unaccompanied minors and, 128–29

Byrd, Robert, 33

Cáceres, Berta, 153

Cahn, Moises, 41

Calderón, Felipe, 151–52

Calhoun, John C., 26–27

California, 99, 129–31, 133–34, 134–35, 150–51, 155. *See also* Flores Settlement Agreement

Carlisle Indian Industrial School, 47, 49, 51–53, 55

Carter administration, 84–85, 89, 191n15, 193n45

Casa Alianza, 95

Catholic Church: abortion rights and, 77; adoptions and, 99–100; Latin America and, 7, 80, 82, 99–100; as sanctuaries for asylum seekers, 173; unmarried mothers and, 99–100

Central America. *See* Latin America; *names of individual countries*

Central Intelligence Agency (CIA): anti-Contra operations, 192n43; drug trafficking and, 98–99, 150–51, 192n43; El Salvador and, 97–98; Guatemala and, 90, 94; Honduras and, 102, 192n43; Nicaragua and, 97–98, 192n43

Chacón, Alma, 149

Chasnoff, Ira, 109

Chavkin, Wendy, 111, 174

Cherokee Nation, 132

child abuse: battered children syndrome, 189n56; child neglect/danger to their children discourse, 8–9, 18–19, 37–38, 156, 168–69, 189n56

children of silence, 99–100

Child Welfare League of America, 42, 188n37
Chile, 80, 99–100
China, 133–34
Chiricahua Apache, 51–53
Choate, John, 49
citizenship: adoption and, 160; deportations of, 144, 146, 160; enslaved Black people and, 17; family reunification and, 134; foster care placement, 160; Immigration and Nationality Act (1965), 134; indigenous people and, 47, 58, 65; Jewish people and, 47; racial nationalism and, 17, 164; whiteness and, 17
civil rights movement: child taking as political punishment for, 33–34, 37–38, 40–42, 74, 126–27, 189n56; desegregation and, 33–34; organizing resistance to child taking, 17, 170; respectability and, 34–36; unmarried mothers and, 112; welfare programs and, 32–37, 44–45
Clinton, Hillary, 3, 153–54, 163
Clinton administration: asylum-seeking refugees and, 4, 10; child separation/detention and, 4, 140–41; expedited review and removal under, 10; Flores Settlement Agreement and, 137–43, 156, 165, 198n15; militarization of border, 131, 135–36; US-Mexico borderlands and, 135–36; welfare reform and, 44, 122–23
Cobb, Thomas R. R., 25–26

Cold War, 10, 76–78, 90, 99–102
Collier, John, 169–70
Collins, Addie Mae, 33, 184n29
Colombia, 5, 12, 151, 192n43
Colorado, 129–31
Comadres (Comité de Madres Monsignor Romero; Committee of Mothers), 14
Committee for Human Rights of the Countries of the Southern Cone (CLAMOR), 80–81
Contras, 12, 89, 97–99, 100, 136, 151, 192n43
Convention on Genocide (1948), 7, 163
Conway, Kellyanne, 162
Cook-Lynn, Elizabeth, 118, 120–21, 196nn46–47
Cooper, Lance, 2
Cowan, Ben, 100
crack cocaine: antiabortion politics and, 110–12; criminalization of drug users, 98–99, 103–4, 106–10, 124–27; drug trafficking and, 12, 98–99, 192n43; fetal exposure to, 12, 109–14, 174; foster care system and, 12, 108–9, 174; opioid crisis vs, 126. See also criminalization; drug trafficking; war on drugs
criminalization: of alcohol use, 106–10, 116–22, 171; of drug users, 98–99, 103–4, 106–10, 124–27, 171; of families of color, 103–4, 106–10; of houselessness, 114; intimate partner violence and, 114; of Native women, 118–22; of refugees seeking asylum, 9, 14, 156–57; Violence Against Women

Act of 1994 and, 114; welfare reform and, 114, 122–24

Critical Resistance, 173

Cruikshank, George, 25–26

Cuba, 10, 134

Customs and Border Protection, 141, 142

Davis, Angela Y., 33, 125, 197n54

Deferred Action for Childhood Arrivals (DACA), 157–59

deportation: citizenship and, 144, 146, 160; early waves of anti-immigrant sentiment, 133–34, 197n7; expedited review and removal, 3, 10, 55; of parents without their children, 144–49, 156–57

desegregation, 32–37, 170, 184n25

detention centers: camp conditions, 4, 138–40, 143, 159, 165; as concentration camps, 8, 173; expansion of, 168; family detention centers, 156, 168–69; Fort Sill protests, 171, 175, 176; strip searches and, 136–38, 142; trans women and, 177. *See also* immigrant child detention

Devil's Lake Sioux (Spirit Lake Sioux), 62–63, 64, 66–68, 71, 73, 189n55

De Witt, Tom, 102

disappeared, the, 3, 14, 79–83, 85, 87–88, 91–94, 102, 174

Discovering Dominga (2003), 93–94

domestic violence, 114, 123, 155–57, 189n55

Dorris, Michael, 116–19, 195n36, 195n46

DREAM (Development, Relief, and Education for Alien Minors) Act, 157–58

DREAM Action Oklahoma, 175

drug trafficking: cartels and, 12, 150–53, 192n43; CIA and, 98–99, 150–51, 192n43; cocaine and, 12, 98–99, 192n43; Contras and, 192n43; gun trafficking and, 150–53; Latin America and, 12, 98–99, 150–53, 192n43; Nixon administration and, 103, 107–8; Plan Colombia, 151; refugees and asylum seekers and, 12; unaccompanied minors and, 136. *See also* war on drugs

drug use: abortion rights and, 110–12; access to treatment and, 107, 108, 111, 114, 115–16, 119, 166; arrest/sentencing disparities, 108; criminalization of drug users, 98–99, 103–4, 106–10, 124–27, 171; drug testing and, 115–16, 174; fetal exposure to crack cocaine, 12, 109–14, 174; fetal personhood and, 110–11, 115–16, 174; house-lessness and, 114; intimate partner violence and, 114; opioid epidemic, 120, 125–26; pregnant people and, 12, 103–4, 109–15, 174–75. *See also* alcohol use

DuBois, W. E. B., 19

Ehrlichman, John, 106–7

Eisenhower administration, 41–42

El Salvador: adoption and, 101–2; anti-Communist child taking, 85–86; Carter administration and,

El Salvador *(continued)*
84–85, 89, 191n15; Central
American solidarity movements,
175–76; child soldiers, 136, 198n11;
child taking as counterinsurgency,
85–88; CIA and, 97–98; Comadres, 14; Flores case, 137–43;
international asylum system and,
10; La Quesara massacre, 85–86;
Reagan administration and,
84–85, 89, 191n15; Serrano Cruz
case, 85, 88–89, 191n26; truth
commissions, 87–88
enslavement of Black people: child
taking as crucial to, 18–28; infant
separation from mothers, 27; a
loophole of retreat and, 22–23;
maternal relationships and, 19–20;
Reconstruction and, 28–29; as
reproductive project, 45; sexual
violence and, 20; slave narratives
and, 20–24; Thirteenth Amendment and, 18, 27, 178. *See also*
abolitionists
Erdrich, Louise, 118, 119, 195n36

Faulkner, William, 8
Fehervary, Helen (Lea Marren),
88–89, 101–2, 191n26
Ferguson, Crystal, 115
Ferguson v. City of Charleston, 115–16
fetal protection: abortion rights and,
110–11, 125–26; exposure to crack
cocaine and, 12, 109–14, 174; fetal
alcohol syndrome, 104, 116–22;
fetal personhood, 110–11, 115–16,
174; foster care system and, 104,
113; mass incarceration and,

115–16; socioeconomic class and,
115–16, 121–22
Flavin, Jeanne, 125
Flemming, Arthur, 42
Flemming rule, 44–45, 184n50,
189n56
Flores, Jenny Lisette, 137–38
Flores Settlement Agreement (FSA),
137–43, 156, 165, 198n15
Florida, 31, 37–39, 47, 51, 98, 150–51
Flynn, Patricia, 93–94
Fort Marion, 47, 51
Fort Sill, 171, 175, 176
foster care system: Black children
and, 39–44, 61, 108–9, 172;
Catholic Church and, 139; child
taking as political punishment, 11,
74, 126–27, 189n56; citizenship
and, 160; fetal protection and,
104, 113; Flemming rule and,
44–45, 184n50, 189n56; immigration enforcement and, 146–49;
lesbian and bisexual mothers and,
172; mass incarceration and,
108–9; parental drug/alcohol use
and, 12, 104, 109–15, 118–19, 174;
racial bias within, 189n56;
resistance organizing and, 170;
state and federal funding for,
44–45, 184n50, 189n56; transnational adoption and, 96–97;
transnational borders and, 145,
147–49; violence against children
and, 189n56; war on drugs and,
108–9; welfare reform and, 39–44,
61; white children and, 37. *See also*
adoption
France, 193n45

Frank, Dana, 154
Frank, Deborah, 125–26

gay and lesbian people, 105, 172, 175–76
Gee, Dolly, 141, 155–56
genocide: use of term, 182n12; Convention on Genocide (1948), 7, 163; Indian boarding schools as, 47–48; Truth Commission of 1999 (Guatemala), 92–93
Georgia, 37, 100–101, 132, 158, 187n21
Gilmore, Ruth Wilson, 108
Gingrich, Newt, 122, 172
Goldwater Institute, 74
Great Sioux Nation: Dakota/Lakota, 50–51; Devil's Lake Sioux (Spirit Lake Sioux), 62–63, 64, 66–68, 71, 73, 189n55; Lakota, 50–51, 64, 118; Oglala Sioux, 64, 68; Sisseton-Wahpeton Sioux, 69, 71; Standing Rock Sioux, 64, 69, 71
Greywind, Elsa, 61
Grisonas, Anatole Julien, 80–81
Grisonas, Victoria, 80–81
Guatemala: adoptions in, 92, 96–97; cartels and, 150; Catholic Church and, 100; child soldiers and, 136; CIA and, 89–91; civil war in, 14, 85, 87–88, 89–91, 102; disappeared children in, 91–94; indigenous genocide and, 92, 93–94; organizing resistance and, 95–97, 173–74; orphanages, 92; reunification of children, 93–97; Rio Negro massacres, 93; sex work and

pornography kidnapping, 96; transnational adoptions, 94–97; truth commissions, 92–93, 95
Guzmán, El Chapo, 151–52

Haiti, 10, 45, 127, 134
Hamer, Fannie Lou, 26
Hard Choices (Clinton), 153
Harlan, James, 18
Hartman, Saidiya, 19, 21–22
Hasta encontrarte/Until You Are Found (Archbishop's Committee on Human Rights), 92–93
Hernández, José Adrían Rochac, 87
Hitz Report, 192n43
Holguin, Carlos, 137
"Home" (Shire), 157
Honduras: caravans for safe passage, 177–78; CIA and, 102, 192n43; Contras, 12, 136, 151; criminal organizations and, 5; gun trafficking, 150–51; Kerry Commission and, 192n43; labor migration *vs.* asylum seekers, 177–78; Reagan administration and, 12; state repression and, 6; US-sponsored regime change, 153–54

illegitimate children: adoption and, 37; Black children as, 9, 11, 30, 33–37, 112; foster homes and, 61; Native children as, 61; resistance organizing and, 39–45; sexual violence and, 35–36; welfare reform and, 34–35, 39–44, 122; white children as, 37. *See also* unmarried women immigrant child detention: camp conditions, 4, 138–40, 143, 159, 165; close-relative rule, 137, 141; family separation, 142–43; long-term detention, 140–41; Reagan administration and, 137–43; strip searches and, 136–38, 142; suitable-home rule and, 63; workplace raids and, 145–46. *See also* detention centers

immigration: use of terms, 9–10; anti-immigrant sentiment, 133–34, 197n7; child separation as deterrence to, 132–34, 160; Chinese immigrants and, 6, 131, 132–34; close-relative rule, 137, 141; Europe and, 132–34; immigrants *vs.* refugees and asylum seekers, 9–10; Immigration and Nationality Act (1965), 134; labor migration, 28–30, 130–31, 132–33, 135, 177–78; McCarren-Walter Act (1954), 134; parental rights and, 146–49; racial nationalism and, 17, 163–64; workplace raids, 145–48

Immigration and Customs Enforcement (ICE): chica trans/trans women and, 177; immigrant child deportation, 144–45; protests against, 161; workplace raids, 145–48

Immigration and Naturalization Service, 10, 137, 141

Incidents in the Life of a Slave Girl (Jacobs), 22–24, 132

INCITE! Women of Color Against Violence, 174–75

Indian Adoption Project (IAP), 188n37

Indian boarding schools: anti-boarding-school movements, 169–70; assimilation and, 51–54, 56–57, 169–70; before-and-after photos, 48–53; conditions within, 48, 56; consent and, 55–56; day schools and, 48, 58–59, 169; as detention camps, 46; erasure of indigenous languages and, 48, 50, 56, 59–60, 74–75; Fort Marion, 47, 51; as indigenous cultural genocide, 47–48; Meriam Report, 57–59, 61; Pratt system, 47–48, 51–53, 55; resistance organizing and, 48, 59–60; Roosevelt and, 169–70

Indian Child Welfare Act (ICWA): overview of, 71–73; coalitions and, 172; grassroots campaign for, 170; parental rights and, 120–21; resistance organizing and, 169–70; Texas ruling (2018), 132; tribal sovereignty and, 71–73, 75; unmarried mothers and, 71

Indian New Deal, 169–70

Indian Peace Commission, 50

Indigenous Environmental Network, 175

infants: abolitionists and, 25, 167, 178; abortion politics and, 117–18; adoptability of Black babies, 37; adoption of Native babies, 27; enslavement of Black people and, 7, 27; exposure to drugs and, 12, 109–10, 113–14, 174–75; fetal alcohol syndrome and, 12, 116–18, 121–22; foster care and, 114–15;

immigration policy and, 6; infant mortality, 104, 109–10, 112, 113–14, 176; kidnapping of babies in Latin America, 77–78, 80, 96, 99–100; Operation Feed the Babies, 41–42; Romero case, 146–48

Inter-American Court of Human Rights, 173–74

InterAmerican Development Bank, 5, 152

Iowa, 146

Jackson, Derrick Z., 113

Jacobs, Harriet, 22–24, 132

Japanese/Japanese American internment, 3, 47, 170, 176

Jewish people, 7–8, 10, 47, 173

Jones, Martha S., 19, 182n3

Kelley, Charlotte, 59–60

Kerns, J. Harvey, 41

Kerry Commission, 192n43

Kind Hearted Woman (2013), 73, 189n55

King, Mary-Claire, 81

King v. Smith (1968), 44

kinship, 18, 71–72, 184n38

Kissinger, Henry, 101

Korematsu case, 47

Krieger, Heinrich, 47

labor migration, 28–30, 130–31, 132–33, 135

Lane, Peter, 126

Laos, 192n43

Latin America: adoptions, 79–80, 79–83; anti-Communism and, 76–78; caravans for safe passage and, 177–78; Catholic Church and, 99–100; Central America solidarity movements, 175–76; child separation, 136–43; child soldiers and, 136; Cold War and, 10, 76–78, 90, 99–102; criminalization of migrants, 156–57; criminal violence and, 150–53; culpability for child taking, 99–102; the disappeared, 3, 14, 79–83, 85, 87–88, 91–94, 102, 174; drug trafficking and, 12, 98–99, 150–53, 192n43; family separation and, 136–43; Kerry Commission and, 192n43; labor migration and, 78; necropolitics and, 78; refugees and, 77–78, 134–36; resistance organizing, 173–74; right-wing militarism and, 76–78; as terror against insurgent populations, 78; truth commissions, 14, 87–88; unaccompanied minors and, 128–29, 135–36, 154–57, 177–78; unmarried mothers and, 100; US-sponsored regime change, 153–54. *See also names of individual nations*

Latinx people, 103–4, 105–6, 130, 158–59

Levenson, Deborah, 150

Lewandowski, Corey, 1

Lincoln, Abraham, 169

Logares, Paul, 81–82

Lomawaima, Tsianina, 53–54

Lone Wolf, 55–56

Lose Your Mother (Hartman), 19, 21–22

Reno v. Flores, 138–39
Report of a Fact-Finding Mission to Guatemala in Relation to Inter-country Adoption (Goicoechea), 96–97
resistance organizing: ACLU and, 167, 170; Central Americans and, 167–68; Central America solidarity movements, 175–76; civil rights groups and, 17, 170, 172; consciousness shifts, 170; Devil's Lake Sioux (Spirit Lake Sioux) and, 62–63, 64, 66–68, 71, 73, 189n55; feminist approaches to, 13–14, 123–24, 157, 172, 174–75, 176–77; Ferguson, 171; fetal personhood cases, 115–16; Fort Sill protests, 171, 175, 176; hunger strikes, 3, 123; Indian boarding schools and, 48, 59–60; international solidarity and, 96–97, 167, 173–74; Japanese anti-internment organizers, 176; jumping scale and, 66, 189n40; LGBT organizing and, 176–77; Native America and, 167, 169, 171–72; neoliberalism and, 105–6; prison abolition and, 124–25, 173; Red Power Movement, 60, 67–68, 74–75, 170–71; religious communities and, 167, 173; reproductive justice organizing, 176–77; silence *vs.* activism, 165–66, 172, 175–76; social movement solidarities, 170–71, 174–75, 174–77; transnational cartel and police violence and, 175–76; against welfare reform, 39–45, 170, 171, 172, 184n43. *See also* abolitionists

Roberts, Dorothy, 44, 74, 108–9, 165
Robertson, Carole, 33, 184n29
Rochac, María Silveria, 87
Rochac, Sergio, 87
Romero, Encarnación Bail, 146–48
Romero, Óscar, 14
Roosevelt, Franklin Delano, 58, 169–70

Salvador's Children (Marren), 191n26
Scalia, Antonin, 140
Schriro, Dora, 181n5
Scott, Walter, 124
Scott-Heron, Gil, 112
The Separation of the Mother and Child (Cruikshank), 25–26
Serrano Cruz family, 85, 86–87, 88–89, 191n26
Sessions, Jeff, 159–60, 181n2
Sevier, Dolly Lucio, 57
sexual violence: against Black people, 20, 23, 25, 35–36, 116; in detention camps, 143, 160, 193n45; Indian boarding schools and, 56; against Latin Americans, 80, 96, 97, 101–2, 193n45; by military soldiers, 80, 101–2, 193n45; Native America and, 56, 59, 73, 74, 119–20, 120–22, 121, 189n55
Sharpe, Christina, 178
Shattered Bonds (Roberts), 45
Shire, Warsan, 157
Sic, Dominga, 93–94
Silent Covenants (Bell), 184n25
Sinaloa cartel, 151–52
slavery. *See* enslavement of Black people

Smith, William French, 192n43
socioeconomic class: AFDC and,
30–32; cross-class solidarity,
122–23; enslavement and, 24; fetal
alcohol syndrome and, 121–22; fetal
personhood and, 115–16; impoverished communities, 105–6; infant
mortality rates and, 113; neoliberalism and, 105–6; orphans and, 30
Southern Border Plan (Plan Frontera
Sur), 156–57
Souvenir of the Carlisle School
(Choate), 49
Spillers, Hortense J., 22, 183n9
sterilization, 36, 65–66, 75
Stevens, John Paul, 140
Stone, Silas, 24–25
Stover, Eric, 81
Stowe, Harriet Beecher, 24, 26
Students Against Mass Incarcera-
tion, 173

taking children: overview of history
of, 2–10; as counterinsurgency
tactic, 12–13, 82–83; as crucial to
enslavement, 18–28; as genocide,
7–8, 47–48, 92–93–94; innocent
children discourse, 177–78;
necropolitics and, 78; neglect
discourse and, 8–9, 18–19, 37–38,
156, 168–69, 189n56; normaliza-
tion of, 104, 120–22, 126–27; as
political punishment, 4, 6, 11,
14–15, 33–37, 37–45, 74, 101–2,
126–27, 189n56; racial nationalism
and, 17, 160–66; for sex work and
pornography, 96; zero tolerance
policy and, 159–64

T. Don Hutto Detention Center, 143
Temporary Assistance for Needy
Families (TANF), 122–23
Tennessee, 125
Texas, 4, 128–29, 129–31, 132, 143,
156, 159
Thirteenth Amendment, 18, 27, 178
Three Affiliated Tribes, 64
Timmerman, Jacobo, 83
Tohono O'odham Nation, 131–32
Tragedy at Pine Ridge (1989), 118–22
Trail of Tears, 187n21
trans people, 127, 177, 200n8
Trump administration: child
separation policy and, 1–4, 6–7,
9–10, 104, 159–66, 168–69;
detention centers and, 1–2, 128–29,
165; Flores agreement compliance
and, 165; neglect discourse and,
8–9, 165, 168–69; racial nationalism and, 8, 160–66; refugees and
asylum seekers and, 1–4, 9–10,
104, 160–62, 168; State of
Washington lawsuit, 182n3;
Trump exceptionalism, 128–29,
168; Twitter dustup and, 128–29;
unaccompanied minors and, 3–4,
128–29, 169; white nationalism
and, 163–64; zero tolerance policy
and, 159–64
Truth, Sojourner, 20
Truth Commission of 1999
(Guatemala), 92–93
Tsuru for Solidarity, 175

unaccompanied minors: as asylum
seekers, 136–37, 177–78; Bush
administrations and, 128–29; child